A Lady Undefined:
From Carriage to Concorde

A Lady Undefined:
From Carriage to Concorde

By
David Knapp

Edited by Richard Fontenot

E-BookTime, LLC
Montgomery, Alabama

A Lady Undefined:
From Carriage to Concorde

Library of Congress Control Number: 2010926632

ISBN: 978-1-60862-158-3

First Edition
Published June 2010
E-BookTime, LLC
6598 Pumpkin Road
Montgomery, AL 36108
www.e-booktime.com

Dedication

A remembrance respectfully dedicated,
with great love and admiration
to the lady who made it all possible,
Gladys Quarre Knapp.

Foreword

Gladys Quarre Knapp, *a Lady Undefined*, began life as a survivor from early-on, living through her dangerous childbirth, where the umbilical cord was tightly wrapped around her neck and she had wedged her fingers in-between the cord and her neck to keep breathing. Her miraculous survival was a sign of her will to overcome obstacles and make the best of what life has to offer, as she eventually came to acquire friends in well-established social and legendary Hollywood circles. Gladys remarked, "it's not important who you know- what is important is who knows you."

The *Lady* this book is about once told the author, "Too much objectivity is a sign of insecurity." She felt to be overly concerned about the other person's point of view indicated an uncertainty in your own position. In assessing Gladys Knapp objectively, her life was a triumph in many respects, a social and financial success, and a gloriously productive run. She went to exciting places, saw fascinating things, knew an endless spectrum of people and pursued eclectic interests. Most of her good fortune, she created for herself.

Attempting definitive analysis, or accurately assess Gladys Knapp's life, would be presumptuous and futile. Gladys was actively married less than ten percent of her lifetime, the reasons are, at once, simple and complex.

As this book affirms, she was the antithesis of reclusive, yet thrived on the solitary. Thoroughly enjoying social interaction didn't negate her being equally happy and comfortable when functioning alone.

Some create their own environment, so far as it's possible, rather than be dependent on outside sources to occupy their minds or to fulfill interests.

This is not to be construed as a rejection of others; it simply means, in initiating activity within one's own sphere, there's less necessity to search elsewhere for inspiration. GQK was one of those genres. She had an enormous capacity for love, and to love, but her self-reliant nature and an overwhelming need for space, wouldn't allow her to be in love.

The demand of a singular-focused sustained commitment was for her, an ideal out of reach. It had nothing whatsoever to do with monogamy, and even less to do with promiscuity, there was no "other person," no clandestine motivation—only perhaps, selfishness about her time. GQK acknowledged and implemented her own reality honestly.

Two decades ago, Gladys Quarre Knapp—Mama—suggested to her son, "God knows you've been afforded ample material and opportunity. Someday, if you can muster the discipline, you ought to write a book."

This is Gladys Quarre Knapp's story. The author simply took notes along the way.

This is for both of us, Mom.

Acknowledging with Appreciation:

The many others who were sources of inspiration and whose influence, energy, effort and presence contributed to the narrative material, those friends and family who supported and encouraged this undertaking and became involved after the fact, and to those who were simply there...

Rupert Allan
Dmitry Bar
Francoise Barton
Kim Underwood Brittain
Larry & Margie Bukzin
Joshua Campbell
William Croarkin
The Delmer Daves Family
James B. Duffy, III
Richard Mark Fontenot
Wayne Johnston
Randal Kleiser
John Laurent
Gen. Frank McCarthy
Stewart & Marianne McAndrew Moss
Carlota Munroe
Charles Quarre
The George Quarre Family
Louis & Arlette Quarre
Oswald & Catherine Quarre

The Phillip Quarre Family
Basil & Ouida Rathbone
Charles Raysbrook
Conchita Raysbrook
Jay Schurman
Dr. Edward & Adele Shapiro
John Simmons
Heidi Dominic Tait
Jean Templeman
Theatre East
Robert Weisel
Paul Woodville

and

The Marianist Order – Society of Mary
Fr. Allen DeLong, Fr. Robert Mackay,
Fr. Lawrence Mann
Bro. Roland Hinger, Bro. John Perko
Mr. James Adams, President of Chaminade
Preparatory School,
with special appreciation to
Fr. David Schuyler

They have been a source of knowledge, inspiration and
compassion and in no way responsible for any errant
behavior or misdeeds, for those I must take full credit.

Chapter 1

A PAST IMPERFECT

Fire in the Cradle

GLADYS RUTH QUARRE was born on the cusp of Taurus and Gemini, May 21, 1901, in Larkspur, Marin County, California, a township nestled quietly in the hills across the bay, north of San Francisco. Her birth on the cusp allowed her latitude in choosing the characteristics of either astrological sign she deemed most desirable; her birth flower, the Lily of the Valley. While her birthstone, and personal favorite, is the most precious gem, the emerald.

She claimed to be a fifth generation Californian. She was in fact, a sixth. It wasn't like her to place herself in an older generation than factual necessity dictated. Perhaps a different interpretation of Genealogy? Accordingly, the author spent most of his life believing he was sixth generation, now knowing he's a seventh, and this turned out to be the least of his misconceptions.

Gladys emerged from the womb with her umbilical cord wrapped around her neck, but she managed to wedge a tiny fetal hand between the cord and her throat, thus, preventing her own strangulation.

Someone present commented, "That little girl will always be able to take care of herself," a prophetic observation. For almost nine decades, Gladys Quarre essentially lived a life she created, combining a daring free-spirited spontaneity, while implementing carefully thought-out overall objectives, she did both with no apologies. Her sometimes-dichotomous nature, contradictory priorities and volatile emotions, combined with a fierce need for an unencumbered personal life, made her—as she was the first to admit—not the easiest person to get along with. A compassionate autocrat, whose imperfections were over-shadowed, often eclipsed, by a personality which ran the gambit, tempered by an omnipresent wry-to-ribald sense of humor, intelligence, strength of character, and an innate sense of right.

She was a quintessentially civilized human being, who pursued a plethora of eclectic interests, stimulating her and those round her. Ingrained or cultivated, she possessed what the Spanish call, *simpatico,* a quality difficult to define, it's just *there,* a certain something that sets some individuals apart from the group—a gift, more than an accomplishment. Gladys Quarre would not be ignored, dismissed or forgotten.

Determining exactly to what degree genetic composition affected her life is difficult to assess. Bloodlines are responsible for many inherited characteristics, while the influences of environment and circumstance are acquired traits. Bloodlines play a major role in defining all species; however, the causes and effects are ultimately dependent on the character of the individual.

Gladys Quarre's parents, CARLOTTA HOWARD JACKSON and EMILE QUARRE, married in January of 1888 at St. Vibiana's Cathedral in Los Angeles. The social pages described the ceremony as being, *"One of the most brilliant that has ever taken place in Los Angeles."* A three-column article named each of the one hundred guests, as well as their wedding gifts. The newspaper went on to say, *"The bride is from one of the oldest and most distinguished families in California. The groom is one of the leading businessmen in Los Angeles.*" The article concluded with, "*They anticipate a European voyage in the spring. Their relatives and friends wish them a continuous honeymoon.*"

The grandiose account wasn't quite accurate, nor was its sentiments fulfilled. Referring to Emile Quarre as a "leading businessman" was an overstatement, and there would be no European voyage that spring, or at any other time during the marriage. A continuous honeymoon would be anything but!

***

Born in Brussels in 1863, Emile Quarre migrated to America in the mid 1880s. His family originally came from the Cote d'Or province in the Burgundy country of eastern France. A church cemetery in the village of Quarre-les-Tombes, a short distance west of Dijon, bears testament to the Quarre forbearers, dating back to the crusades. Emile's grandparents, along with *their* parents, fled France during the bloody revolution in the 1790s, one assumes, to avoid the guillotine. They crossed the border into Belgium, settling in Brussels, apparently prospering to varying degrees. Why Emile elected to leave a familiar, purportedly comfortable, secure life, for an uncertain future in a faraway land, is to speculate. Nothing indicates his departure from his homeland was due to necessity or expediency. The threat of beheadment also appears not to have been a factor.

Europeans were aware the California Gold Rush had long since declined, pretty much ruling it out as a possible reason. Perhaps, a need to get away was an incentive— resisting complaisance?

Grandfather Emile arrived in California literally a foreigner, and departed as one, figuratively. Despite becoming a naturalized U.S. citizen, a husband and father, Emile illustrated his elusive nature not many years later when, not having found the frontier panacea he'd imagined, or the financial security he'd envisioned—possibly feeling burdened by a wife, toddler son, and infant daughter. Thus, Emile became disenchanted with California, and pulled up stakes to seek his fortune in Alaska. The expeditionary premise for the venture was, in fact, tantamount to abandonment.

Once in the land of the midnight sun, he established some sort of *fur 'n pelt* trading business and became involved in local politics. If success can be gauged in terms of family financial support, his business must have been an abysmal failure.

To call Emile's adventuresome wanderlust a euphemism for irresponsible windmill-chaser, might be harsh. Another grandson, my first cousin, CHARLES QUARRE, [1923-2004] sent me a photograph of Emile taken in a rugged Alaskan setting at the turn of the century. A kinder image is that of a *Falstaffian* figure, a rural boulevardier in fur coat and boots. Charlie's father, OSWALD QUARRE [1896-1974], Gladys' brother, bore a strong physical resemblance to the father he barely knew. In other respects, they were totally dissimilar.

To give Emile his due, given the transportation restraints of a century ago, his ostensibly siring a family in California while running a business two thousand miles away in a virtual wilderness, took super-human tenacity. Several other factors come to bare, involving chronological discrepancies, which may negate or affirm key elements in this chronicle thus far. The actual date of Emile's initial California departure varies; the most credible source has it at 1899. His daughter's birth in May of 1901 would indicate one of three things; either he returned to California briefly in the early Fall of 1900 [unrecorded]; or, Gladys's birth date was tampered with so as to put it in the twentieth century [I recall a crude attempt to alter her passport to make '190*1*' read '190*7*']; or, the most probable scenario, if least desirable—Emile was her father in name only.

Adding more uncertainty, according to recently obtained documents, Emile Quarre's death in 1908 at age forty-five—ostensibly in Alaska—actually occurred in Los Angeles! One assumes, unexpectedly.

Rumors he didn't go quietly in his sleep were inevitable. The family never knew the exact circumstances. At that point it's doubtful they much cared. Grandpapa's legacy would be as a husband in absentia to my grand-mother, and a nonexistent father to my mother and her older brother, Oz. His death fourteen years prior to the birth of his oldest grandchild precluded his role as a grandparent. The author acknowledges, had it not been for Emile there may, or may *not*, have been anyone to write this book about, or anyone to write it? Then too, what you don't know, you don't miss.

***

Proving disparity in genetics, later generations of Emile Quarre's family graciously took Gladys, other members of the American Quarre family and me to their bosom on various visits to their beautiful home in Brussels, the Chateau Larraldia. Cousins Louis and Arelette Quarre gathered family members for dinners and outings. If I wasn't certain exactly what my relationship was to many of them, they would patiently explain.

My never having heard of those relatives was irrelevant. The discovery, the European Quarres knew even less about Emile than those in California, was of some consolation. It's reassuring to know one's ignorance is shared.

The cousins I've met are delightful, articulate, attractive, whom I'm fortunate to have, and proud to call family. Regretfully, this has not always been the case with kin living on the west side of the Atlantic.

***

A Girl's Gotta Do, What a Girl's Gotta Do

Gladys Quarre's maternal ancestry, approached in a cursory manner, is a colorful romantic saga; however, if scrutinized with an eye for subtext, and genetic accuracy, it becomes more colorful and *far* more romantic.

Gladys' mother, Carlotta Howard Jackson, hereafter referred to as *Lottie*, was born in 1869, into an aristocratic California dynasty, with solid social credentials, which were put to the test in her case.

Lottie was the eldest child of Dolores Carrillo, born 1852, just seventeen years before her daughter. Lottie's father, Charles Howard, a fellow whose identity is shrouded in a lingering fog, was another enigmatic figure. A century and a half after the fact, no official records of Dolores Carrillo's marriage to Charles Howard have been found—which isn't to say they didn't exist, but no one has ever seen them. Dolores' granddaughter, Gladys, claimed, the documents were destroyed in the San Francisco earthquake and fire of 1906, which challenges credibility. Lottie's birth, thirty-five years *prior* to the catastrophe was ample time to locate any records—plus the fact, she was born in *Los Angeles!*

It appears Charles Howard's parental involvement was solely biological.

After the Howard affair, great-grandmother Dolores married John Jackson, an Englishman, in a more conventional manner, by whom she had a son Andrew, and a daughter Ruth—born Estella.

Mr. Jackson eventually left on a voyage to Australia, from which he never returned. Lottie, her half-brother and half-sister, were joined by another half-brother, Gerald Craner, when Dolores married Henry Craner, a union which also caused angst in a traditionally Catholic family. Henry

Craner's father was the first rabbi of note in Los Angeles—a founder of the Temple Emmanuel.

Between Lottie's father, stepfather, and husband, it would seem her luck with men was questionable, however, her daughter would surpass her. Gladys' grandfather, father, *three* husbands—and a son—arguably, left something to be desired.

To describe Gladys' grandmother Dolores as, *ahead of her time*, is an understatement. She fueled enough gossip to headline any tabloid. Dolores shunned traditional social mores of the period, or most periods, considering them restrictive and bothersome. Intimidation by conventional standards was unacceptable. She did what she wanted, when she wanted it, and with *whom* she wanted. Gladys inherited some of her grandmother's characteristics, but her approach was less vigorous and in a far more traditional fashion. What she described as her grandmother's "liberated libido," was not part of the inheritance. Gladys would set her own course, but in a circumspect manner.

In all fairness, great-grandmother Dolores was born with justifiable expectations of personal wealth. Her parents were given the island of Coronado as a wedding present!

Dolores didn't break new ground or set a family precedent. Decades earlier, her mother was gifted with a solid rosewood piano from General John C. Fremont, a leading military and political figure in early California, as well as the nation. Fate, rather than achievement, thrust success on General Fremont, who, as many of his political successors, was savvy enough to spend a great deal more time cultivating an image, than dealing with substantive matters. In 1856, Fremont was the first presidential candidate of the newly-founded *Republican Party*, heretofore, known as *Federalist* and *Whigs*. His candidacy proved to be an inauspicious beginning for the G.O.P. Fremont somehow managed to lose the election to an innocuous Democrat, James Buchanan, whose mark in history is etched as, "the President before Lincoln," and as the only bachelor to hold that office. His most significant achievement was being one of the few presidents to leave office *less*-known than when he entered.

Fremont's extravagant *seventy*-eight-key gift, having been passed down three generations, stood fully functional in our ranch living room for twenty years, until Gladys donated it to the Santa Barbara Historical Society in 1977. I naively asked her, "Why did General Fremont give your great-great aunt such a lavish gift?" Gladys rolled her eyes, "*Really* darling, you sound as if you just fell off the pumpkin truck."

***

Dolores' grandfather, Don Juan Bandini, the founding father of the California Bandini family, was the son of Jose Bandini, one of two younger sons of an Italian nobleman, who, upon his demise bequeathed his entire estate to his eldest son, as was the custom, leaving Jose and the other younger son to fend for themselves. The two younger brothers took demonstrative umbrage, causing enough unrest and commotion to warrant banishment from Italy and were exiled to Spain. Spain's King Carlos III, a close friend of the Bandini family, welcomed the errant brothers, but not indefinitely.

Jose and his brother did not go gently into that good night either, continuing to create discord from the west end of the Mediterranean, becoming political liabilities to a point of threatening diplomatic relations between Spain and Italy. King Carlos was finally forced to get the Bandini brothers out of his political hair, but did so in a most gracious and generous fashion.

His Majesty gave Jose and his sibling each a ship to sail around the Horn to the new world, along with land grants to properties along the Pacific, equivalent in area to the state of

Vermont, ultimately making them infinitely wealthier than their elder brother with his inherited Duchy in the old country. The younger Bandini brothers decided to put pride and principle aside, placing property and pragmatism in the forefront.

Leaving behind all they held dear, Jose and his brother valiantly embarked on two tri-masted ships, virtually alone, but for their families, aides, servants; and with but a few basic possessions stuffed into numerous wardrobe trunks, along with boxes of jewelry, their furnishings, laces and linens, gold and silver service and Castilian-steel weaponry. In this Spartan mode, with only a handful of soldiers and the ship's crews to protect them, the brothers Bandini sailed off to an uncertain future in an unknown frontier, clutching little more than title to many thousands of acres of land.

The Bandinis arrived on Pacific shores in 1769, for reasons ethereal or entrepreneurial, one brother elected to drop anchor in Peru, whether as access to Inca culture, or due to acute seasickness, we don't know. As it turned out, he was able to blend temporal and spiritual needs when he became archbishop of Lima. Information as to why, when, and where brother Bandini took "Holy Orders" is sparse. The more tenacious Jose sailed north, guided by instinct, good judgment, and state-of-the-art charts. He bypassed everything from Panama to Guatemala, then, up the Mexican Riviera to Baja California, where he apparently took a detour up the Baja's East Coast on a very successful pearl-seeking quest in the Sea of Cortez. Leaving a few dead bodies and a great deal of ill-will in his wake, Jose departed with his pearl treasure, many examples of which would soon be hanging from the necks of royalty and ladies to the manner born, on two continents. The Spanish ship returned to the open sea and continued north to a more temperate climate where it dropped anchor. Jose Bandini, leapt ashore, laying claim to large chunks of the prime property he'd been granted, located in what is now San Diego, Riverside, Orange and Los Angeles counties.

Jose replanted his roots, married, with the inevitable results, one of which was a son, [Don] Juan Bandini, who not only managed and increased the real estate empire, but found the time and energy to sire ten children. Juan had three daughters by his first wife of the Estudillo family. She died young, perhaps intentionally, foreseeing seven more children her husband would have with his second wife of *La familia antigua* Arguello.

The Bandinis further solidified their socioeconomic position when Don Juan's eldest daughter, Josepha Bandini, married Pedro Carrillo from the even more socially, if not financially, established Carrillo family. Any confusion in assimilating this background information will be cleared up on knowing, Pedro and Josepha's daughter was Gladys Quarre's grandmother, Dolores.

The Bandini-Estudillo-Arguello-Carrillo consortium proved as fertile as the land they owned. The producers of produce and cattle were equally adept with progeny. The Bandinis and Carrillos producing more males resulted in their names dominating future generations.

Once sufficiently proliferated, concern over possible contamination of family bloodlines resulted in tacitly discouraging over-fraternization with outsiders. A tacit effort was made to keep things pretty much in the four-family format, marriages between first and second cousins were quite acceptable. Gradually, as blood thinned, so did judgment.

One year a draught wiped out thousands of head of cattle, so, when liquidity diminished, "Pay 'em with land," became the credo. Federal law by then, required landowners to prove ownership, but documents, especially those on parchment, had been lost, destroyed by earthquakes or fires, or literally eaten by rats.

Boundaries were vague, described, "From the west side of the creek, 1000 meters, to a great boulder," rather than surveyed with specific lines drawn. Lawyers demanded outrageous fees to authenticate land titles. Patrick O'Melveny charged $100,000 per large ranch for legal services, resulting in his establishing one of the biggest law practices in America. Meanwhile, family members paid off $2000 to $10,000 debts with up to a hundred acres of land— land which now represents substantial chunks of Santa Monica, West Los Angeles, and the Cities of Industry and Commerce.

"We should be the richest family in California—hell, in America!" Gladys bemoaned. By the time she came on the scene the vast holdings, potentially worth billions [up until fairly recently a billion dollars was considered a substantial amount of money] were virtually depleted due to a void of business acumen on the part of a great number of her progenitors, and subsequent Bandini and associated generations.

Still, the family could take pride in coming to America on *their own* ships—not as political refuges, religious dissidents or victims of bad economies, and not shackled in steerage! The Bandini-Carrillos didn't schlep across prairies in covered wagons; they dined on beef, not buffalo stew; wore tailored *haute couture,* not animal hides punctured by bullets and arrows! Those newer arrivals with more consonants than vowels in their names, soon avenged any transportation disparity in future business transactions with the landed aristocracy, leaving many of the latter with just their aristocracy intact, sometimes not even that. Many interlopers and carpetbaggers subsequently rose to exalted heights in California's social pecking order. This was especially true in the northern sector. Mother and grand-mother often referred to the San Francisco contingent as *Irishtocracy,* maintaining that two generations ago they were gold prospectors, card sharks, peddlers, washerwomen and ladies of questionable virtue. The younger friskier members of the Bandini-Carrillo clans, who did over-fraternize with the rabble, frequently ended up supporting the prouder family members.

Human nature, practical reality necessitated the family become a more gregarious and accessible lot—a possibility of eyes being too close together, may also have been a factor.

Another of Don Juan Bandini's latter progeny, Arcadia, born in 1827, married a friend and business associate of her father's at age fourteen. Her husband, Abel Stearns, a Yankee with Mexican citizenship, was almost four decades older than his bride, older than his father-in-law and, according to all accounts, *much uglier*—a prototype of *Beauty and the Beast*. Young Arcadia may have taken solace, knowing her beastly husband was also richer than her very rich father. Don Juan was consoled, in that, his older son-in-law was richer than *anyone* in proximity at the time! Newspapers profiled Don Abel as, "*The richest man in the state. Twice as wealthy as any man in the County* [Los Angeles.]"

Stearns' generosity compensated for any chronological and physical deficits, he named a ship after his wife, dispatched it out of Boston, around the Horn to California, laden with cargo intended to enhance his child-bride's lifestyle. He auspiciously demonstrated his affection by giving a downtown commercial block her name, along with the street it was located on. To further affirm his devotion, he honored her by naming a project he was working on, the City of Arcadia.

One can only hope Stearns' material magnanimity wasn't to off-set parsimonial benefits in conjugal matters.

Stearns finally died in 1877, but the name gift-giving continued from another source. Arcadia's susceptibility to older, wealthy, powerful types again manifested itself, when she found refuge in a second marriage to Colonel R. S. Baker.

The former Mrs. Abel Stearns, never comfortable in role of "the little missus," deciding being *Mrs. Baker* was a step in the wrong direction, reverted to her original title-of-address, while respectfully acknowledging the existence of new husband. Henceforth "Mrs. Baker" would be known as Dona Arcadia Bandini De Baker.

Not to be outdone, Colonel Baker built the finest hotel in Santa Monica at the time, naming it after his bride, on property formerly owned by his marital predecessor. However, he cleverly diffused his subsequent tributes by giving them *their* name, hence, the "Baker Block" in downtown Los Angeles, the desert town of Baker and the city built on *Baker's Field*—thus fueling his own ego, while keeping the peace at home. It appears Arcadia had a serious rival for Colonel Baker's love, *Colonel Baker!* Anyone who has been to the three locales might consider having any of them named after you a dubious honor.

Years later, Dona Arcadia de Baker donated the land on which the Sawtelle Veteran's Hospital complex now stands in West Los Angeles, next to the Federal government building, for the care of war veterans. Conveniently sand-wiched between Westwood and Brentwood, the property was given with the stipulation it only be used for the care of veterans, should it cease to be used for the intended purpose, it would revert back to the family. One hundred years later, it serves many non-related purposes, the primary one is the Federal Building on Wilshire Boulevard, now hosting regular "anti-everything" demonstrators who derive vicarious pleasure blocking traffic and creating havoc for futile causes.

Arcadia's generosity didn't end there, she died childless in 1912, *in testate*, thus, handing the rest of her thirteen million dollar estate to the government as well. I can't emphasize enough that was 1912! Today, in West Los Angeles, the value of that estate would be closer to four hundred million, which may not be much to many folks in the Twenty-First Century. Washington hasn't seen fit to compensate the family. When we suggested a measly fifty million dollars as a token of goodwill, the powers-that-be decided the money could be more productively spent on a study to determine the feasibility of utilizing hangar decks of decommissioned aircraft carriers as shelters for the homeless.

Attorneys advised the family, with so many heirs, taxes, legal fees and government shenanigans, the net financial benefits per member, would be so diffused, it hardly seemed worthwhile.

A small percentage of relatives, less cavalier in financial matters, occasionally managed to stem the tide of property depletion and diminishing family coffers, over the expediency-oriented protestations of the majority, even reversing the trend to some degree, but the potential opportunities to accrue monumental fortunes were gone. Family members with a head for business were an anomaly; astute males in particular, were greatly outnumbered by the less-astute ones. Expediency took precedence over future planning. Gladys reasoned, "That's why so many are poor, so few are rich." Mother opted for with the minority, but then, who sets out to acquire poverty?

Brittle Branches

We think of family trees in vertical configurations. In fact, the genetic progressions in either direction are not symmetrical, balanced or consistent; they more resemble a tumble-dried wig, horizontal, diagonal, bare spots, and dangling ends.

Multiple children by multiple marriages add to the disarray, resulting in *half*-this, *step*-that, various levels of *removal*—his, hers, and ours, with wives younger than their step-grandchildren, et al. The task made more difficult by members naming their progeny after themselves, a tradition proliferating our family—a custom redundant, unimaginative, confusing and smacking of ego.

Why would a young father age himself prematurely by being, "Joe Jones, *Senior*?" What if *Junior* turns out to be a major schmuck? Who wants a serial killer named after him?

Researching origins can be hazardous; significant revelations are rare, pilfering through the past hoping to find a famous, distinguished, even notorious, predecessor, is futile. Rest assured, any family member of note has been long since identified and thoroughly publicized, and the brittle branches of many family trees make limb-climbing inadvisable. Those vertical lines and arrows could be aimed in the wrong direction.

Conclusions drawn on genealogy charts, don't make them so. He informs you, "I'm a quarter German, Norwegian, and Dutch, an eighth Portuguese and Hawaiian." Oh, yeah? That's a lot of ports o'call.

Gladys observed, "Better a bastard by birthright, than to have earned the title," unless there is lot of money or property at stake.

Those with Italian and/or Spanish blood coursing through their veins are inclined to give vent to passion over propriety. When birth dates don't gel with papa's whereabouts at the time of conception, when the coloring and features of the new arrival are unlike any on either side of the family's recorded history, the brown-eyed child of blue-eyed parents, a genetic impossibility. Discrepancies invariably attributed to recessive genes, looking so much like a great-grand parent, but whose? Or, "If you look real closely, his eyes are more hazel than brown."

Gladys further observed, "Love babies tend to be happier, healthier, and better looking than those resulting from an obligatory, once-a-month, alcohol-stimulated tryst."

That Was Then

During the first decade of the last century, Gladys and her brother, Oz, learned to walk, talk and behave without the benefit of scientific reports, manuals and illustrated brochures explaining every step of the way. Child psychology was based on the parent being older, wiser, and bigger, with a broader base of experience than the child. Common sense dictated three-year-olds don't have the same voting privileges in family affairs as mom and dad. Children in their formative years were rarely a part of the decision-making process. They were not consulted, they were told.

Some feel, if you don't encourage children to express their ideas and thoughts freely, they'll be repressed, intimidated and reluctant to communicate—which was the whole point!

When the family didn't wish to include the children in a conversation they spoke Spanish, so, instead of encouraging bilingual skills, they used language as tool for exclusion. In light of future cultural demographics, this would be monumentally short-sighted.

In years gone by, youngsters getting out of hand received corporal punishment, their bottoms smacked pink to red, depending on the gravity of the offense. Today, hordes of unmotivated teenage Neanderthals roam school corridors, preventing others from getting an education, advocating gang membership, dealing, vandalizing, threatening with weapons of death, and worse, giving attitude. Are these slugs sending a subliminal message by wearing their pants so low, half their buttocks exposed? Could they be subconsciously inviting the corporal punishment some of them so richly deserve?

In days of yore, intimidation and the fear of repercussions acted as a preventative. Gladys and Oz played by the rules out of respect as well as possible retribution. The vast majority of bad kids have bad parents. If mom and dad don't have the confidence and respect of their children, you can be fairly sure they haven't earned it, either by commission or omission.

Gladys was convinced values and ethics don't come through osmosis, they are acquired through example. You learn what you've been taught, fundamental good and bad are not subjective or relative abstracts, they exist.

Uncle Oz, father of five, would be a disciplinarian traditionalist, often referred to by his progeny as the "Belgian Drillmaster." I half-jokingly asked him about it, he conceded, he probably deserved the title, "I was their *father*, and they could make their own *friends*." Despite some degree of retrospective bitterness, all five turned out to be productive and responsible adults. Other family branches, spared the metaphorical rod, turned out with less favorable results in many areas—the author being a classic example.

***

In 1906, Gladys Quarre, her mother and brother, witnessed the San Francisco earthquake and fire, from a bluff across the bay, the only means of family-owned transport were a horse and buggy, and brother Oz's goat-drawn cart. Prior to construction of the Golden Gate Bridge thirty years later, barring the ferry, the surface trip from Larkspur, around the Bay area to downtown San Francisco, in climate weather, could take nearly as long as it did for that little girl, to fly from New York to London on the Concorde, seventy years later.

***

Gladys and brother Oz, five years older, grew up in a genteel atmosphere with more social respectability, than financial stability. Mother would regale me with the ordeal she underwent to attend school each day—the mile walk from the house to the ferry landing, crossing the bay under typically drizzly overcast skies, choppy water in cold windy weather, barely having enough money for the cable car and trolley. This account was embellished over the years, the walk lengthened, the choppy seas and wind became *hurricane force*, while the cable car trolley fare almost forced her to work the Tenderloin District.

Gladys talked of having to accept hand-me-down clothing from Lottie's sister, her irrepressible aunt Ruth [Mrs. Harry] Hill, reminding me her aunt was short and full-bodied, while she was tall and statuesque. It's true, Gladys was physically blessed at birth, while her aunt had to put in hours of hard labor for less results.

Hand-me-downs might imply threadbare, discarded moth fodder—not the case. Aunt Ruth passed along articles in excellent condition, rarely worn, superior in quality, design and well worth a few alterations.

Gladys adored and revered Lottie, but would emulate her Aunt Ruth's lifestyle, rather than her mother's more modest and financially restrictive one. Gladys attributed a sage piece of advice to Lottie, "Never learn to cook, or you'll marry a man who can't afford to hire one." Lottie failed to heed her own consul, but her sister and daughter applied it with commiserate results. Aunt and niece adhered to Lottie's principle effectively with five marriages between them; however, the bond between Lottie and Gladys remained the strongest. They were a mother-daughter team, consummate friends, a relationship no one could drive a wedge between, speaking or thinking ill of one became a double negative.

Gladys Quarre's early life wasn't always a picnic in June, nor was it a chapter out of Dickens. The implication of somewhat deprived circumstances wasn't entirely accurate. Aunt Ruth's second marriage to Harry Hill made her a wealthy woman compared to her sister, on the other hand, there is no indication Lottie and her two children were gravely suffering economically. A person having a lot more money than another doesn't necessarily put the latter in the poverty category.

Eccentricities Not Withstanding

Gladys had *selective memory syndrome*, elaborating and embellishing the recollections she chose to. Other events were dismissed, erased, or taken to the grave. She exorcised certain periods and episodes in her life, while retaining others with vivid clarity.

Mother's generation by and large was more communicatively circumspect, not just due to technological restrictions, but by desire and choice. To kiss and tell, was to have no one to kiss and nothing to tell. Secrets held and guarded for a purpose are understandable, simply knowing something another doesn't, isn't. One person can keep a secret from others, but everyone trying to keep a secret from one person is all but impossible.

I believe Gladys carried *secrecy by omission* to an extreme, at least where I was concerned. If I tried to pin her down on issues I had every right to know about, she became evasive and/or fatalistic. "Why look for answers you don't want?" Very simple, I *did* want answers. How could I know I *didn't* want to know until I knew?

Often, when facts were finally uncovered, there was no logical reason for secrecy. Protecting, sparing, and sheltering were frequently-used excuses to justify exclusion. But from what? From who? At age ten, maybe, but an adult?

Questions pursuant to past events proved awkward; there was no compunction about relating a totally nonsensical fabrication—evasive contradictory fairy tales would have to suffice. Mysteries ceased to be the primary focus. *Why* they were treated covertly became the real issue.

Inquiries regarding present and past relatives were frequently met with; "Well, he wasn't really an uncle," or "We called her 'aunt' for the children's sake," or "Actually, your cousin was adopted." Imperceptible curtains were drawn if serious personal matters became the topic, older family members exchanging apprehensive glances, tacitly asking, "Has that been declassified?"

In my thirties, a reference at a family get together became a major source of angst. Someone mentioned an *Aunt Lois*, of whom I'd never heard. Mother's reaction on hearing the name caught my attention. Later, I asked, "Who was Aunt Lois?" Mother's hapless response, "The term 'aunt' gets bandied about, it could mean anything, literally or figuratively," was typically ambiguous. I'm thinking, "Okay then, forget about the 'aunt' part, who was Lois?"

"Lois? Oh, she's been gone a long time, why do you ask?"

"Because of your reaction when I do. Mom, did you have an aunt you never mentioned?

"No, *I* didn't!

Did I imagine emphasis on the first person singular? "She must have been somebody's aunt." This assumption was met by a look that made my mouth go dry. Should I pursue this? I'd done enough leaving well-enough alone! Mother's cautionary expression only exacerbated my need to know. Was she denying or baiting me? Suddenly the fog lifted, "Oh, dear sweet Jesus! Do I have an aunt I never knew existed?" The silence was eloquent.

"Is this your way of telling me, *you* and Uncle Oz had a sister you haven't mentioned for *thirty* years?"

"She died before Ozzie and I were born. We never knew her," Mother offered with a sigh of finality. She sensed I had a problem with that.

"David, she died at birth."

"Dammit Mother, someone who died at birth isn't referred to as *Aunt* Lois!"

"She died forty years before you were born, why are you so upset?" Mother sounded genuinely puzzled.

"Her name was Lois, not *she!*"

"Why was I lied to?"

"No one lied to you. It just never came up." Mother rationalized.

"In catechism class we called that a sin of omission," I exploded.

"I'm surprised you paid that much attention." Mother had a dismissive edge when she added, "She died long ago, David, let's not belabor it."

"Her death isn't the issue, it's the fact she *lived!*"

"She—*Lois*—didn't live! She never had a life!" A masterpiece of ambivalent innuendo.

"This isn't about Lois anymore, Mother; it's about your thinking I have to be treated like a retarded child. Why bother to lie, and then make a point of letting me know you are? If you're not going to tell the truth, at least come up with a convincing alternative!"

"Rave and rant all you want, David, but I haven't uttered one untruthful word. There's nothing more I can tell you."

"Nothing more you *will* tell me."

"Anyway you want to put it, that's all there is!" The lid was closed and sealed. As she stepped away, I snorted, "Lemme guess, poor Aunt Lois was liberal democrat!"

Her exit line, "At least it would have been *something.*"

Years later, I discovered Lois Quarre survived her birth in the mid-1890s, by forty-five years, dying in 1940, in my lifetime! I feel a sense of frustration at never having known the truth, while wondering, if it was such a concern, why hadn't I made a more concerted effort to find out?

I suspect Aunt Lois was institutionalized since early childhood, possibly retarded or even psychotic. In those days families often dealt with troubled members by declaring them dead long before they were.

Curiosity lingers as to how a person as family conscious as Gladys Quarre, could dismiss a sister of more than forty years, as a non-person?

The only clue came in her observing animal behavior, commenting on how mothers of most litters and multiple offspring, don't waste time on sickly or deficient newborns, but concentrate their energy on nurturing the healthy ones. One could argue that's what separates humans from animals—on the other hand; other human flaws more than compensate for the disparities.

Gladys was bothered by a couple we knew obsessing on their hopelessly retarded child, to the emotional neglect and detriment of their two perfectly normal ones, the latter suffering throughout their formative years as a result.

In hindsight came the realization, I wasn't alone in thinking Gladys more of an ephemeral image than a hypostatic entity. Family and friends would wistfully reminisce over colorful and amusing experiences they had shared with her, but rarely, if ever, offered any personal insights, or volunteered in-depth analysis or hazard a guess, let alone, draw any conclusions, as to her persona.

Imperious Idiosyncrasies

It seemed odd someone as independently strong-willed as Gladys, contemptuous of what she considered bourgeois, compassionately liberated in her approach to human behavior, could obsess over minor infractions in social decorum? So liberated, yet such a traditionalist.

A cousin asked me to be an usher at his late-morning-February wedding, stipulating the groom's party wear black-tie with white tuxedos. Gladys was appalled, "You don't wear a dinner jacket [she never said 'tuxedo'] in the morning, and certainly not *white* in mid-winter, unless you're near the equator!"

In a more tolerant tone, she conceded, "I know they live in Orange County, but still…"

I once accused her of snobbery, she noted, vernacular changes had given "discrimina*tion* a far different connotation than discrimina*ting.* "

The traits people tend to dislike most in others are those they themselves possess—we both could be terrible snobs.

***

Gladys would review a large itemized receipt in minute detail, taking great satisfaction in discovering she'd been overcharged three dollars on a three hundred dollar bill, then, minutes later write a large birthday check to a relative she hadn't seen for decades, but who had been kind to her in the past.

Her investigative antennae kicked in on receiving a bill from a general store she and her first husband shopped at near a lakeside lodge they'd rented during the summers in New Brunswick. The bill arrived in November, she was positive it had been paid months before, and her husband's secretary confirmed it had.

When she called the store, they were most agreeable, explaining, "We always double-bill our summer customers. You'd be surprised how many pay twice."

Another bit of curious logic reared its head when she went to buy a popular item, and was told the store no longer carried it. "I thought it was one of the most popular items your sold?" she said to the clerk. Indeed it was, the clerk confirmed, explaining, "It was just too much trouble, it sold out so fast, we had to be constantly restocking it, so, we decided not to bother." The clerk probably went on to manage retirement funds.

Gladys often found dumb behavior amusing, rather than annoying. Ignorance was another matter, not knowing something you should, or worse, pretending to know something you don't, caused a volatile reaction.

Watching election returns, resulting in a victory for a candidate she despised, Gladys ruefully concluded, "Never underestimate the stupidity of people in large groups. Before you lead a horse to water, teach him how to swim."

Chapter 2

MORNING, NOON & NIGHT

The longer you know, and the closer you become to an individual, the more protective armor is shed. Helmet and breastplate removed, quite often one discovers you're not as familiar with them as you thought. Gladys said, "The closer you get, the greater the threat." A false sense of security is a fragile defense against insincerity.

"The alleviation of aggravation serves as compensation for frustration."

A bonding thread in this tapestry of non-sequiturs is a fondness for alliterations, analogies, and metaphors. This was classically illustrated when this book was in barely an embryonic stage, one which the author might not see through gestation. A reason it went to full-term, came in San Francisco when fate intervened in the form of a *pariente especial*, Jacob "Jay" Schurman, a second cousin, whose grandmother, my Great Aunt Ruth, was Lottie's half-sister. Jay and I rarely see one another, communicating primarily by phone or mail; He's pure San Franciscan. He's is a gentle, caring, sensitive soul, while I bring to mind a different image. The four hundred miles separating us, could be light years in some respects—we're foreigners in a sense—yet, with significant things in common. I suspect, our congenial relationship may be, in part, attributable to the infrequency and the lack of proximity factors. The Northern California branches tend to think of Los Angeles as somewhere between Fresno and Tierra del Fuego.

Traditionally, San Francisco denizens take great pride in showing off their city. It is of no matter the visitor, having been there dozens of times—knowing where you can't make a left turn and to bring warm clothing—remains a tourist in their eyes.

Indicating a particular house, the host gives you a brief history, reaffirming its ownership and any skeletons of note it had the last ten times it was pointed out.

Apparently, Gladys desperately wanted to loosen family shackles, and break way from restrictive small town parameters. With the big city so close, yet rarely in reach, it was frustrating for a girl on the brink of adulthood. With brother Oz away, a sergeant with the American Expeditionary Forces in the trenches of France, Gladys persuaded her mother Lottie to share a small apartment in the city. Lottie would leniently chaperone her daughter's first bid for freedom outside the family confines. With a solid job prospect, they'd have a modicum of financial independence. Small world that it is, they took an apartment on Broadway, in a building which happened to be owned by a fellow named, Harry Hill, who happened to be Lottie's brother-in-law.

Gladys was hired by *I. Magnin's*, a prestigious department store with a top-quality reputation. The venerable institution with its upper-echelon clientele was an ideal workplace for ambitious girls, aspiring to future financial security, social acceptance, through marriage or arrangement. Conversely, it seemed a safer working environment for a young lady *with* social credentials, whose financial resources, if not demanded, suggested, she seek employment—a theory largely dependent on a customer's ability to discriminate, then behave accordingly.

Gladys knew the key to handling herself was the ability to handle others. Things went smoothly, until her wealthy, prominent and well-connected Auntie Ruth, got wind of her niece's involvement in retail sales, horrified, the grand dame took it as a personal affront, reflecting darkly on her matriarchal status and position in San Francisco society. No niece of Mrs. Harry Hill would be on public display for men who'd be better suited in a brothel! No matter her niece stood behind the counter, not on it!

Jay described his grandmother descending on I. Magnin's, demanding Gladys' immediate dismissal! Fearing her formidable wrath, the management complied.

My accusatory reaction, "You're telling me, *your* grandmother had *my* mother fired!"

"Don't make it so personal. Gladys wasn't *your* mother at the time she was dismissed from her job."

"Jay, you get *dismissed* from jury duty. My mom was *fired.*"

Jay attributed our exchange to semantics, "First you were shocked your mother worked as a sales girl, now you're incensed because she lost the job."

"Involuntarily,*"* I pointed out. "It must have been awkward, people wondering was she too good for the job, or not good enough."

Jay took the high road, "It may have been the best thing that ever happened to Gladys."

"What's impressive about Mom's reactive role in the whole affair?"

"Her *reaction* to her 'reactive' role was to turn it to her advantage," Jay explained.

I still didn't get the subtext.

Slowly, succinctly he elaborated, "Motivation. It gave Gladys the impetus to make her own way—not to be dependent on anyone in the future."

Was he putting too big a handle on her being dismissed from a menial job?

Jay tempered his hypothesis, "I thought perhaps, it may have played a role in your mother's approach to life?"

Jay's theory, *negative-motives-often-beget-positive-results*, was born out in the Foreword of a best seller. The author listed several people, expressing his appreciation; *"Without their negativity and lack of faith in the author's literary skills, this book might never have been completed."*

However, let it be noted, proving the opposition wrong, doesn't necessarily make you right, but it's a step in the right direction.

Ironically, the company's head, Grover Magnin and his wife Jean became close friends of the short-tenured former employee later on, and remained so for decades.

Free, Fresh Wind in Her Hair

Gladys Quarre didn't burst forth a *raving beauty*—a tall, very pretty girl with good features, but short of spectacular, who nevertheless made an impression. As with all of us, her formative years were not idyllic, but things would change. By her early teens, she was exceptionally attractive, and in a few more years, she was marked for life as a classical beauty. Many women *look* beautiful, Gladys *was* beautiful. Hers wasn't a carefully manicured glamour; it was a gift from God.

The "raving beauty" description applied by the time she Charlestoned into the roaring twenties. Her ever-growing list of beaux and admirers left no empty spaces on her dance card. Life was a party, to which she was more than welcome, living it to the fullest. After a Saturday night out, Gladys would return to the apartment on Broadway, as Lottie was leaving for Sunday Mass.

Gladys Quarre's persona and background, combined with intelligence, affability and a wicked sense of humor, placed her in the lap of San Francisco society, without her having to aggressively seek it. She made an auspicious debut in 1921 with a full page photograph in the Sunday, March 27th *San Francisco Chronicle,* proclaiming her, "The most beautiful debutante in San Francisco.", the subsequent article expanded the quote with, "…in California."

Gladys later reflected, "It was a lovely thing to read, but it doesn't make you popular with the other debutantes."

Paul Dougherty, a renown artist whose works hang in New York's Metropolitan Museum of Art said, "Gladys Quarre possesses the classic lasting visage seen in portraits by [Thomas] Gainsborough and [Joshua] Reynolds." A portrait of her, painted in the mid-1930s, other than her gown, could have been eighteenth century England, or a century later on a canvas by John Singer Sargent.

The portraitist, Howard Chandler Christy, described Gladys as, "One of the very most beautiful women in America," to which she responded, "It was a great compliment, but why did he have to qualify it with the national boundary part?"

I was never quite sure if she was serious or being flippant on these occasions.

***

Gladys Quarre "crossed the Rubicon" triumphantly—expectations now realities, dreams materializing, life was at her fingertips, she would now begin the selective process. A criterion subtly established at the outset, she never had "boyfriends," only *beaux.*

Too much too soon, may have been a factor, but Gladys was beginning to sense San Francisco was a tad smaller than she'd realized.

She made frequent visits to Los Angeles as a house guest of Southern California family members, who acted as unofficial chaperones, should the need arise. Despite numerous opportunities and temptations, she could be trusted to use good judgment in sensitive situations. Gladys' overall objectives would not be compromised by fleeting impulses. She couldn't be exactly sure in what shape or form they might present themselves, but she'd know one when it came along.

Her sights were set on the big picture—ironically, soon that would cease to be a metaphor.

The Chic and the Sheik

At a dinner party in Los Angeles, Gladys was introduced to a darkly handsome young man at the apex of a brief but spectacular film career. Rudolph Valentino and Gladys apparently hit it off. She knew about him, but had little idea as to the astronomical heights his career had soared. Valentino was educated, articulate, knowledgeable, and a gentleman. The San Francisco debutante and the international movie star idol had an immediate rapport, which she attributed to her *not* being in awe of him. She found him charming and fun—bottom line, she simply liked the guy.

Valentino asked her to dinner the following evening, and unable to come up with a good reason not to, she accepted. At dinner the following night, Valentino expressed his wish to see her again, when she explained her logistical and family situation, he suggested, if she didn't come South regularly, he'd go north to visit her. She was sophisticated enough not take things too seriously.

San Franciscans tend to be blasé about motion picture personalities, who are frequently looked on in a condescending light. Mother would discover a dichotomy in that some San Francisco hierarchy would covertly maneuver and finagle a film star to their dinner table. Decades later Gladys observed, "If those people [in San Francisco] could get just *one* of the guests I entertain regularly in Los Angeles, they'd send out invitations six months in advance."

Two weeks after Gladys returned to San Francisco the phone rang, Lottie answered, after a brief exchange, Gladys heard her mother say to the caller, "You *are*? Really? Well, what an odd coincidence, I'm Mary Pickford!" Gladys rushed to the phone, "Rudy, its Gladys, I'm so sorry. No-no, that was my mother, she thought it was a joke. Yes, I know you did, but I didn't expect you to."

Lottie listened dumbfounded as her daughter made a dinner date with the legend for the following Saturday evening. His validity confirmed, Lottie was eager to know, "What was the occasion warranting the screen idol's visit to San Francisco?"

"To see *me*, mother," and asking Lottie, "Please, mention it to no one, he is coming up for a quiet weekend."

When Oz got home, Lottie informed him of the big event, he was skeptical, thinking it a joke the girls had cooked up, yet he too, swore not to repeat it.

Lottie made certain everyone else she told was sworn to secrecy, they in turn relayed the need for secrecy to those they told. Once everyone knew of Valentino's forthcoming secret visit, a feeling of inclusion prevailed, the movie star and the San Francisco debutante had a delightful evening. He got the evening off to a thundering start, when being introduced to Lottie, he remarked to Gladys, "I see beauty comes naturally to you." Mother's like to hear that sort of thing.

The next day Valentino took Gladys, Lottie, and Oz to lunch, their Italian blood acted as a catalyst. In future years, Gladys could have written a manual on "What to expect when going out with celebrities."

***

On subsequent visits, Valentino was given "the man's-man seal of approval." Oz awarded him with, "I'm glad you don't act like you do in the movies, all that prancing around in funny clothes, with all the makeup. I thought maybe you were. . . Y'know?" With Gladys and Lottie trying to silence him with subtly frantic gestures, Oz went on, "Anyway, Rudy, I don't care what they say. They don't know what the hell they're talking about. I think you're a fine fella."

Possibly that male affirmation meant more to the super-superstar, than the adulation of female fans. It struck a cord with Gladys as well. She claimed to prefer a *man's-man kind of guy*, who enjoyed hanging out with the guys, as opposed to a "ladies man," who feels uncomfortable and threatened by his own gender. In retrospect, although it's hard to visualize Valentino roping steers, apparently he didn't come across as a sissy. Gladys never understood why some wives get ballistic if their spouses have a night out with the boys. "She should realize, if she clings for dear life, there's a good chance they'll both go under."

Most wives of the men I hung out with seemed to agree, they not only condoned an occasional night out, many encouraged it, no doubt reasoning, their husbands were less apt to skirt-chase when in the company of someone not so inclined. Of course, there's a flip side.

On Gladys' future visits to Los Angeles, hosting family members were delighted to have the idol of millions arrive at the house to take their cousin for an evening out. One in particular, her young cousin, Estella del Valle, then an exotically beautiful little bird of a girl in her teens, enthralled by celebrities, was a designated "greeter." On his first visit Estella hovered by the front door in near hysteria. Gladys and several family hosts the living room, heard the doorbell, the door being opened, then a shriek from Estella. They dashed into the entryway to see her gawking at Valentino. Gladys stepped into view, Estella, thoroughly flustered, informed him, "This is my cousin Gladys."

Estella enshrined the encounter, prim and proper, but never a prude, she exemplified lady-like dignity, along with a naughty sense of humor.

***

Straining credibility during the Valentino period was Gladys' quiet insistence on the platonic nature of their relationship. The man every woman wanted, with the woman so many men wanted, and not indulging, some thought a waste. Valentino was protective of Gladys, confining most of their social life to private dinners and relatively small unpublicized parties. The few occasions the couple attended large film industry functions, the fan's behavior caused Gladys to pragmatically consider the monumental scope of Valentino's popularity. The release of *"Monsieur Beaucaire"* intensified the hysteria. Public appearances became a terrifying ordeal. Screaming mobs of frenzied women presented a real danger to a point where police cordons had to surround them to prevent being knocked down and trampled. Like lion taming acts, daring, dangerous, death-defying at first, then deadly dull—but still dangerous.

The friendly ending to the relationship was made easier as being *in* love wasn't part of the equation, but what was, Valentino was about to embark on a marriage of expediency. The timing worked to Gladys' advantage. The public's smothering adoration beyond rationality, she could only sigh with relief.

Valentino gave Gladys a book of his poetry, entitled *Day Dreams*, with a note expressing his appreciation, "...allowing him to be at ease and not having to be *Valentino* off screen." He concluded with words to the effect, their friendship helped him maintain a balance between reality and myth. It was signed, *"With Deepest Affection, Rudy."*

On finishing his book, Gladys concluded, he was better at prose than poetry. To all intents and purposes, the letter would also seem to confirm the platonic nature of their relationship.

Eagle in a Parrot's Cage

Gladys now in her mid-twenties, family pressure was mounting, in the minds of some, she would soon make the transition from "still-single" to "spinster." This wasn't due to lack of opportunity or proposals. Photographs, sketches and renderings of her appeared in newspapers almost weekly, with captions reading, *"San Francisco's great beauty, stunning, exquisite, radiant*—all about, *Miss* Gladys Quarre."

The prospect of marrying a nice innocuous account executive-type in a *Wilkes Bashford* suit, with a good bond portfolio, settling down, having two-point-three children and living a pleasantly predictable life in her native city, was too obtainable an objective.

Gladys didn't much care for nice bland fellows, preferred blue chips to bonds, children weren't on the immediate agenda and the "pleasantly predictable" concept made her nauseous. She loved her immediate family, however, domesticity in the Norman Rockwell sense held no allure, or as she put it, "I feel silly in an apron."

***

Brother Oz had a diametrically different concept of marriage when he took Catherine Mohun, *Aunt Kate*, as his wife. They wed in February of 1922. Their compatibility was established when they produced their first son that December and the second in November of the following year. They had three more children in the next seven years, a consummate marriage lasting until Oz's death in 1974.

The parallels between siblings angled off sharply in their martial modes. Brother Oz had one wife for fifty-two years, five children and thirteen grandchildren, while Sister Gladys, had three husbands, totaling eight years, one child and no grandchildren.

Lottie and Aunt Ruth advising Gladys not to learn to cook, was juxtapositioned—her brother married a lady who had never learned to either! Kate did learn to cook, with little choice or enthusiasm, as she and uncle oz presented Gladys with four nephews and a niece, my five first cousins—George, Charlie, Phillip, Peter, and Ann— produced a baker's dozen of grandchildren.

I remarked to Aunt Kate, "After four sons, it must have been nice to have a daughter." In a moment of candor she responded, "I wanted a daughter very much, but we never seemed to have much in common." There was no rancor in her reply, perhaps just a hint of regret.

A half century later one of their sons confided, his mother and father's commitment to each other, superseded their role as idyllically loving parents.

There were times Gladys hypothesized over her brother and sister-in-law's relationship, wistfully comparing its solidity and enduring nature to the lifestyle she had chosen. I'd listen, nodding at appropriate moments, and we'd then exchange bemused smiles.

I analogized, "Like an eagle adapting to a parrot cage." She considered a beat, "I suppose, maybe, if you clipped its wings." We both knew clipped wings wouldn't change a thing.

Chapter 3

SHE KNEW WHAT SHE WANTED

In 1926, with hope evaporating, spinsterhood looming, Gladys Quarre met Frederick Griffith Peabody. He bore some similarity to a number of Gladys' past suitors, post-preppy junior executives, heirs-to-family businesses, and boys-about-town with more expensive toys. In Fred Peabody's case, it was stretching parameters, he was *well* post preppy, a senior executive, a man-about-town, and if a Rolls-Royce qualifies as a toy, he had one.

Fred was the vice president of a leading clothing manufacturer, *Cluett & Peabody Corp.*, best known for *Arrow Shirts*, *Jockey*-brand shorts and as inventor-patent-holder of *Sanforization*, the non-shrinkage process for cotton goods. Fred and the company having the same name weren't coincidental, the company's cofounder and president, Frederick Forrest Peabody, was Fred's father.

Fred, the younger, was born in Evanston, Illinois in 1890. The social pages had him as a resident of New York and Santa Barbara, he was actually living in Chicago. Fred, Senior built the Peabody estate, arguably the most renowned home in Santa Barbara at the time.

Gladys's engagement to Fred Peabody was received with contained enthusiasm, some felt the chronological difference literally doubled in visual terms, Gladys had the blush of early spring about her, while Fred had the aura of mid-autumn and there were other low-hurdles to clear. The more Catholic family members were concerned about his staunchly Protestant background—and the fact he was divorced! These were overlooked by the more modern thinking members, taking solace in his ability to provide Gladys with a *very* secure future and if worse came to worst, a merry widowhood.

Lottie rationalized her misgivings by "annulling" her future son-in-law's previous marriage—as they were Protestants.

The lady responsible for Gladys' dismissal from I. Magnin's a few years earlier, Mrs. Harry Hill, had reverted back to her role as supportive Auntie Ruth, wholly in sync with her niece's priorities in picking a husband. She defended the choice by letting it be known, the first Mrs. Peabody, Gertrude Widener, was from a most distinguished and influential family in Philadelphia, and about the richest. Aunt Ruth felt, "Marrying a man whose first wife was a Widener is to be in very good company."

Newspaper articles describing the groom-to-be's father, Fred, Senior, as "*... one of the richest men in America, and rich as Croesus,*" may have played a role in consolidating support for the nuptials, putting things in a more tangible perspective, thus, easing potential moral dilemmas.

Although Fred Peabody looked middle-aged, however, being eleven years older than his *twenty-five* year old bride-to-be hardly put him out to pasture! He was not an unattractive man, and he carried his social-pedigree and privileged background with ease, never shirking the responsibilities of his birth right.

Being *in* love isn't a prerequisite for marriage, Gladys believed relationships built on more substantive considerations have a better chance for a long survival, close friendships are more apt to withstand the trials and tribulations, than those born out of obsessive passion and hurly-burly of the boudoir.

"Being in love with no food on the table may be romantic—but sitting down to a feast with someone you are genuinely very fond of is more resilient to time."

Gladys was also attracted to this worldly man because he had a marvelous sense of humor and was fun to be with. She would sheepishly confide to me forty years later, "His blue eyes twinkled—when they weren't bloodshot. Thinking back, he was actually kind of sexy in his own way."

All that aside, paramount in her mind, he would be her liberator!

On August 7, 1926, with her family's qualified unanimous approval, Gladys Quarre became *Mrs. Frederick Peabody*, in a small ceremony at her Aunt Ruth's home.

***

I was led to believe during my formative years that Fred Peabody was my father, which I eagerly accepted. In a chronicle about a lady who took his name for twenty years, and her son, who carried it for his first eight years, he warrants more than passing attention.

Having no recollection or knowledge of ever having seen or spoken to Fred, who I suspected in my heart wasn't my dad, I wanted to believe otherwise. The only visual images of him are an 8"x10" posed formal sepia photograph taken in New York in 1930 and few faded black and white snapshots in a disintegrating scrapbook, taken during their marriage. The factual information is mostly from a half-column in *"Who's Who in America, Business Edition"*, 1930-31 editions, and faded news clippings. The impressions and antidotes are based on select bits and pieces Mother chose to impart through the years.

Gladys and Fred had a belated honeymoon in Europe, one oft-told episode took place in Paris. The newlyweds were dining at the famed *Tour d'Argent*, before it became a highlight of the tour-bus circuit. The bride ordered a bottle of vintage Montrache. The sommelier cradled the dusty bottle to their table as one would a newborn heir apparent. Fred stared in disbelief when the bill arrived, handing it to his bride, "You're better with French, take a look at this, it can't be right." Gladys studied the bill, confirming the amount. "That's impossible," her husband protested, an outrageous sum in terms of U.S. dollars. The bride pointed out, the bottle of wine alone was sixty percent of the bill. A grain-over-grape man, Fred examined the bottle, asking his wife, "Didn't you like it, sweet-thing? There are still three-quarters of a bottle left."

"If it makes you happy, I'll have one more glass," the bride sighed.

"What would make me happy, at that price, sweet-thing, is an *empty* bottle."

"I can't drink the whole bottle, Fred, and please, stop calling me, sweet-thing."

"We're going sit here until you finish *every* drop," he emphasized, "Sweet*ness*."

Some time later, the Maitre d' helped Fred carry his young wife to a taxi. On arrival at the Ritz Hotel, husband and doorman carried her into the hotel—husband and a *femme du chambre*, tucked her into bed.

The American couple would reverse roles in the future.

The first two years of the Peabody marriage were spent in Chicago, where Cluett & Peabody's Midwest division was headquartered. Chicago is a magnificent city, made more so, if moved to a better climate. The quintessential *American* city, New York and Los Angeles, are no longer indigenous to America, they are worlds unto themselves, international DMZs. This in no way demeans the status of those two cities; it's simply the way things are.

Gladys rarely had anything positive to say about Chicago, or the Midwest in general, despite a beautiful apartment on Astor Place, off *The Loop*. The fringe benefits included a staff of three Finish girls, and a chauffeur-driven Rolls-Royce; a super hospitable sister-in-law, Rachel Peabody, with a magnificent home in the posh suburb on the North Shore, Lake Forest, for weekends—an entree to the best the city had to offer, which is an enormous amount, still, she considered it an extended engagement on a national tour.

"Freezing winters, scorching humid summers and the St. Valentine's Day Massacre," summed up her impressions of the *Windy City*. She also hated the wind. She was savvy enough not to verbalize her impressions at the time.

The Chicago press, however, held Mrs. Frederick Peabody in high esteem, society pages made a point of rolling out a welcoming red carpet, extending it throughout the two years they lived there. Photographs, illustrative sketches and articles, epitomizing her style and grace with vigorous print-praise, her gowns were described in detail, along with her figure. Gladys was a big girl by the standards of the day, statuesque, without being Rubenesque, at almost five feet-eight, one hundred and thirty-eight perfectly distributed pounds, a thirty-seven inch bust, and unlike most, she photographed ten pounds *less* than she was—however, and that would not be the case indefinitely.

Fred adored his mother-in-law, Lottie, welcoming her visits from San Francisco. He cared much more for her, than his own mother. The reason was simple, Gladys explained, "Fred's [step] mother was the bitch from hell."

Gladys' disenchantment with Chicago peeked during their last months there. Lottie hadn't been well, suffering from a kidney disorder and her daughter and son-in-law insisted she stay with them to be better cared for. Lottie came east, remaining at the Astor Street apartment for several months. Externally, her condition seemed to improve, but internally, her kidneys were gradually deteriorating. Lottie's demise wasn't thought eminent, when, one morning, while chatting with her daughter, she died suddenly.

Her mother's death at fifty-nine from Bright's disease, had a shattering effect on Gladys, it meant not only the loss of her mother, but a big sister and most beloved friend. Her grief was resurrected a few years later, when a cure for kidney degeneration, by simple injections of cortisone, came about. Knowing her mother could have been easily saved had the drug come a little sooner, was a source of frustration for Gladys throughout her life.

One can surmise other factors were involved in her reaction to the mid-west city, when all is said and done, she apparently concluded, Chicago wasn't quite like playing with the varsity.

From what I gather, Fred Peabody was essentially a *man's man*, an urbane sportsman who thoroughly enjoyed roughing it first class. He could net a thrashing ten-pound fish in a raging river with a three ounce Hardy rod, drop a bird at 150 feet with a .16 gauge, sail a yacht while both were three sheets to the wind, and maneuver pack animals, or the four door convertible Rolls-Royce, through an uncharted wilderness. He and Gladys trekked to the wilds of northeastern Canada, "where no white men had been," the two of them, a guide, the pack man and, on occasion, the Rolls loaded with gear from *Abercrombie & Fitch* and/or *Hammacher Schlemmer.* Fred anticipated basic camping needs by having a buoyant waterproof padded bag designed to hold four quart bottles [presumably scotch], protecting them from any whims of Mother Nature.

Gladys took a photograph of Fred standing by the Rolls at the edge of a wilderness lake, the lower front end of the car partially submerged in the water, done to keep the magnificent machine out of harms' way, as a result of a sudden forest fire. More extraordinary, how they managed to extract the big car from the lake without a tow truck, then get it back to civilization—a testament to British engineering, as well as the fellow capable of pulling off a feat like that.

Digressing

The author compared that outdoorsman ship to his white-water rafting adventures decades later, down the Salmon [River of No Return], Snake [Hells Canyon], Colorado, and Columbia Rivers. Filling out forms, questionnaires, health reports, waivers, liability releases, writing a big non-fundable check, then, voluntarily spending three to six days exposed to the elements, paddling endlessly under a merciless sun, subjected to fresh water tsunamis and circumventing boulders. Once ashore, exhausted, toting huge gear bags from the zodiacs to a campsite, always up a steep incline, through brambles and poison ivy, while all of God's little creatures try to take a nibble at your parched flesh. Democracy in action, statutes now prohibit reserving a campsite. It is first come first served, so, in recent years, it means, discovering another group got there first, and then having to negotiate further down river to a less desirable site.

Ostensibly pitching your own tent, groping through your gear bag for relief, realizing you've miscalculated, your generosity towards fellow group members has resulted in the last bottle being almost empty, with two days to go! Thank God, you had the foresight to keep a bottle stashed, only *you* know where it's hidden—the problem now, *you* have to find it!

Manly meals of succulent filets grilled over an open fire, are no longer the milieu, now a cellophane sack of premixed pasta is your reward. No lavatory facilities are a given. The obvious aside, five days without a shower, the ecology disallowing soap when washing in the river or even handy wipes, all of which, no amount of *Eau de This or*

That can conceal. Mother Nature comes into play, when everyone smells badly, nobody notices.

The "natural" hot springs of old are now fed by concealed pipes and temperature gauges, nudity is no longer tolerated, that applies to the river too—young otters may be watching.

Campers have a canvas-rubber-like weatherproof bag for gear, all your needs must be contained in this punching bag facsimile. When full, it stands almost four feet high, four feet in circumference, weighing up to sixty pounds, seventy in my case, bottles being heavier than T-shirts and underwear. Shorts don't seem to be an issue, most wear the same pair the entire trip.

You're told, if packed with organized efficiency, you reach in, pull what article[s] you need without having to unpack the whole load. Regrettably, for many unskilled in survival school procedure, a good part of any trip is spent foraging through ninety-eight percent of the contents to find a tube of insect repellent or a dirty book.

The element of danger on these treks shouldn't be entirely ignored, there are moments of stress. The author prefers not knowing it at the time, then having it brought to his attention after the fact. Several months after undergoing a second angioplasty he was rehabilitating down the Columbia River Gorge, when our three zodiacs hit the biggest, steepest, and meanest set of rapids I ever encountered. The first two went over the falls on one side of a mammoth cluster of boulders, but the current forced the third, carrying most of the heavy supplies and the author, to divert to the channel on the other side. Plunging vertically down the falls it seemed we would flip over completely into the swirling rapids below with our gear boat landing on top of us, the author clinging and thinking, "No way, these people know what they're doing, it's all part of the adventure." I wasn't badly-shaken until the head of our group, riding in another zodiac, informed us, our inadvertent detour down the wrong channel, almost cost us our lives! Once again, Shakespeare summed it up, *"The best laid plans of mice and men oft' times go astray."*

A Noble Man's Failing

Although Fred Peabody didn't pull himself up the corporate ladder by his bootstraps, he was by no means along for the ride. He functioned effectively and successfully enough to make 1928 a significant year for his young wife, in a positive sense. Gladys' hopes materialized when he transferred to the company's main office and relocating to a new home at 1035 Fifth Avenue, New York, New York. The tenth floor, ten room apartment, located at the corner of 85th and Fifth Avenue, a block north of the Metropolitan Museum, had a spectacular view overlooking Central Park. 1035 Fifth Ave. would be Gladys Peabody's primary residence for the next twenty years—Fred Peabody's tenure was appreciably less.

In the twenties, through the late forties, New York City was an even a more wondrous place than it is today, but without the overcrowded, congested, and slovenly conditions. A large percentage of the residents spoke English back then, though it was the mecca of an evolving cultural socioeconomic era.

The stock market crash in October of 1929, and the subsequent depression, had a minimal effect on the Peabodys. Fred was a salaried executive of a company which had little difficulty riding out the lean years. It remained a glamorous era, formal events meant white-tie and tails, black-tie was acceptable for dinner parties, restaurants, and nightclubs. Prohibition was a farce; Fred knew every speakeasy from Harlem to the Battery, a priority patron at every gin-mill from East River Drive to the Westside Highway.

The marriage was still in working order, when they met another couple they immediately connected with, becoming a social foursome. The wife's given name was *Anna*, and her last name was that of her husband—naturally. In a whirl of activity and parties, and not paying too much attention to biographical details, it was weeks before the Peabody's realized, Anna's maiden name was Roosevelt, or that her father, Franklin Delano Roosevelt, who would be the next President of the United States, serving longer than any in history.

Gladys said years later—after her political animosity ripened, and when he'd been in office a few years—"Anna was such a darling. I still can't believe that man was her father!" However, Gladys masked any monarchist leanings long enough to attend his first inauguration in January of 1933, as a guest of his daughter. Hidden away is a grainy 16 millimeter clip Gladys filmed from a second floor window of the White House of the incoming President-elect, FDR, and out-going President, Herbert Hoover, in top hats, leaving for the inaugural ceremony at the capitol building in an *open car,* today that seems inconceivable! Later, Gladys would hiss FDR when he appeared in newsreels.

By 1931, on the home front, the honeymoon was well over. Fred's affinity for alcohol was no secret; he was an upfront steady drinker long before his second marriage. By contemporary standards in that time, he was in the mainstream.

To Fred's peers, water was a thirst quencher, but only as a last resort; its primary function was as a mixer, or for bathing—not a labeled entity unto itself.

Pre-dinner cocktails were the "hard stuff," wine was served with dinner, *rarely* before. Half a century ago a fellow ordering water, *lemon peel, no ice*, might be looked on with suspicion in the men's locker room.

Fred got silly at times, tipping hat-check girls fifty dollars, wearing funny hats, but for the most part, he was a gentleman accustomed to holding his liquor. A steady drinker's subtle progression to dissolute alcoholic, is harder to detect, a noble man's failing, becomes the failure of a noble man.

A year later it was official, he moved out of the apartment, an arrangement which was satisfactory for a time. Gladys didn't file for a Nevada divorce until the end of 1934, then, after spending the compulsory six week residency in Reno, the divorce was granted, on grounds of mental cruelty, in 1935. Legally, the Peabody marriage lasted seven years—the actual *marriage* lasted only five.

Ironically, Gertie Widener [Peabody] and Gladys became good friends over the years, even house-guesting at one another's homes. I asked Mother, if the two ex-wives compared notes. "We never really discussed Fred," was all she had to say.

This attitude manifested itself in non-verbal ways while going through scrapbooks covering their married years. The dozens of photos and news items were about *Gladys Peabody* and/or *Mrs. Frederick Peabody,* rarely a word, and never a picture of *Mr. Peabody.* As of this printing, not a single picture of them together exists that I could find. There *were* many, I'd seen them, but not one remained in her personal effects. Her photo collection was comprised of drawers filled with unorganized stacks tossed in at random, without order or much interest. The few involving Fred had vanished.

I would come to understand Fred Peabody's weakness, harder to understand, was Gladys' unwillingness or inability to lend a more supportive hand, to at least reflect on him in a more compassionate way, in light of the number of men in her own family, before, and long after their marriage, who shared his failing to various degrees.

In spite of his innumerable flaws, imperfections, addictions, knowing we had no biological ties, and Gladys' negativity, I wish I might have spent a few hours with Fred, sharing a bottle of Scotch during the good times, talking of *"ships and shoes and sealing wax, of cabbages and kings."* I'm not sure why, but in interpreting subtext, at times, when Gladys spoke ill of him, a tinge of fondness crept into her voice.

Fifty years later, lying in bed in the early stages of dementia, she grasped my hand, murmuring, "Where have you been, Fred?"

Chapter 4

PLACES TO GO, PEOPLE TO MEET

Following the divorce, Gladys sublet the New York apartment and further expanded her geographical horizons. Figuratively, she'd been "single" for quite a while before becoming a divorcee.

Will Rogers and his wife, prevailed on her to chaperone their daughter, on her first trip to Europe. Gladys foresaw no difficulty with Mary Rogers, the daughter of the wholesome folk hero, the embodiment of all that's good in America. Mr. Rogers claimed, he'd *"Never met a man he didn't like,"*—unfortunately, that applied to his daughter as well! Unbeknownst to Gladys, her ward intended the trip as an exercise in liberation, away from what must have been a very repressed existence as the daughter of a living icon. Mary was hell-bent on making up for lost time. Gladys first *smelled the coffee* en route to Europe on a Cunard liner. Returning to their cabin late one morning, she found the steward making Mary's bed—with Mary in it!

Compassion prevailed, after they arrived, Gladys took her ward to a dinner party given by an Earl and Countess at their country estate outside of London. Story has it, Mary took one look at his Lord and Ladyship's son, a lusty strapping public school boy in his teens and decided to forego strawberries and *crème double* for dessert, in lieu of the young peer. He graciously took her on a tour of the grounds, an hour later, anxiety having built to a fever pitch in the drawing room, Mary and the heir rejoined the others. The Earl admonished his disheveled son, "Good God, boy, it normally takes twenty minutes!"

Some of the lady guests gave the Earl's wife a sympathetic nod, where upon the Countess noticed the back of Mary's dress, gently suggesting, "My dear, before you sit, do let's brush those leaves and twigs off your lovely dress."

By their second week abroad, Gladys cabled the senior Rogers, "She could no longer take responsibly for their daughter's behavior." Mary Rogers' future headline-making lifestyle would more than substantiate Gladys' position.

**

During the Thirties, Gladys made frequent Atlantic crossings, establishing lifelong friendships in Europe. She rented a mews house in London off Farm Street and began collecting 18th Century English furniture. Her affinity for that period wasn't solely based on aesthetics, there was a practical side. 18th Century English, and *Early-American* [English, made in America] furniture works effectively with other styles and periods, as well as in contemporary surroundings.

She attended two Wagner Festivals in Bayreuth, Germany, where the *"Der Ring"* was performed in its entirety, beginning at five in the afternoon, a dinner break, finally, ending after midnight. Gladys said it was such a glorious experience, the audience would have sat through it a second time if given the opportunity. I don't know if she actually polled the audience on that—especially those smart young S.S. Officers in their snazzy black uniforms that *stood* in the aisles at every fifth row throughout the entire evening. It would be gratifying to think they concluded their military careers on the Russian front.

In any event, she got a good look at Adolf Hitler, above in the center box. She couldn't image how, "such a common-looking odious little man" could gain so much support. "He was the type you wouldn't even hire as a butler," she recalled.

Gladys dined in Rome with Ambassador Joseph M. Davies, author of *"Mission to Moscow"* Having just returned from Germany, where she hadn't been able to sleep due to the constant noise made by mechanized army units on cobbled streets all though the night. She asked the influential diplomat what precautions were being taken in light of Germany's military buildup. The Ambassador gently suggested she not worry her pretty head, patiently explaining why a country the size of Germany, with its population, its dire internal economic problems, still in recovery from the last war, couldn't possibly pose a serious threat—this, in the spring of 1937.

***

On lighter note, a favorite Gladys incident several years later, involved another U.S. Ambassador named Joseph. While dining at Marjorie Merriweather Post Hutton's Palm Beach home, Mar-a-Lago, Gladys was seated next to Joseph Kennedy, just relieved of his ambassadorial duties to the Court of St. James for his pro-Nazi leanings.

What occurred was confirmed by Mrs. Frances Heinz Diehl, seated on the other side of Kennedy. During the meal his hand wandered under the table and on to Gladys' knee. The hand was discreetly returned to its rightful place, only to return again and was firmly removed again. The patriarch's tenacity went unabated, minutes later his hand again trespassed, this time the attractive lady leaned over to him, the former bootlegger with salacious intentions tilted an ear in her direction, into which she whispered, "Mister Ambassador, I don't fuck Irish."

With No Apologies

An aura of mystery surrounded Gladys' last prewar visit abroad. Based on incremental bits and pieces she wistfully alluded to, I had the distinct impression she wanted to tell me something—but didn't want to talk about it. She was well-on in years when she finally decided to get it off her chest, her way. Something about "the handsomest thing she'd ever seen."

I took the bait. "Who, Mom?"

"Not important. Long ago and far away." Her sigh exaggerated.

"*Who* was long ago and far away? Anyone I knew?" I asked.

"No," Gladys assured me, then, a dramatic pause, "Ironically."

This would be a cliff-hanger!

I was able to extract the subject in question was a Scotsman she *encountered* aboard ship.

"Encountered. Is that like bumped into? Played shuffleboard with? Did you ever see him again?"

"Oh, God, yes."

"And, did he have a name?"

"Douglas."

"First or last?"

"First, his other names were more complicated."

Was I too dumb to absorb a hyphenate I asked?

"It wasn't that," she explained, "There was more involved."

Aha! Rank and title? Half right, I learned his father was a Viscount—that's somewhere between an Earl and a Duke—and that his family had an estate outside of Edinburgh with gardens, lots of dogs, horses, and sheep grazing in meadows. There was a big pond filled with ducks and swans."

It sounded like a John Constable painting.

"How long did you stay in Edinburgh?" I hadn't meant to sound peevish.

She weighed her answer, "For the weekend."

I knew a little about long European weekends!

She continued with a defiant nonchalance, "on my first visit."

Least I get the wrong impression, mother emphasized their 'friendship,' her status as *house guest,* and that Douglas was a gentleman.

"Is that a euphemism for gay or asexual?"

"No dear, nothing could be farther from the truth," she smiled, without a hint of subtext.

"So, it wasn't all leisurely strolls in an idyllic setting, reading Wordsworth?" I surmised in an accusatory tone.

Gladys down-shifted, "Not that it's really any of your business, but try to understand, it wasn't a sordid clandestine liaison. There was no reason to hide the relationship."

"This happened before the war?"

"War clouds were on the horizon."

"How long before the war?"

"David, are you interrogating me?"

"No, I'm *responding.*"

She gave me a clinical once-over, "You remind me a little of Douglas. He was better looking, had more charm, less flawed—but when you're nice, there are similarities."

I wanted to know, "Was there a happy ending?"

"In those circumstances, there are no happy endings, just endings." A haunting ambiguity.

My cynicism reached an apex when I proffered, "Now, let me guess, Douglas was shot down during the Battle of Britain or killed on the beaches at Normandy?"

Rising above my cheaper-than-cheap shot, Gladys replied, "He didn't get that far. Two months after I returned home, his father cabled me, he'd been killed in a bombing of an R.A.F. base, while in flight training."

Mother evaded further queries for whatever reasons. Her motive for finally sharing this episode so candidly, might not be as obvious, or obscure, as it appears. A news clipping has her back in New York the first week in February of 1938. How long before that she returned is unknown, another missing piece of a puzzle the author chose not to solve.

Name Drops Keep Falling on My Head

Officially a New York resident, Gladys Quarre Peabody was drifting West by the late 30s. Los Angeles has been depicted by some as a pop mecca, lacking in cultural tradition. Orson Welles described it as, "A hundred suburbs looking for a city." Not so detracting as the majority of Welles' significant work was directly connected to Hollywood, where he settled in his final years.

An era beginning in the 1920s, flourishing through the 1950s, Los Angeles played host to the founders and creative forces of an American cultural phenomenon, motion pictures; but also included leaders of industry, pioneers in technology, and acclaimed international figures in the world of literature and art. These cultural icons lived and worked for substantial periods in Los Angeles, many with permanent homes, and some died there.

People don't make an issue of living in Los Angeles—they just do. Where others *do* make a point of *not* living there, especially expatriates in the movie business.

Weather, scenic variety, movies, and World War II were visceral causes for the city's continuous boom, but a plethora of intangibles enter into the equation as well.

In the final analysis, in spite of earthquakes, fires, floods, mudslides, racial riots, gang warfare, runaway illegal migration, its status as the front-runner in mindless trends, air pollution, jammed freeways, beaches you don't dare swim, Los Angeles has that indefinable *"it,"* which makes it about the most exciting and agreeable place on earth to live, if not to visit.

The City of Los Angeles suffers the slings and arrows of scornful resentment, accepting it with a tolerant unflappability. The City of Angels doesn't retaliate or try to compete, it simply doesn't have to. If the second biggest city in America isn't gung-ho enough to have a football team, it isn't going to worry about ridicule. Some Angelinos, including the author, encourage and promulgate the negativity directed at our home town, in the sincere hope it will discourage others from coming here.

Los Angeles isn't a city so much, as a state of mind, which is why in 1937, Gladys Quarre Peabody decided on a change of venue, opting to give her native state another try, but this time, primarily the southern part.

The next half decade is best depicted in a collage of black and white photographs now hanging in my pub. A sleek, slender, and extraordinarily beautiful young divorcee in a simple unadorned black or white evening gown, more than holding her own, could be found seated between Hedy Lamarr and Marlene Dietrich, or surrounded by Douglas Fairbanks, Senior and Junior, Artur Rubinstein, Leslie Howard, Basil and Ouida Rathbone at a dinner given by the Rathbones. Other times, Gladys would be flanked by Leo McCarey, Edward G. Robinson, and Charles Boyer, indulging in a political confrontation with Charles Chaplin, while a bemused Errol Flynn and an attentive Erich Maria Remarque were in the background. On a sofa again at the Rathbones, this time with Bette Davis and the legendary Dorothy DiFrasso, looking daggers at the beauty seated between them, then girl-talk with Olivia de Havilland.

There were other functions in the early forties with Ronald Colman, Greer Garson, Brian Aherne, and then-wife, Joan Fontaine, supporting the British War Relief Fund.

Weekends hosted William Randolph Hearst at his castle-ranch in San Simeon. Pictures taken at a costume party there with Mr. Hearst, Marion Davies, Atwater Kent, Dolly Green, whose father, Burton Green, founded Beverly Hills. Norma Shearer, George Raft, a young aspiring cowboy singer-actor, Roy Rogers and a man named William [Billy] Wessel appears in a clown outfit—more about him later.

Louella Parsons, in a column March of '39 covering the Turf Club Ball, listed a dozen glamorous movie stars and celebrities present, ending the article, *"The prettiest woman at the Turf Club was Mrs. Gladys Peabody, who should be in pictures. That's all for today, see you tomorrow."*

When I asked Mother what she thought of Louella's article, she replied, "I don't know about *prettiest*. We weren't at the county fair."

"Nevertheless, I bet it got you on a few more guest lists."

"And scratched off a few," she shot back.

Gladys, meantime, far from scratched San Francisco off her list. Now as a *hometown-girl-made-very-good,* her carefully timed visits became mini-events in the social pages. One edition in March of 1939 devoted an entire page to the *"Outstanding white-tie supper dance Gladys Quarre Peabody hosted in honor of the Basil Rathbones in the Room of the Dons at the Mark Hopkins Hotel. The 100 guests agreed that the party was the high spot of the season,"* wrote society columnist, Lady Teazle. Another noted, *"The grandees who look down from the walls of the Room of the Dons have never seen a more colorful and distinguished gathering than that which greeted their painted eyes."*—striking a familial cord for Gladys.

Guest Ina Claire wore, *"…emeralds as large as pullet's eggs."* Mrs. Pierpont Morgan Hamilton and Muriel Vanderbilt Phipps were also described in very favorable terms, as were several other guests, among them, the paper's publisher and his wife, William Randolph and Millicent Hearst.

***

If She Had It to Do Again

As a new decade approached, it was known by many, Charles Dana, founder and head of *Dana Corporation*, was very much in love with Gladys Peabody, making no effort to conceal it. Dana was a cut above most of the men in Gladys' life, or most lives. Sinclair Lewis could have had Charlie Dana in mind when he wrote his novels, *"Dodsworth"* and its sequel, *"World So Round."* Dana's similarity to *Sam Dodsworth, the leading character,* was striking. Both men's characters were classic Americana, imbued with the virtues, ethics and simplistic philosophy, which societies are founded on. The kind of self-made men of integrity you want to see as president, but would never stand a chance of being elected. Men of Dana's genre make many uneasy; we're more comfortable with those we can easily identify.

Twenty-plus years after-the-fact, knowing Mother's investment in Dana Corporation was responsible for a substantial section of the large roof over our heads, I asked her why she hadn't accepted his proposal[s] of marriage. A question not wholly based on his wealth, or rustic good-looks, but as a person. She seemed uncertain how to answer, something to the effect of his being, "A diamond in the rough, needing polishing," and something about peanut butter on his necktie.

"Regularly?"

"No, not regularly," she conceded.

"Mom, are you telling me you didn't marry Charlie Dana because he had some peanut butter on his tie *once?*"

"Well, if you must know, I wasn't in love with him."

Biting my tongue, "That might be a valid reason for some women, but, from you? You really should have married him."

"No, I did the right thing," adding with disarming candor, "Charlie deserved better."

"I'm not sure that kind of objectivity becomes you, Mama."

"Which is why I rarely bother with it."

Charlie Dana remained Gladys' champion indirectly, if he couldn't give her marital security he'd help her achieve substantially more financial independence by giving her stock in his company as a parting gift, advising her to buy as many shares for herself as she could afford. She did just that, in the ensuing years the stock in Dana Corporation doubled, then tripled, split, doubled again, split, and just kept rising. Her barely five digit investment in 1940, accrued into well over seven digits by 1980.

I believe a deep-seated anxiety lay at the core of her decision, with the realization, becoming "Mrs. Charles Dana," meant a real marriage in the full conventional sense, not a nuptial arrangement. No separate bedrooms, they would attend social functions as *a couple*, travel *together—* not as two individuals sharing a roof. In short, the prospect of being a traditional wife to a man like Dana, simply overwhelmed her. Consciously or unconsciously, she reacted accordingly—to her credit, she demonstrated her love by not marrying him.

Gladys faced the same dilemma with other men at the top of their profession. Being a great admirer of the late conductor-arranger, Nelson Riddle, I was astounded at lunch one day when he confided, "I was crazy about your mother, and I'd have married her in a second, if she'd have had me."

"But then, I wouldn't be around," my jocular response.

"Don't flatter yourself, David, you're not *that* young, you were already around at the time," Nelson informed me.

Although Gladys still voted in New York, she closed out the 1930s by buying a second home in a Los Angeles suburb. This time there was a specific reason Gladys chose a more bucolic atmosphere.

~~ PART TWO ~~

Chapter 5

AND BABY MAKES TWO

The author was born; *Robin Howard Peabody* at 6 p.m., on September 25, 1938, at Mercy Hospital in San Diego, California. Not yet familiar with the ways of the world, he had the innate good taste not to screech onto the scene at a god-awful, pre-dawn hour, opting to make his first entrance during cocktail hour. In years to come, this would serve as a glib rationale, as well as prophetic.

***

The first home of my memory was in 1940 at 301 North Cliffwood Avenue in Brentwood, a not-too-shabby suburb in West Los Angeles. The spacious yet cozy one-story house sat on a full acre, half of which was an avocado and apricot orchard, Southern California at its unpretentious best. Mother furnished, draped, and carpeted it perfectly, all from Sears Roebuck—in sharp contrast to 1035 Fifth Avenue.

She further expanded her family with three cocker spaniels—father Beau, mother Gerry, and son Dadun—the latter, my crib-mate, along with a teddy bear named Dindy. Three score and five years later, Dindy remains tucked away in his box bed in a corner of my closet.

This fondness for creatures great and small initially included sharing the dog's food, along with live snails off the garden wall, and a sweet-tooth occasionally satisfied with a taste of sweet green liquid from a jar of ant-poison. These dietary supplements were not out of neglect, he also received three normal meals a day.

Perhaps I should qualify my love of furry and feathered creatures, some a helluva lot less than others. Nocturnal hours were laced with vivid nightmares of peacocks! Mother passed along many helpful and precautionary bits of information, none more emphatically than her conviction that those non-flying, screeching, narcissistic birds were inherently evil birds, and bring bad luck. If that seems out of the Dark Ages, watch a past-middle-aged man freak out at the sound of a peacock wailing or at the sight of its garish tail feathers fanned out! I loathe the way they sound and strut about, looking and behaving like ornithological drag queens. They're not an endangered species, but it would be a step in the right direction, short of extinction.

The first indication of a less than idyllic world occurred on an early December morning, while peddling a little red fire engine around the patio. Mother and my nanny, *Bingie*, a woman worthy of beatification, came rushing out of the house to tell me people from a country I knew nothing about bombed some place I'd never heard of on a Pacific Island belonging to us. The proximity alarmed me as my only frame of reference was a trip to Catalina Island.

My geographical knowledge of Pacific Islands improved dramatically over the next four years, via the print media, radio and newsreels; Hawaii, Japan, the Philippines, Guadalcanal, Midway, Tarawa, Okinawa and Iwo Jima became household words.

Our generation's familiarity with the carnage wrought by war, had an advantage over future generations; morale, clearly defined objectives, and the certainty we *were* the good guys, doing the right thing. It was black and white, no shades of gray.

Man's inability to learn from history, the repetitious cycle of lessons taught, and then ignored, will continue to prevail. An interesting perspective was expressed on the issue of war and peace at a seminar I was privileged to attend at Columbia conducted by Colonel Alexander Kerensky. The interim leader of Russia after the overthrow of the czar and the communist takeover eighteen months later, Kerensky explained to the assembled audience, "Wars don't interrupt the peace—peace is only a period *between* wars. War will exist as long as two men walk the earth Gladys advised her son, "The important thing is to be on the right side. At least if you die, it will be for something."

Do Dogs Go to Heaven?

An inkling of mortality came another morning in Brentwood. A beautiful young woman, in tears, stood at our front door holding Beau's lifeless body. The father spaniel, having gotten out of the yard, ran in front of her car. Her bringing him to us, his blood on her clothing made a profound impression on mother and me. The young lady was a rising star at Twentieth Century Fox named Linda Darnell. A far greater loss occurred years later when she perished in an apartment fire in Chicago.

Beau's death left his mate Gerry and son Dadun. The household now became a pair of mothers and sons. Over the ensuing forty years Gladys raised, loved, and eventually buried over a dozen dogs. Many were born at home, spending their entire lives with her. All were laid to rest on her various properties, in some instances, on the same place they had been conceived. A small ceremony, flowers and some form of marker, a grave stone, bush, plant or a tree were placed to indicate their final resting place. The author continued the tradition. His present home of twenty years is the burial site of seven dogs and two cats.

As a youngster, I confessed guilt that the loss of a dog often affected me more than the passing of friend or relative. "That's perfectly natural." Mother explained. "Dogs don't complain. They're never critical." She personalized her thoughts. "Dogs keep their opinions to themselves, they don't call at odd hours, ask for money, forget to flush, and they're rarely boring. How many people can you say that about?"

I would add, "They don't fret when you forget their birthday. On the other hand, they do expect you to prepare their meals and open doors for them."

"When dogs die, do they go to heaven?" I asked.

"They must. It wouldn't be heaven without them."

Her answer made perfect sense. Even most agnostic dog-lovers tell their children that if the question comes up.

A friend thought Golden Retrievers were overrated.

"Why?" I asked.

"They're terrible bed-hoggers," he explained.

Having shared my bed with six of them over the years, all I could say was, "Amen to that."

***

Prelude in C Sharp Minor

Gladys was hosting a small party at the house, when her four year old son crept out his room undetected to watch the guests dining. I was familiar with most of those present, Count Maximilian de Henckel-Donnesmarck, a close friend and oft-time escort of my Mother's until his death in the early seventies and his sister, the Baroness Bina de Rothschild, a gifted oil painter and the most aristocratic woman imaginable. [Director George Cukor agreed. And though not an actress, he cast her as the queen in the film version of *My Fair Lady.*] Maximilian and Bina's family were premiere examples of European Aristocracy. The Nazi's exiled them from Germany rather than imprison them because the Third Reich feared repercussions, as the family was considered sacrosanct.

I didn't recognize the strange elderly man seated on my Mother's right. The stranger spotted this four-year-old maneuvering for a closer look, and my mother turned with that admonishing resigned look parents get when their precious offspring unexpectedly appear after *beddy-bye* time. I was waved in, introduced to the mystery man, a composer. Sensing a little kid's uncertainty, the man explained, in a heavy accent, "I write music." When I asked, "Do you write songs?" he smiled, without condescension. "Not yet." As I was about to be whisked away, the man extended his hand, holding mine for an extra moment, and I sensed someone special.

Tucking me into bed for the second time, Mom told me, "You've been touched by greatness," hoping it might rub off. "In years to come, Robin, you'll hear a piece of beautiful music, knowing the hand that wrote it held yours."

Six decades later, I feel a tingling sensation on hearing Sergei Rachmaninoff's, Second *Piano Concerto* or *Prelude in C Sharp Minor.*

My first time in Carnegie Hall was to hear Vladimir Horowitz play, the not as frequently performed, *Rachmaninoff's First Piano Concerto*, with Leonard Bernstein conducting the New York Philharmonic. The performance left the audience in tears of euphoria. After the pianist and orchestra struck the last note, there was no applause, only a moment of dead silence—then a thundering human explosion, followed by a ten minute standing ovation. The erupting affirmation would not allow Horowitz, Bernstein, or the orchestra to leave the stage.

I was puzzled by that momentary silence, before the reaction. Mother observed, "When an audience is in awe, it takes a moment to sink in. Meaning, it was as good as you thought it was."

Pretty Rich Kids Who Kiss a Lot

Since the 1940s, Brentwood has continued as a celebrity enclave, split in half by Sunset Boulevard as it winds its way to the ocean. It gained popularity as an ideal blend of urban and rural living, its residents rustically centralized, the feeling of country in a cosmopolitan atmosphere, with the virtues of both with the vices of neither.

Famous parents in the area supplied a plethora of indulged, beautiful little playmates for Robin Peabody. Joan Crawford's brood, Lloyd Nolan's kids, Allen Jones and Irene Hervey's son, Jack Jones, who in the '70s became more famous than his dad. Another Robin, son of [Gilbert] Adrian, the premier MGM dress designer and his wife, the first "Best Actress" Oscar winner, Janet Gaynor; Mary Lee and Doug Fairbanks, Jr.'s three daughters were regulars. A few years later another junior beauty joined us, Frances and Edgar Bergen's daughter, Candice.

Other junior smart-set members were imported from Bel Air and Beverly Hills, like Basil and Ouida Rathbone's daughter, Cynthia, Tony and Gil Smart, whose father, Richard Smart owned the Parker Ranch on the big island of Hawaii, the largest privately owned ranch in the world.

These gatherings were under the tight control of nannies and governesses to make certain the expensive kiddie clothing didn't get too smudged and knee scratches kept to a minimum.

These parental surrogates were put to the test each spring when Easter Egg Hunts had to be organized and meticulously pre-planned to insure everyone found their fair share. A dozen greedy aggressive kids searching for three dozen colored eggs can turn into the Oklahoma Land Rush, creating lifelong animosities, potential tyrants, and political leanings.

Gladys theorized, the reason for "Cadillac commies," "Lincoln liberals," and "Rolls-Royce radicals," in the entertainment industry, were a direct result of childhood trauma caused by kids seeing others with Easter baskets full of eggs, when they came up empty!

Less-scrupulous nannies brought secret stashes of extra eggs, covertly slipping them into their charge's basket if things weren't going well during the hunt. This unethical approach is intensified in adulthood, when moguls revert back to childhood, searching manicured grounds for Easter booty. God help the rising actor, director, or writer ending the hunt with a fuller basket than the studio head! Winning can impede success, but to see a career sabotaged over a few lousy hardboiled eggs dipped in dye?

Getting There was Half the Fun

Throughout most of the 1940s, Gladys Peabody & son were bicoastal, going from the Brentwood house to the New York apartment. By age ten, I'd made eight transcontinental round trips by train and two by car. Chronologically reconstructing events through photographs, the first journey east was in 1942. There was [is] no direct rail service between East and West Coasts. Santa Fe Railroad's the *Chief, or Superchief* took you from Los Angeles to Chicago. There, you switched trains to *the Twentieth Century Limited, Commodore Vanderbilt, or Trailblazer* continuing on to New York or the reverse. Commercial air travel wasn't the norm until the fifties. During World War II, armed forces personnel, big shots, the R.A.F. and Luftwaffe, logged most of the air time.

The Chicago train transfer was expedited for Gladys on "through-cars"—those uncoupled from the first train, transported across town, then connected to the other train. Passengers in those cars avoided packing, unpacking and re-packing. The less fortunate passengers transported their luggage across town by any available means.

Let the Amtrak generation be informed, in addition to remaining on the track more consistently, those trains were owned and operated by the private sector. The competition resulted in superior service and more spacious accommo-dations. This was the mode of travel for the rich and famous, as well as us regular folk. Appearance was in vogue back then, the well groomed luminary passengers were accessible to an adorable precocious little brat running helter-skelter from car to car, under the watchful eyes of Pullman porters—a proud fraternity of trained, tireless, and dedicated men in black and white uniforms—a lost breed. The primary reason for this independence was my maternal traveling companion.

Dining cars with tables, linen and silverware, excellent food, conscientious waiters in a civilized restaurant atmosphere, earned the slogan, *"Getting There is Half the Fun."* Progress and economics now offer mobile carts with dry sandwiches, wrapped in labeled cellophane, tasting like they were prepared in the 1940s! Now, *"Getting There is Pure Hell!* Travelers accept the astronomical costs, endless lines, delays, cancellations and cramped "cattle car" atmosphere, taking it in stride as standard procedure.

A Tale in Two Cities

Gladys' ability to adapt to constantly evolving technology—environmental transitions and all matter of people, or give the impression she had—was in many instances, a matter of *adapting*, rather than *adjusting*.

Gladys believed the decline in civilized amenities was attributable to air travel. "Now, everyone can go everywhere," she bemoaned. "Some people are innately superior—being aware of it, but appearing not to be," Mother felt was the key to interacting. She elaborated, "Let people find out for themselves what you are, don't tell them."

"Trying to be 'one of the guys,' when you are not, can backfire if there's an element of condescension."

With all due respect to Thomas Jefferson, Mother insisted, the phrase, "*All men are created equal*" was utter nonsense, misinterpreted and misunderstood. "Nothing is further from the truth," she observed, "Maybe, in the eyes of God, but equality ends there. *Liberty and Justice for all* are ideals, not practical realities."

"We can strive for a more perfect world," I remarked as devil's advocate.

"A perfect world, could you imagine? Would you want a utopian existence without conflict? If everything is hunky-dory, why bother to live? If there's nothing to achieve or aspire to, what's the purpose? Where do you go from there?"

Frankly, I'd never thought that far ahead.

***

With the war raging on two fronts, rationing was in effect. Appliances were scarce, when available; they had to be ordered months in advance, replacing parts became difficult-to-impossible. Meat was limited to special occasions, butter replaced by sacks of colorless oleomargarine; parachutes took priority over ladies stockings, rayon filled in for nylon. The only automobiles rolling off assembly lines from '42 through '45 were destined for military use, civilians had to wait for a new car until '46, maybe '47. Gasoline, rubber, and parts rationing were less of a problem in New York, but more apparent in car-dependent Los Angeles. The 1940 Buick Mother drove throughout the war served us reliably, but required fuel, tires, and occasional parts.

Gladys had planned to buy a Cadillac, before the war, but downgraded to a Buick, so she could give the difference in cost to a close cousin, Helen Young, in temporary financial straits with four children. Mother's generosity was repaid shortly after, Helen's husband, Paul, a construction engineer, came up with the most efficient method of constructing prefabricated housing, which the government badly needed. In so doing, Paul Young's family was assured they'd never have to live in one.

Gladys worked long hours with Ouida Rathbone and Bette Davis at the Hollywood Canteen, where many celebrities hosted armed forces personnel to some R&R. To a young serviceman, returning from a bloody beach in the Pacific, or about to be sent to one, having sandwiches, soda-pop and coffee served by Rita Hayworth, sharing a conversation with Greer Garson, dancing with Betty Grable, or getting a flirtatious smile from Veronica Lake, was a well-deserved elixir.

In a less glamorous, more significant mode, Gladys volunteered to drive army ambulance trucks off Detroit assembly lines to military destinations. Driving big cumbersome military vehicles, designed for discomfort with minimal suspension, inadequate heating and no radio, was a tangible war effort. The driver sat on an unpadded stool with no backrest for days at a time, constantly shifting gears, in all kinds of weather and road conditions—automatic transmissions, power steering, and air conditioning weren't options.

She did get to visit places otherwise undiscovered, military instillations in Winnemucca, Prairie City, and Los Ojos, New Mexico, a stone's throw from fun-town, Tierra Amarilla. Members of the Army Medical Corps sometimes accompanied her on these junkets, as did Max deHenckel on one occasion.

The image of Mrs. Gladys Peabody and Count Maximilian de Henckel-Donnesmarck driving a vehicle resembling a U.P.S. delivery truck, across wastelands and gravely mountain roads, I thank God, I wasn't old enough to accompany them.

***

Gladys rented the Brentwood house to English actress Jill Esmond, Laurence Olivier's first wife, who had appreciably more off-screen charm than her ex-husband. Meantime, Mama saw fit to dispatch me to the Ojai Valley School. Boarding school wasn't an agreeable experience for a highly-strung and spoiled six-year-old. Most of his tenure there is blocked out, except for omnipresent homesickness, despite not having settled in one home long enough to miss it.

One event in April of '45 sticks in my mind. While waiting by the school gate for Mother to pick me up for the weekend, there was a commotion from fellow students and faculty members. Franklin D. Roosevelt, the only president in my lifetime, died in Warm Springs, Georgia. The news blaring on the car radio as we pulled away, Mother commented, "Now the country is run by a failed Missouri haberdasher."

The Brentwood house rented and the New York apartment sublet to the *British Information Service*, an intelligence gathering organization, we and the two spaniels sought shelter at the Beverly Hills Hotel, Bel Air Hotel, and the Huntington in Pasadena. These hotels had three things in common, all top quality, all accepted dogs, and were run or owned by good friends—Hernando Courtwright in Beverly Hills, Evelyn Sharpe in Bel Air, and Steve Royce at the Pasadena location.

Dadun and Gerry were exemplary guests. The only moment of discord occurred at the Huntington, when Dadun took a flying leap at the bellman's backside. With a solid grip on the man's pants, he held on as the tearing process continued down to his ankles. The sight of the terror stricken bellman fleeing down the hotel corridor with Dadun tenaciously dangling from his shredded pants sent Mrs. Peabody into convulsions.

***

By early spring of 1945, the war was rapidly winding down. The New York apartment had William Hale Harkness as a tenant, whose legacy is left in Yale University's Harkness Pavilion. When his sublet expired, Gladys and son were back in the apartment in time to celebrate the end of the war in Europe. We watched the VE Day parade along Fifth Avenue from the apartment with a large group of Mother's friends—all happy *half* the war was over and to have her back in their midst.

When Japan surrendered four months later, the marching bands on VJ Day had a more tempered sound, though equally significant. It came as almost anticlimactic. The war in the Pacific virtually ended several weeks before the actual surrender, with the deployment of the atom bomb over Hiroshima and Nagasaki.

Gladys felt it a shame Harry Truman didn't apply his aggressive decision-making, ending WWII, five years later during the Korean conflict.

Chapter 6

POLITE AWAKENINGS

William Wessel came from a wealthy Danish family in the import-export business. I vaguely recall a rather handsome man with wavy hair, well in his forties, in a gray business suit and brown suede shoes. I wish I remembered Billy Wessel, the man, as clearly as his shoes. Now, there is only a hazy recollection of a man Gladys loved deeply and might have found happiness with, of whom I'm aware—so, this episode in her life I can only piece together. He and brother, Tito, ran the family business. Tito was *hands on*, while Billy, essentially a man of leisure, approached it in a more cavalier fashion.

Over a period of several years, although we never actually traveled together, Billy would appear on either coast shortly after we arrived, or, was there waiting for us *when* we arrived. Billy's omnipresence was taken for granted, everyone seemed to like him, I don't honestly know his reaction to having a kid tagging along, but as I have no scars or psychosis as a result, it must have been okay.

There are more photographs of Billy and Gladys together, than she and her three husbands combined. What I do remember vividly is the day Mother and I saw him off to Europe on a TWA Constellation at La Guardia Airport. It was to be the last time Gladys would see her lover.

A week later, she sat slumped in a chair, holding a cablegram from Tito Wessel, informing her, Billy died during minor surgery in a Paris hospital. I had not seen my mother as truly desolated as she was that day—nor would I ever again.

An afterthought expressed by many, the one we never have the opportunity to find ultimate happiness with, is the one we like to think would have made everything all right. Not having stood the test of time, and ignoring the reality, in certainty, we'll never have the opportunity to find out.

Just When You Thought it was Safe

Mother whisked us off for two wet summers in Southampton, where a red flag was hoisted on the beach when swimming conditions were unsafe. The continuously flapping flag became a part of the landscape. Surviving choppy seas, undertows, and riptides was no guarantee of safe passage—danger awaited an inquisitive seven year old on shore. The little red tag-like flags cylindrically placed in the sand adjacent to the club's beach looked as though the big red flag had indiscriminately self-reproduced. When left on his own recognizance for a few minutes, he immediately went to investigate. Several steps into the patch of beach surrounded by the little flags, he found himself sinking, fun at first, but easily bored, he tried to extricate himself, but the only direction he could move was down. Not able to differentiate sedentary sand from quicksand until he was waist-deep, stark terror time! Rescued by lifeguards with knotted ropes, with half the beach club now in attendance, came another moment of terror as Mother raced to the scene, overcome with joy that her son was alive and furious he'd wandered off. Her chin quivering, she whispered lovingly, "If you ever scare Mommy like that again, you'll be very sorry."

Gladys made it a point not learning to play Bridge, fearing she'd have to play it all day during a typical Southampton summer, while her little trooper gambols through poison oak to pick blueberries and learns the manly art of self-defense from the old boxing pro at the club, who set him straight, "Forget the self-defense crap, you're here to learn how to kick the shit outta 'em."

As neither of us was getting any younger, Mother thought it an ideal time to learn to ride a bicycle. My athletic ineptitude failed me; I mastered the two-wheelers in a matter of hours. Three mornings after that, the instructor was still walking down country lanes alongside Mother holding the handle bar. He instructed her repeatedly, not to *think* so much about balance, let it become second nature. I quietly suggested to him, if he'd let go of the handle bar she'd have to gain her own balance. Wanting to keep his job he demurred, so, I volunteered to do the dirty work.

I guided Mother until we reached a patch of drizzle-softened foliage, unaware it was camouflaging a ditch, I gently let go of the handlebar. Mother plunged directly into the ditch. The panicked instructor and I, rushed to her side.

"You were just being a naughty little boy, weren't you, darling?"

"No, Mom! I wanted you to do it on your own!"

"Lucky for Mommy, we weren't crossing a bridge," she responded.

Redeeming those Hampton summers is a posed black and white photograph of a seven-year-old kid nestled against his Mother, dressed all in white, sitting on a lawn. The picture remains the most haunting of hundreds taken of the author and his Mother.

Hassles on the Hudson

In contrast, Gladys decided to place me in a select boarding school fifty miles north of New York City directly across the Hudson River from the United States Military Academy at West Point—The *Malcolm Gordon School.* The forty male students, grades three through eight were virtually guaranteed entry to Choate, Groton, St. Paul's or Philips-Exeter schools, which in turn meant Harvard, Yale or Princeton. *Au rigueur* were blue blazers with the school crest on the breast pocket, ties with diagonal school colors, gray flannel pants, sweat socks and brown loafers.

The school was housed in an old mansion, a gothic fire trap, squatting on a hill overlooking the Hudson, the view I had to enjoy through the courtesy of classmates, as I was assigned rooms facing the other direction. Classrooms, dormitory, faculty residence, dining and recreational facility were one compact facility, enhanced by rolling green lawns, playing fields, and forested acres. At far side, a rustic hockey rink, its surface contingent on Mother Nature. When temperatures froze, it froze, in steady conditions it was flat and smooth, harsher weather turned it into a bumpy hazardous obstacle course.

Students were divided into two teams, "Hudsons" and "Highlanders," not just for athletic purposes, but academic and behavioral competitiveness around the clock, half the student body pitted against the other half. Californians were anathema at the Gordon school, my allies defended me by pointing out, "Robin can't help where he's from!"

After high tea with the Gordons, Mother concluded, "They have a certain provincial old world charm," wondering if they've ever been west of the Adirondacks. It seemed a good time to ask, "Why do I have to go here?" She suggested I take the attitude, how *fortunate* I was to be there, attending the same school as..., and she named several prominent alumni. I couldn't let that slide by, "I'll bet there are ten times as many prominent people who *didn't* go here."

I knew why I was there. It was a path to the citadels, who prepare the young low-profile heirs to vast fortunes, from old money, the American aristocracy, you rarely hear or read about, bred to live quietly and unobtrusively, secure in the knowledge they will one day play an intricate, behind the scenes, role in the power infrastructure. A role I was ill-equipped for in every sense. The unobtrusively low profile aspect was an insurmountable hurdle. Putting a saddle on a donkey doesn't make him a horse.

On the positive side, ol' man Gordon made history come alive, not because he'd been around for so much of it, but his ability to convey an interest and enthusiasm for the subject which is still with me today. My fascination with the American Civil War prompted Mother to give me the three volumes of *Lee's Lieutenants* by Douglas S. Freeman as a fifteenth birthday present. I read every word of it, in increments, over a two year period.

***

Breaks from Malcolm Gordon became more treasured events when mother introduced me to the Broadway theater during the '46 - '47 season. A diabetic's dream revival of the operetta *The Chocolate Soldier,* frothy and fun; the original production of *Annie Get Your Gun* with Ethel Merman; Lerner and Loewe's first collaboration, *Brigadoon*; and *Finian's Rainbow* with Ella Logan and David Wayne. Radio City Music Hall's Christmas and Easter spectaculars became an annual event, as did the productions at the Roxy Theatre with the Rockettes. Other movie houses had entertainers and/or live bands on stage between screenings; uniformed ushers with flashlights to assist, etc. Theaters were visibly staffed and catered to the customers. Now, with theater complexes, the only people you see are those who take your money at the box office and behind the confection counters.

Chapter 7

DEPENDS ON WHO YOU TALK TO

All events were eclipsed on an autumn afternoon in 1946, when I stood witness to a small private ceremony in a New York City judge's chambers, as Gladys Peabody became, MRS. THEODORE JACKSON KNAPP. I'd only met my new stepfather three or four times prior to the nuptials, nonetheless, I was delighted. Mother, true to form, gave me no inkling of her plans to remarry until the last minute.

I recall Teddy Knapp as vaguely resembling Theodore Roosevelt, only taller. He was referred to as *Teddy*, never *Ted*; conversely, her first husband was *Fred*, never *Freddie*. Gladys' two husbands contrasted physically, and Teddy had no ex-wife, having been a bachelor for over five decades.

The similarities began with the diamond engagement rings both husbands gave her, with the same cut and mounting, although Teddy's was several karats larger. Teddy, also a decade older than his bride, was the fourth of five children by Harry Kearsarge Knapp and Caroline Burr. Two of Teddy's older brothers died at infancy, the third passed away two years before he married Mother. His only living sibling was a younger sister, Caroline Knapp Post. The Knapp forbearers settled in Massachusetts in 1643, over a hundred years before the Bandinis arrived on the opposite coast. The family produced subsequent generations of educators, physicians, bankers, brokers, lawyers, Presbyterian ministers and staunch Republicans.

The Knapps, like the Peabodys, were affluent, socially prominent and for the most part, pillars of the community—at least, so the record would indicate.

Teddy, no slouch in achievement, held a seat on the New York Stock Exchange; served on the Board of Montgomery-Scott, a major Philadelphia investment house; the executive head of the Long Island Hunt Club; and president of Aqueduct Race Track. Not as versatile a sportsman as Fred Peabody, Teddy was ranked the second best man at shotgun-hunting in the nation—first actually—number one was a lady from Kentucky. He didn't have a Rolls-Royce, but he owned the first post-war Fleetwood Cadillac off the assembly line *and* a chauffeur to drive it!

Teddy Knapp was past his child-rearing years, nor had he ever experienced them. Reserved even imperious at times, he wore stiff collars, but never a stuffed shirt.

I was excited to have someone to call *Dad*, for the first time. Teddy was ill-equipped for parenthood but got high marks for sincere effort. I asked if I could take his name, and he seemed genuinely pleased; the timing seemed propitious for another change. Not anticipating a favorable reaction, I worked up enough courage to tell to mother I didn't like the name she'd given me. Robin was a *sissy* name.

"I never liked mine either," Gladys commiserated. Then catching me completely off-guard, she asked, "What do you want to change it to?"

"You mean it is okay?"

"As long as I have veto power," she qualified.

Not thinking it would come to this, I hadn't planned ahead.

"You'll have to live with it the rest of your life," she pointed out. The pressure was on. "I like men's names beginning with a consonant." Meaning, forget about, Athol, Otis, and Ute.

With diminished options and no idea why, I blurted out, "David!"

Mother thought a moment, "All right, from now on it's *David*, but never *Dave*, and *Howard* stays." She never called her son Robin again.

Gladys and Robin Peabody, would henceforth be; Gladys Quarre Knapp and David Howard Knapp.

***

Every other Saturday, Gladys and Teddy drove, or were driven up to the school by Tom Sheffield, Teddy's aide-de-camp, man-for-all seasons, and chauffeur. We'd lunch at the *Bird & Bottle*, the local "'in" place. I did enjoy riding in that big new Cadillac, although it fueled some of my school-mate's animosity. One scion to a lot more money than I'd ever see, thought the car a bit *nouveau riche,* I reminded him, his parents drove a spanking new Lincoln Continental. "Lincolns are subtler than Cadillacs," he countered.

I eagerly awaited summer vacation, family outings, tossing the ball, romping in the sand and getting to know my stepdad. Instead, I was packed off to summer camp at Lake Placid, while he and Mama opted for a belated honeymoon in California.

Rethinking the idea of Theodore J. Knapp, and his eight-year-old stepson, slam-dunking balls in a vacant lot or over a volleyball net was ludicrous, given my intense dislike for both games. Ping-pong or checkers would have been nice though.

***

Godparents, Basil and Ouida Rathbone, sold their house in Bel Air and moved to a magnificent townhouse on East

91st Street, hoping to escape Basil's *Sherlock Holmes* film image. After playing the world-famous character in *fourteen* successful films, Basil's having a professional identity crisis was understandable—although many actors might welcome such a fate.

The first play on his return, *The Heiress,* with Beatrice Straight, was a solid hit, reestablishing his theatrical reputation. Unfortunately, over the next twenty years he was never again involved in a play of that quality, except to replace Raymond Massey in Archibald MacLeish's *"J.B."* On a ironic note, having fled Hollywood to get away from his *Sherlock Holmes* identity, circumstances and finances eventually dictated he co-produce and star in a play about the super sleuth, which ran ten performances.

The lavishness of Ouida and Basil's entertaining, on both coasts, was legendary, and deservedly so. Basil, on and off camera, was magnificent person. A gentleman in the true sense, kind, erudite, extraordinarily conversant, he possessed a wonderfully broad sense of humor, adored animals and the New York Yankees! Ouida was Ouida, spoiled, selfish, extravagant, at times a headache, but rarely a bore. I adored her.

Mother observed, "Ouida should have been born at the beginning of the nineteenth century, not at the end."

Basil's autobiography was disappointing commercially. A bitter reflection, *Hieronymus Bosch* turned author. Mother was a little hurt after all the years of close friendship and diverse experiences to be summarized in one sentence, "I stayed with friends in Huntington Palisades in a house overlooking the sea."

***

Teddy's Christmas present that year was a two foot long motorized submarine from F.A.O. Schwartz. The submersible was functional, with a remote control, a perfect miniature example of advanced post-war ingenuity. After a short submerging test in my bathtub, it was time for a real test run. The Central Park pond was the domain of exquisitely detailed wood-crafted model sailboats, up to four feet in length, gliding gracefully across the pond, sails billowing from masts, as Tom Sheffield and I launched the mechanized marvel. The sub responded lethargically, partially submerging, and heading erratically into deeper water. Suddenly, another vessel under full sail appeared from out of nowhere on a collision course! The sailboat's wooden hull impaled itself on the metal bow of my hapless submarine, the puncture allowed enough water into the hull of the much larger craft to cause it to sink into the pond's murky waters. Only its masts were visible above the surface.

Confused eye-witnesses claimed the sub struck the sailboat amid ship. I maintained the sail boat was underway at a reckless speed, resulting in self-inflicted damage from the bow of my vessel. Without benefit of a formal inquiry, I became the sacrificial goat, paying the irresponsible sailboat owner full restitution. Compounding the injustice, the sub was banned from the pond and its *skipper* told not to hurry back! Subsequent attempts to obtain miniature floating mines for the park pond came to naught.

***

In the early spring '48, Gladys and Teddy missed a Saturday visit. I was told mother had the flu, but would be up the following Saturday. When she came, Mother was with Tom Sheffield at the wheel sans Teddy—"*He was away on business.*" Two weeks later Mrs. Knapp arrived again, but still no Mr. Knapp. There was no hint in mother's behavior, or in Tom Sheffield's, or by the school's faculty, that anything was seriously amiss. When Teddy hadn't appeared by May, I feared they'd had a major spat. I learned the truth several weeks later at the end of the term. Tom picked me up. I was so elated to be out of there, I didn't think too much about mother not coming up, or about Teddy's lengthy absence.

On the drive back to the city, Tom, a super guy, asked me all the appropriate questions about school. After a perfunctory exchange, I sensed something was very wrong. I tried to sound off-handed, "I'm really looking forward to seeing Teddy after all this time." Tom forced an awkward smile and didn't say a word during the rest of the trip into the city. At 1035 Fifth Avenue, the doorman and elevator man greeted me in an overly effusive manner.

While mother welcomed me home with reserved solemnity, I found myself postponing the inevitable by feigning naiveté, looking around the apartment for any remote sign of Teddy—knowing there would be none. Then, sick of the entire pretext, I asked as to his whereabouts in a demanding manner. "What's going on?"

I remember mother's resigned sigh as she sat on a decorative antique regency chair in the entrance hall, the kind you don't normally sit on. "There's been a terrible accident." She didn't have to go on; it was easy to supply the rest.

"Teddy's dead, isn't he." It was rhetorical statement. Mother nodded.

My only emotional reaction was of momentary disappointment, then a detached feeling you have when a relative you barely remember passes away. We were both surprised at my response.

***

Mitigating Factors

I heard the widow's version of what happened at dinner. Two months earlier Teddy had been to a bachelor dinner at the Long Island Hunt Club, where they'd all been drinking and carousing in manly fashion. After dinner Teddy went into another room to clean his shotgun, it went off accidentally, wounding him seriously in the shoulder, where upon he collapsed. Then, according to GQK, by the time the others found him, he had bled to death.

GQK didn't say a thing about rampant rumors regarding the incident, which offered a more plausible theory, those I heard about later. I was offered little choice, but to accept her version of the tragic events, but even at age nine, something didn't wash. The bigger mystery, how did Mother, even with the school's cooperation, manage to keep Teddy's death a secret from me for over two months? His prominence, the circumstances surrounding his death, and the substantial news coverage it generated, made the secret no less than a black miracle.

What actually happened at the Long Island Hunt Club that night, I would try to sort out in future years. Acquiring knowledge of guns rendered the version I'd been told highly improbable. How could an indoor shotgun blast not alert everyone in proximity? How could an expert with that weapon, regardless of how much liquor he consumed, accidentally shoot himself? His shotgun's barrel also served as shell chamber. To clean it, they must be opened; the barrel is then separated from the firing mechanism in the stock, rendering it inoperable.

The "collective panic" theory was an attempt to cover up what? A conspiracy on the part of scores of members, men of stature, and friends of the deceased, didn't make sense. If someone else fired the gun accidentally, or purposely, surely members of a prestigious club wouldn't condone a cover-up of that nature—nor, would there be a reason to. Teddy had to be dead, or near-dead, by the time they reached him, immediately after they heard the shot. The odds against it being an accident are so remote, it has to virtually be ruled out; leaving only one rational conclusion—Teddy took his own life, intentionally.

Gladys' marriage to Teddy Knapp was more of a mutual arrangement, than a marriage in the generally accepted sense. Based on a pragmatic premise, it served both spouses. GQK was additionally fond of his sister, Caroline Post. GQK's account is indirectly substantiated in a published diary, *Family Memories* by Shepherd Knapp, a first cousin and contemporary of Teddy's. The book is a detailed and extensively researched the Knapp family chronicle in which Teddy's name appears once, in the genealogy chart.

Teddy chose a strong woman, one not easily intimidated, malleable, or submissive, perhaps anticipating a confrontation with his relatives after his demise. This doesn't explain why his death occurred so soon after his marriage. A coincidence? Something happened, whether disenchantment, too radical an adjustment after fifty-four years of bachelorhood. An inability to perform the intimate duties expected most husbands, wasn't an issue, certainly not a surprise, that was understood and agreed to pre-nuptially.

Forty years later, I was not unable to find a single photograph of Teddy Knapp among GQK's effects, nor could I recall having seen one in the intervening years. I did come across several snapshots that might supply a piece to the puzzle, taken at the school during visits, between the time Teddy died and my learning about it. There were photos of Mom, I, and Tom Sheffield. Tom's actual physical appearance had eluded me, a vague recollection of a faceless man of indeterminate age in a dark suit, a part of our lives throughout the brief marriage and during the aftermath. The Tom I saw in the photos was anything but innocuous-looking; he was appreciably younger than I remembered, in his late twenties. I was surprised to see how exceptionally handsome he was. Decades later, it seemed to offer a possible subtext in reconstructing that period.

That eighteen month relationship was the basis for my reaping a half century of posthumous benefits. In retrospect, I remain grateful to Teddy Knapp, a man I barely knew. I've never regretted taking his name. Hopefully, it was a bright spot in the murky closing chapters of his life.

Speculation over Teddy's death, the animosity on the part of some of his former colleagues over his widow's role, if any, contributing to the tragedy, created a taut atmospheric undercurrent. Gladys finally decided to give up the lease at 1035 Fifth Avenue. We moved out bag and baggage, loaded up the Cadillac, several moving vans, and then headed back to California. I wouldn't return to New York for six years.

Chapter 8

PAINTING WITH BROAD STROKES

Proceed at Your Own Risk

Uncle Oz and Aunt Kate's eldest son, George Quarre, fresh out of a naval hospital, accompanied us on a leisurely six week motor trip west across the country, stopping at sights of interest en route. Two years earlier, Cousin George, a junior naval officer, was blown off the deck of a destroyer by a Kamikaze plane and awarded the Purple Heart. The after effects of that incident would plague him physically the rest of his life, but not mentally or psychologically. He and his future wife, Betty, raised three fine well-adjusted children. Now seeing them as adults—Carlotta named after her great-grandmother Lottie, and Lisa and Christopher— it's hard to accept, a generation *after* mine beginning to get gray around the temples. I had no gray hair until was well past the age they are now—I attribute that to clean living and *Clairol*.

 With Cousin George riding shotgun, Mama and I zigzagged across the country in record time. We managed the three thousand miles from New York to Los Angeles in just thirty-two days, a week *less* than it took ox-drawn pioneer wagon trains; and we did it all adding only six thousand miles to the odometer!

Niagara Falls, south to Williamsburg, Chattanooga; through Alabama, Mississippi; west to New Orleans; across Texas, north to Mount Rushmore, Yellowstone, Sun Valley, and Crater Lake; with stops in places I don't think really existed.

Driving through the Southern States in the late 1940s, past chain gangs, speed traps, and cafés marked, *"Whites only,"* and rest rooms designated *"Colored Only,"* it still seems incredible that kind of discrimination could have existed in my lifetime. A hit song from a Broadway show *Texas Is the Rear-End of the U.S.A,* resulted in sugar being poured into the gas tank of the big ol' Cadillac with the New York license plates in Big Springs, Texas. It was *proceeding at your own risk.*

In the days before bucket seats, the back seat filled with luggage, I sat in the front seat between Mother and George the entire trip. The two lane highways in the heat of summer with no air conditioning, was made more palatable in knowing thousands of God's tiniest flying creatures selected *our* windshield as their final resting place.

To those who've only seen most of this great country from thirty thousand feet, be aware of the variety of scenic backdrops available over the vast majority of it; flat desolate prairie as far as the eye can see; if barren arid desert is your thing, there's an abundance of that; for those who prefer a more austere setting, parched wastelands are right around the corner.

In areas inaccessible to radio frequencies, we started singing, *"Ninety-nine Bottles of Beer on the Wall",* by the time we crossed South Dakota we were down to nineteen-bottles-of-beer.

***

Within a month after arriving back in California, Gladys Knapp bought a two-story Monterrey colonial house in Pacific Palisades, in a section referred to as Huntington Palisades. The fifteen room house at 14954 Corona del Mar, stood on a cliff overlooking the Pacific Ocean. Several large pine trees framed the view, so she named it, *"Pinecliff."* GQK purchased the house from actor-director Charles Laughton and his wife, Elsa Lanchester, although we lived there twice as long as they did, it would always be referred to as, *"The Charles Laughton house."*

On the beach below, people would invariably point up to the first visible house on the bluff, proclaiming, "That's Charles Laughton's house."

"No, it's not. His was four houses north of there. It is set back, you can't see it from the beach," I'd explain. "Anyway, Charles Laughton doesn't live there anymore." Then the inquisitions began. They'd ask, "How do you know?"

"My Mother bought the house. *We* live there."

"So you live in Charles Laughton's house?"

"Something like that."

***

A week after moving into the Pinecliff, amidst unopened boxes and crates, we celebrated my tenth birthday. While Gladys' friends welcomed her back, she wasted no time in acquiring new ones, reestablishing herself socially. Cobina Wright, Sr. became a welcome figure at our home. Cobina, an energetic columnist with the *Los Angeles Herald Examiner,* knew everyone—except a good dentist. Her dentures never gave her a moment's rest, or anyone else within earshot, but she was a fun and delightful woman.

Another staunch ally was her magnificent cousin, Princess Conchita Sepulveda Pignatelli, a quintessentially elegant grand dame, who happened to be the social columnist for the *Herald-Examiner,* and a dear friend of its owner-publisher, William Randolph Hearst. Princess

Pignatelli's family, the Sepulvedas, paralleled the Bandini–Carrillos, intermarriage had made us all *parientes*. She was a noble and courageous woman, the embodiment of California aristocracy. After Prince Pignatelli departed, she single-handedly raised their daughter, as well as two daughters by her deceased first husband, George Chapman—Little Conchita and Carlota. More about the latter two later on.

Conchita Pignatelli, as a reigning *duena*, was one of the most respected women in the state. Her funeral mass was celebrated by James Cardinal McIntyre, archbishop of Los Angeles. Those who bid her a final goodbye at St. Basil's, filled every pew, the church couldn't have held another soul that day.

Louella Parsons and Hedda Hopper, the two most powerful movie columnists of the Hollywood Fifth Estate, were both good friends of GQK's, both the competitive ladies treated her, and her son, generously in years to come.

The grace and ease with which Gladys Knapp cultivated interesting people from all walks of life, never ceased to amaze. There was never an obvious effort on her part to pursue fascinating people; she just seemed to attract them. She was selectively eclectic in her choices of who she considered worthy of the time and effort. GQK was a snob with values and priorities, more impressed by achievement than ancestry. When someone got uppity about another successful individual's lowly background with, "Did you know his mother took in laundry," Gladys responded, "More power to him."

Gladys never considered others of her gender as competition or potential threats. She valued them as much, if not more, than the men in her life—they seemed to sustain longer. Her longtime friendships with legendary women who achieved the pinnacle in their profession; Mary Pickford, Rosalind Russell, Irene Dunne, Merle Oberon, Corrine Griffith, Dolores Del Rio and yes, Zsa Zsa Gabor. Her steadfast relationship with Renaissance-lady Clare

Boothe Luce, aviatrix Jacqueline Cochran, Gladys' life long ties with women who couldn't be dominated, Doris Stein, Jean Howard [Feldman]; Dolly Green, a surrogate sister; and Barbara Hutton; as well as the remarkable wives; the Begum Khan, Dorothy Hammerstein, Jean MacArthur, Blanche Seaver, and Kay Spreckels Gable; not to mention many less known but equally accomplished ladies who stood testament.

From 1948 to 1952, the not-so-little trooper was in the trenches again, enrolled at Urban Military Academy in Brentwood—resplendent in a gray uniform, eventually, with all the trimmings. I received a solid foundation in military parade basics, making a proficient cadet captain in the final year. It was scholastically innocuous, militarily, and what could have been absorbed in four weeks of boot camp, was stretched over four years. It paid off, to this day I can salute, perform an "about face" or do a "manual of arms" as proficiently as any Marine sergeant—however, an obstacle or endurance course might prove problematic.

GQK's guest book through the late forties, fifties, and into the sixties, reads like a *Who's Who.* Our cliff-dwelling neighbors, Roger Edens, MGM's musical man for all seasons, "Dutch" Kindelberger, head of North American Aviation and an avid admirer of Gladys, who confided to her, "God, I wish I'd met you before my wife," understandable to those who knew Mrs. Kindelberger. I think possibly Mother wishes he had too. Further down the street, a former R.A.F. hero, Tony Bartley, and his wife Deborah Kerr were frequent guests. Deborah, already a major star in British films, was just beginning her American film career at MGM.

The view from Gladys Knapp's terrace overlooking the ocean was often enjoyed by Randolph Scott in Stetson and boots, or a dinner jacket—always a charmer—as were Antonio Moreno, Philip Reed and Nigel 'Willy' Bruce, Basil Rathbone's crime solving partner 'Dr. Watson,' in the

Holmes pictures, regrettably, the two men weren't speaking by then. Couples who dominated film society, Doris and Jules Stein, Mervyn and Kitty Leroy, Mary Pickford and Buddy Rogers, Rouben Mamoulian, King Vidor; then spicing it up further were Tony and Beegle Duquette, unique artists *extraordinaire;* designers Billy Haines, Jimmy Pendleton, Orry-Kelly and Broadway's Norman Bel Geddes.

***

Back at Pinecliff

GQK's musical coterie included, the *Music Man*, Meredith Wilson; Louella Parson's beaux, composer Jimmy McHugh; Ira Gershwin, Burton Lane and Nelson Eddy, with his steady, Gail Sherwood. Gossip had it, Eddy's musical partner, Jeanette MacDonald found him even duller off-camera than on—and that's saying a lot. The classics represented by Artur Rubinstein and his wife, Nella; L.A. Symphony's conductor, Alfred Wallenstein; Isaac Stern, a friend from Mama's San Francisco days; Yehudi Menuhin and diva Dorothy Kirsten [French], all spent hours around Gladys Knapp's dining table.

Living down the road in Santa Monica Canyon, was a show-stealer, Cousin Leo Carrillo, known as *"Mister California."* Effusive and colorful to a point of flamboyance, his carefully cultivated Spanish accent used in public was pure affectation; Leo believed his public expected it, as ninety percent of his life was spent "in character" anyway, so he obliged them. Leo's gaudy '48 wood-paneled Chrysler convertible, a promotional gift from the manufacturer, had cowhide upholstery, horns protruding from the grill and an air horn that could do any horny bull proud. It was *mini-float* in a never-ending parade. When well-paid and motivated, Leo Carrillo was a wonderfully versatile actor. He served as grand marshal in two Rose Parades and was awarded by civic groups, political bodies, and charitable organizations—and a hero's medal for saving three lives aboard a sinking excursion boat on Lake Michigan. Leo's only source of depression was in realizing, his primary legacy would be TV's *Pancho* in *The Cisco Kid.*

***

Mama's social triumphs became more of a feat as she lacked karma with servants. When I suggested she refer to them as "*help*," she responded, "If I need *help*, I'll ask you, dear. Servants I'll hire." GQK believed the nutritional value of food was secondary; its primary function was to be inspected and used as leverage. Sharpening knives took a backseat to nerve-ends in the kitchen. It wasn't a matter of discovering something poorly prepared, it was *knowing* it must be, then, finding it!

True, many servants GQK hired and fired regularly, were not cut from the pre-war Evelyn Waugh school cloth, their dedication and deference had given way to disregard and defiance. A number of them had a propensity for nipping at the cooking sherry. Spirits-induced stimuli was illustrated by one bloodshot-eyed butler sauntering over to his employer and her guests wanting to know, "Hey Ladies, how's life with the idle rich?"

One couple, Willard and Astrid, were a piece of work. It looked like a middle aged *Porky Pig* had teamed up with *Tugboat Annie.* When Willard and Astrid slurred words, with glazed eyes and a pungent breath, it was due to "medication." To add zest to her meals, health-conscious Astrid was prone to use large amounts of *medication* in her cooking. Her brandy bouillon was tantamount to a stiff pre-dinner drink. Willard having consumed several bowls of soup would emerge. His condition further deteriorated when he reappeared giving the impression of serving dinner at sea in rough weather. If a guest took a moment choosing from the serving platter, Willard might lean down, in a loud whisper and say, "Let's not take all night. Ya' know, chop-chop."

Willard and Astrid were dishonorably discharged weeks later.

Another couple, Mama dubbed "the lurkers." Every time you stepped out of a room or turned a corner, you'd see them scurrying off. Their brief tenure ended one morning when GQK heard the front door bell, followed by persistent knocking, when no one answered, she hurried downstairs to find out why. Spotting the couple in the utility room, she demanded to know why they hadn't answered the door, the husband stammered, "Lady, they're cops!" It turned out, the cops were backups for the FBI agents, who dropped by to take our butler and cook into custody, two principal members of a drug ring!

The exceptions to all this were two *housekeeps* from Scotland, Jean Templeman, a former employee of Barbara Hutton's during her marriage to Cary Grant, and Mona McClive, two "ladies of the thistle" who remained in Mother's employ, in various homes, for three decades, as *femmes du chambre,* housekeepers, nannies, cooks *or* confidants. Jean and Mona were pillars of dependability, tolerant and kind to a spoiled loathsome brat from his grammar school days through near-middle age.

Breakfast with Wall Street

I recalled an incident in my pre-teens at the Palisades house that occurred during a period when GQK was walking an emotional tightrope and over-reacted to minor infractions with major responses, the reasons for this I didn't under-stand. I had some classmates over and was told to keep them outdoors. I failed to do so, resulting in a fine porcelain piece being smashed. I was given such hell, I ran upstairs and started packing. GQK appeared at the door, wanting to know what I was doing. I told her I was leaving. "Where was I planning to go," she asked academically. I didn't know, I just wanted to get away.

"Then you'd better pack carefully, you might not be coming back," her voice flat and steady frightened me. I tearfully continued stuffing my suitcase, "If you don't want me back, then you don't want me here now!"

"Be sure you think about it," was all she had to say. Striking back with repressed hurt, I yelled, "I've been thinking about it since I was six, when you put me in boarding school!" She looked at me thoughtfully, "Have you been saving that for a rainy day?" I was choking too much to respond.

"David, look at me. I did what I believed was the right thing at the time."

"Same as when I was seven, eight, nine?" I croaked.

A moment later she had her arms around me, "Sometimes it's hard to know what to do, you'll find out someday."

Was this the same mother who when asked, "What do you regret most *not* having done in your life," thought a moment before replying, "When the British gave India its independence in 1947, I was invited by the Nizam of Hyderabad to the last durbar given for Viceroy Lord Mountbattan."

"Why didn't you go, Mom?"

"I didn't want to leave you."

I was so touched, my chin quivered. Later, it occurred to me, I was in boarding school at that time!

Regardless of mudslides or waves of salt across Pacific Coast Highway below, Gladys Knapp had breakfast in bed. Orange juice, poached eggs, soft, on wheat toast and a cup of cream-laden coffee, with the *Wall Street Journal* and *Financial World,* nourishing the body as well as the coffers. She'd become an authority on the stock market, her advise was taken very seriously by those who profited from it. A conservative investor, primarily in blue chip stocks, which would be locked away in her safety deposit box and "forgotten,"—an *investor*, not a speculator. Brokers were told what to buy, they didn't tell her. "Of course I'm interested in their suggestions, I just don't follow them often." She reasoned, "Stockbrokers make their commissions by buying and selling your stocks. Not a good way to get rich in the long run."

GQK based her investment portfolio on a simple premise. "Look around your house, buy what you use on a regular basis—items being sold everywhere, companies whose products are household names—products you use daily, directly or indirectly. She conceded, "Sometimes these companies have problems, but they're not going to go away. Figure how many people use some product manufactured by *Johnson & Johnson* or *IBM*. The most important hard and fast investment rule is diversification, *never put all your eggs in one basket!*"

To Touch an Idol

In the early fifties, Mother took me to a large reception at the Ambassador Hotel in Los Angeles. Several hundred movers and shakers were chit-chatting over drinks, when abruptly, with no prior announcement the honoree entered and a hush fell over the ballroom. A sense of a presence swept over the crowd.

All eyes focused on a man in a gray suit and his wife, as they made their way through the room, graciously acknowledging the assembled guests. The man who led the rainbow division in World War I, a recipient of the Congressional Medal of Honor; the youngest commandant of West Point and Army Chief of Staff in our history. As the Allied Supreme Commander in the Pacific, he led hundreds of thousands of men to victory in World War II and brilliantly governed the defeated nation. Then, well into his seventies, he again launched a major strategic victory with the Inchon Invasion in a third war. General of the Army, Douglas MacArthur, was a deity to my generation.

The General wasn't as tall as I'd imagined, but he exuded an aura of greatness, which awed every soul present. His wife, Jean, at his side, his aides introduced each person in the long reception line by name. As we approached him, I began to tremble, an aide gave him our names. To a kid barely in his teens, shaking the hand of Douglas MacArthur was to touch the face of God. His eyes looking right into mine, he said, "Mister Knapp, how nice of you to be here." *Mister* Knapp, how nice of *me* to be here? What made it harder, he seemed to mean it! I was so overwhelmed, the words I'd practiced choked in my throat, and wouldn't come out. With an understanding paternalistic smile, he extended his hand, I clasped it for a moment, then moved on. I didn't wash my hand for three days.

GQK had a better handle on the situation, and became a good friend of Jean MacArthur's. Whenever GQK was in New York while the General served as Chairman of the Board of the Remington Rand [Sperry Rand] Corporation, she and Jean would rendezvous at the MacArthur's apartment in the Waldorf Towers, go to dinner and the theater. Their son, Arthur MacArthur, and I became friends in later years. Arthur was extremely intelligent, often delightful, but a seriously neurotic young man. His father's giant shadow overwhelmed him. He allowed his birthright to be a curse.

Hung-over to Hawaii

Dadun and Gerry, our aging spaniels, were joined by an adopted English Setter, *Tica*. Utterly feminine, shy and graceful, she shared our lives for fourteen years. A fourth addition was on the horizon. In 1950, Mother, I, and her first cousin, Jackson Baird [Aunt Ruth's son by her first husband], went to Hawaii for the first time, aboard the Matson liner *Lurlene*, out of San Francisco.

Louis Benoist gave GQK a going-away party at his Almaden Vineyard northeast of the city where the author had his first glass of champagne—his second and third, along with encouraged sips of red and white wine from other guest's glasses, during and after dinner. Boarding the ship to Honolulu the following day was the most hung-over twelve-year-old in recorded history. Having sufficient credentials to speak authoritatively, there is no beverage capable of inflicting more residual punishment than champagne.

Our arrival in Honolulu five days later, was out of a period travelogue. The harbor's clock tower above, dozens of happy young Hawaiians swimming around the ship diving for coins the passengers tossed over the side. On the dock, lovely brown-skinned girls in authentic grass skirts greeted the new arrivals with songs, undulating hips, and fragrant flower leis, which they would drape around your neck with a kiss on each cheek. It wasn't corny then, just welcoming. Anyone surviving a swim in the harbor today, would either be attempting suicide, or a terrorist saboteur, and receiving a lei and a kiss from a stranger means, forget about your wallet.

Five decades ago, the only buildings visible on Waikiki Beach were the *Moana*, the *Halekalani* and the *Royal Hawaiian* Hotels, the latter was GQK's choice.

A year later, Mama, Cousin Jack, and I made our second trip to Hawaii. It was Mother's first commercial flight and my first time in an airplane. The nine and half hour flight on a Pan Am Stratacruiser, departed Los Angeles around 11 p.m., arriving in Honolulu the following morning. The belly under the main deck, served as lounge bar, then converted into a first class berthing compartment. At a cruising speed of 275 mph, you woke up the next morning for an early breakfast, then landed in Honolulu. The problem, having first traveled in that mode, made it all downhill from then on.

Apropos of Nothing

In 1952 Mother broke down and bought a television set, not out of interest in the relatively new media, but because her son was spending all his time at neighbor's houses watching their TVs. The TV cabinet was placed on the large second floor landing between Mother's bedroom and mine. As I wasn't old enough to attend her dinner parties, the TV served as a diversion. I was allowed to greet the guests briefly, then banished to the second floor. A guest one evening was the star of my favorite film of all time, *The Third Man*, Joseph Cotton.

Another night, watching TV in exile, with party voices drifting up from below, a lady guest came trudging up the stairs, informing me, in a husky voice, "Your Mother said I could come up and see the rest of the house—and I want to pee."

"Yes, ma'am. My name is David."

"I know, your Mother told me."

I'm thinking, "Well, the ball's in your court."

"Oh. My name is Greta Garbo."

The lady who knew when to quit while she was still ahead! At the time, I knew the name but had never seen her in a movie—she hadn't made one in over ten years. I lied, telling her how much I liked her pictures.

"Where's the bathroom," she asked, keeping the conversation at a fever pitch. I pointed, she continued on into Mother's room. Miss Garbo returned minutes later, paused, and asked what I was watching on TV? It was a

Western with Roy Rogers and Dale Evans. Never knowing when to leave well enough alone, I indicated Dale Evans on the screen and asked her, "Did you make any Westerns?" Miss Garbo looking at Dale Evans on the tube, muttered, "No, but I'm often confused with her," then went back downstairs.

GQK laughed hard when I told her about the episode. I asked what was so funny, "the Garbo-Evans tie?" "No, the fact Garbo has a sense of humor," she chortled.

That was challenged years later at a dinner at Dolly Green's when Gaylord Hauser reintroduced me to Miss Garbo as "Mrs. Brown" as if I'd just gotten off the bus from East Jesus, Arkansas. I looked at the screen legend a moment deadpanning, "Mrs. Brown, has anyone ever told you, you look like Greta Garbo?" She and Hauser didn't react. At dinner, Miss Garbo, with no inflection or timing, told what must have been the longest, dullest joke in recorded history.

***

Mother and I drove up for a visit up to Uncle Oz and Aunt Kate's ranch in central California's San Benito County. Their spread was near Paicines, which is near Gilroy, a few miles from Hollister.

A no-frills working ranch with orchards of walnut trees and rocky pastures, where they raised sheep. Oz worked from five in the morning until dark, often single-handedly, when sons Charlie or Peter, couldn't be there to help out. The main house was simple, a parlor with a screened porch, kitchen, two bedrooms and one bathroom. The kitchen may have been designed for the couple in Grant Wood's painting, *American Gothic*. Referring to a refrigerator as an "ice box," literally applied in this case.

Gladys thought it a bit too rustic. One morning, watching her brother and sister-in-law chasing some wandering sheep out of the walnut orchard, she wondered aloud,, "Have they gone stark raving mad? The only thing they know about sheep is cooking a leg of lamb—and Kate doesn't do that terribly well either."

Mama was curious about the walnuts, "How do they collect them? Do you suppose they stand under a tree all day with an open bag waiting for one to drop?"

With grasp of horticulture, I suggested, "They probably shake the tree first."

The day of our departure, Mother confronted Uncle Oz with "You simply have to have another bedroom and bathroom." Her brother informed her that they had a big mortgage then and couldn't afford to—well, his sister could. Six months later, Oz and Kate had a *three* bedroom, and *two* bathroom-ranch house with a refrigerator. Years after Oz and Kate passed away, their youngest son, Peter, told a family gathering, "The day they sold the ranch and moved back to San Francisco was the happiest day in mother's life." Unbeknownst to most of us, Aunt Kate quietly loathed the rural life, but she loved her husband enough to stick it out.

***

Back at Pinecliff, Mother and Jean packed a steamer truck of required gear for my summer at Catalina Island Boys Camp [C.I.B.C.] located, oddly enough, on Catalina Island. It wasn't the kind of place they sent underprivileged kids to get them out of the city, none of the campers were on summer scholarships. Located north of the isthmus, the camp was owned and run by "Grumpy" Gus Henderson, a cross between Wallace Beery and Wilfred Brimley. He'd been a coach somewhere, but found his niche in pitching his camp to affluent daddies and mommies, thus getting their tiresome, easily bored kiddies out of the house for most of the Summer without causing much trauma. The old bastard

Henderson pulled it off, C.I.B.C. was a blast. Seven campers to a tent with a councilor, we called ourselves the "Goon Platoon."

Henderson's wife looked like a retired hooker. She spent the Summers either sleeping in their cabin, or wandering around in a bathrobe, in curlers, her face covered with adhesive patches that supposedly removed wrinkles. Regretfully, for Mrs. Henderson, at some point the adhesives had to be removed and therein lay the gist.

On one occasion, GQK appeared in the camp's harbor on a large chartered yacht, with her nephew, my Cousin Phillip Quarre, and assorted guests—parents of other campers. She came ashore in a wide-brimmed hat with dark glasses, the counselors, mostly college undergraduates from modest backgrounds, found it a hoot. I overheard one say, "It's *Auntie Mame* on the Q.E. II." GQK didn't give a tinker's damn, it was just her style.

During the weekend GQK was moored in the harbor an event occurred. It happened, the only challenge to the *Platoon's* supremacy was a band of Hollywood brats led by a nasty little prick called *Ricky*. He and his ever-present entourage of sycophants, took an acute dislike to me personally, they gave me a hard time verbally whenever they caught me alone. I developed a seething hatred for Ricky.

C.I.B.C. held weekly exhibition boxing matches in which I participated with decent results, thanks to the tutelage in Southampton. This Sunday evening fate paired me with my nemesis, Ricky, in a three-rounder.

Gladys, Cousin Phil, and her yachting guests were invited ashore by Coach Henderson and seated ringside. I had pre-fight jitters so badly we could barely tie on the gloves. Ricky and his smirking cronies in the opposite corner didn't realize they were handing me an advantage in motivation.

Halfway into the first round, I realized Ricky's punches felt like a fly-swat. Ricky also sensed things weren't going quite as he had anticipated. Between rounds, I saw GQK carefully watching my opponent in his corner! She whispered to Phil, who then walked casually to my corner, quietly relaying, "Aunt Gladys thinks you ought to aim for his face, not his body."

Ricky burst out of his corner in round two with bravado, his buddies screeching support. We danced around a few moments, I then realized, he not only couldn't punch, he didn't know how to protect himself—he was mine! Five decades later I still relish the sensation of knowing you're in total command of someone you despise.

By the end of round three, tears rolled down Ricky's face, his mouth went from a smirk to a quivering blotch of uncertainty, his ringside cronies silenced, I returned my corner victorious. The harassment ended that evening—one weasel gone from the barnyard.

Mentor from a Mountain Top

Throughout this period I'd assimilated into a second family, one Mother encouraged. Delmer and Marylou Daves had been part of the scene since the mid-40s, and to me, they were the embodiment of an idyllically unified, wholesome, solidly based lifestyle, in lieu of Gladys' more flexuous quixotic approach. Their son, Michael, my age; daughter, Debby, who became my "adoptive sister," and their kid sister, Donna, were the kind of family I'd only read about in the *Saturday Evening Post.*

Marylou would fondly reminisce over her two older children and I having shared a sandbox, and how I had thrown sand in Debby's face. Marylou made my ungallant behavior sound endearing. I have no recollection of having done that, which isn't to say I didn't, but I just don't remember it. The Daves' attitude towards me never reflected any misdeeds on my part, I was as one of their own. Whereas, GQK was very fond of the younger Daves, she was never able to extend herself to them, as their parents did to me. I'd receive big genuine hugs from Delmer and Marylou, but Michael and Debby had to settle for a peck on the cheek from Gladys.

Delmer Daves was a Renaissance man, his interests and accomplishments covered a panoramic canvas. As a writer-director-producer of motion pictures, his films included; *Destination Tokyo, Task Force, Broken Arrow, Dark Passage, Never Let Me Go, Cowboy, 3:10 to Yuma,* and *Kings Go Forth,* starring cinematic legends; Cary Grant, Gary Cooper, Humphrey Bogart, James Stewart, Clark Gable, Alan Ladd and Frank Sinatra. Delmer was a master film craftsman and an actor's director, with a voracious appetite for knowledge in general. A scholar in etymology, an expert at script, pen and ink drawing, whose geological rock collection surpassed most institutions, which he bequeathed to his alma mater, Stanford University.

The Encyclopedia of Film describes Delmer as *"...a meticulous craftsman. His films always interesting to watch and were often imbued with humanity and sympathetic understanding for characters in conflict with their environment."*

Delmer was a gregarious bear of a man, with a pugnacious face and a voice that could derail a train—rarely necessary—he made his point by *lowering* it, you knew then, ominous clouds were gathering, and to best mend your ways. His generosity of spirit, compassion, and charismatic character made one eager to absorb and benefit from his company. I worshipped Delmer, more importantly, I *liked* him. If he sounds too good to be true, take consolation in knowing, he was a lousy driver.

Marylou was a vivacious precious gem, a wondrous bundle of directed energy and commitment; a devoted wife and mother, a steadfast friend and a talented actress in her own right. She could well have served as a role-model for two of her closest friends, actresses, Jane Wyatt and Donna Reed, in preparing their successful TV characters. Marylou went on to become a successful author and editor of art books with commentary by significant personalities. She was a wondrous human being. GQK described them as, "That rare breed you can call at three in the morning."

Debby Daves became "Mrs. William Richards" quite awhile back. Time seems to move at supersonic speed, and as the years pass it's going at *Mach 2!* Geographics aside, I think of the Richards as being among my closest and most valued friends.

Chapter 9

A LILY IN THE VALLEY

Gladys Knapp's concept of a ranch differed from her brother. Her stock portfolio added enough girth by 1952 to purchase a second home from director John Cromwell. The ranch was located in a pastoral oasis called Hidden Valley, an hour's drive from the Palisades house, located across the Ventura County line, northwest of Thousand Oaks—then, a sleepy town of six thousand. You drove past undeveloped flatlands with grazing sheep—now Westlake Village—then took a winding road around Lake Sherwood and descended into a kind of California-Kentucky-Connecticut hybrid.

Gladys' fifty-acre-weekend hideaway had sloping pastured fields enclosed by white wood-slat fences, clusters of pine and oak trees, with a back drop of rocky foothills and a creek running through it. The sprawling main house, with high beams and pine paneling, looked down on a swimming pool and pool house, a tennis court, foreman's cottage, stable, feed barn, and assorted out-buildings.

She named the show place, *Rancho Gladavida*, a contraction of our given names which she insisted meant "happy life" in Spanish. *Vida* was valid, but in its entirety, it means nothing in Spanish.

Up the road, the only neighbor beyond us was a delightfully eccentric lady, Eleanor French, who shared her hacienda-type house with seven dogs. Rumor had it, Eleanor's deceased husband, Colonel French, had been secretly buried on the property. In future years, being buried behind the house in the pine forest wasn't a repelling idea to Mom, except, she worried about subsequent ranch owners, "Would they be the kind of people you'd want share space with?"

Down the road a piece, Sue and Alan Ladd had their ranch getaway, *Alsulana Acres*. Over the years our Hidden Valley Association included; George Brent, Thora and Tex Thornton, founder of Litton Industries, Eve Arden and Brooks West, Dean Martin, his producer, Greg Garrison, Richard Widmark and Rupert Murdoch. Across the road from our place, for several years, Roy Rogers and Dale Evans were neighbors.

Over twenty-five years, ranch denizens included nine dogs, and Buddy, an Arabian-Palomino mix, who was exactly what his name implied. The pastures became home to other horses, given to us by friends who no longer had the facilities, it became a retirement home for aging skittish polo ponies and Shetlands, former pets of indulged kids who *grew out of them.*

Four steers made up our cattle empire. We also had chickens, ducks, pheasants by the score and two particular favorites of GQK's, two sows referred to as, "The Girls"—making damned sure they never became the source of anyone's barbecue! In the right environment, pigs are clean, personable and delightful pets.

Gladys and I had an affinity for ducks, which have more personality than any other winged species. A mama duck with her ducklings waddling in line behind her, makes any heart melt. We started with two mallard drakes and four hens as a commercial venture. Stupidly, we named them, if you do that, you're dead—chances are *they* never will be! A large naturalistic enclosure was built for our web-footed friends, with cozy protected areas for nesting and a pond for their enjoyment. Their enjoyment produced twenty more ducks in no time and it geometrically progressed from there. The duck population grew to around eighty, not one ever went to market, all died of old age, or as a result of occasional nocturnal visits from local predators. Surprise night visits with my twenty-gauge shotgun saved a few ducks.

Only one bird from GQK's turkey enclosure ever made it to the Thanksgiving table. The twenty-pound bird was cooked to perfection, but we couldn't eat a bite of it.

Meanwhile, Back in Town

Ouida and Basil Rathbone stayed at the Palisades house for two months the Summer of '54, while he made his movie comeback in *Casanova's Big Night* at Paramount with Bob Hope. Gladys and Ouida were dear friends, but living under the same roof put their relationship in grave peril, Catherine the Great and Marie Antoinette sharing quarters was potentially volatile.

The following Summer, Basil came West again, *sans* Ouida, for a Danny Kaye film, *The Court Jester*, then a third California Summer to work with Humphrey Bogart, in *We're No Angels*. During these work-treks, Godfather and Godson managed to spend quality time together, some of it on studio sound stages. My pre-conceptions, Danny Kaye, as a fun guy and Bogart, an ogre, were reversed; the "tough guy" was a lot nicer to be around, than the "funny guy." I found this to be a rule-of-thumb.

Many actors, primarily known for their villainy, make a point of countering that image off-camera; while nice guys often don't sustain their image.

***

At fourteen, GQK allowed her son a .22 caliber, single-shot rifle. While in the gun shop she zeroed in on a snub-nosed .32 revolver. I cautioned her, the two-inch barrel was only good for big targets at short distances, in dire self defense—compatible with her needs, she bought it. I showed her the basics in operating the snub-nosed, stressing its inaccuracy beyond ten yards. Weeks later, GQK, hearing what sounded like a reptilian Mariachi band, found herself confronting a coiled rattlesnake. She nailed it with one shot at forty feet. Was it luck, or done for my benefit?

The Alan Ladd family became good friends, with houses in Holmby Hills and Palm Springs, the ranch was a third home. Alan and Sue's two eldest children, Carol Lee and Alan, Jr., were from previous marriages. The younger two, Alana and David, were from theirs. If the odds against all four turning out extraordinarily well are slim, Alan and Sue beat the odds. You'd be hard-pressed to find a more solidly-rooted, nicer lot, than the Ladd family. The year we became neighbors, Alan made *Shane*. At the peak of his career, he was the genuine article, remaining so the twelve years we knew him.

Mom thought it a shame Alan never had an opportunity to lighten up on screen, in a comedy. He could be very funny when the mood struck him. Comedic moments and situations with Alan Ladd would be a lot funnier than with Jerry Lewis. Alan seemed to take his enormous success in stride. Inwardly, he had his demons like everyone else. His death came far too soon. Alan Ladd left a legacy and scores of friends.

His daughter Alana was a down-to-earth enchantress, our occasional dates were fun, at least for me. I hope they were for her. Alana married the *right* Michael Jackson, one of the greats of talk-radio, who dressed conservatively and wasn't in the least androgynous.

Machinations with a Matriarch

Great Aunt Ruth Hill was still going strong in her mid-eighties. Gladys and she were alike in many respects, neither believed in the nobility of poverty, assiduously avoiding it throughout their lives. They were shrewd businesswomen, who fought to keep the few original remaining pieces of family property intact, trying to dissuade relatives wanting to sell out. Those *needing* to sell were bought out. In several instances they gave the relatives back their shares, gratis, for their children's sake.

Ruth and Gladys had an enduring alliance, rather than a close relationship. They respected and loved one another as much as their individual natures allowed, always a competitive undercurrent, both were dynamos in their respective spheres.

Ruth's apartment on Nob Hill, next to the Mark Hopkins Hotel, was a museum. Her beach house, an hour or so south of San Francisco in Aptos, was the site for a number of summer weekends for Gladys and son over the years.

In the 60s, Ruth still had her 1947 Fleetwood Cadillac, driven by her Filipino houseman, Rosario. Rosario kept a baseball bat under the front seat for protection against other motorists, justified by Ruth's insistence he not drive over 35 mph, even in 65 mph zones. Impeding traffic, screamed expletives, and obscene gestures from fellow motorists were of no concern to her. The situation intensified when turning off the freeway onto the two-lane road to Aptos. The ever-increasing line of cars behind them, unable to pass the old Cadillac, might stretch back as far as the eye could see. The chorus of horns grew to a Beethhovenesque crescendo. The hour-plus trip to Aptos could take half a day, requiring a stop for luncheon—Aunt Ruth never *had lunch*, she only *luncheoned*.

Aptos weekends usually included Ruth's son, Jackson Baird, more of a brother to Gladys than a first cousin. Born only months apart, they shared a special telepathic rapport through their adult years, both having naughty natures, they reacted to people and situations with a secretive amusement only they were privy to, lost on the rest of us. They adored each other. Jack was a superb chef, as dinners at Aptos were gastronomic events. Normally the gentlest and humorous of men, when I tried to assist him in preparing a meal, Jack would always tell me fondly, "Get the hell out of my kitchen!"

GQK was at his bedside as he lay dying of throat cancer in a San Francisco hospital at age sixty-one.

Disney at Disneyland

Walt and Lily Disney invited Mother to the grand opening of *Disneyland*, "The eighth wonder of the world," and far better known than the other seven, despite thousands of years headstart. Being transported around Disneyland in the Disney's specially designed fringed cart was a thrill for even the most jaded and sophisticated of guests. Its mini-bar served as an additional spirit-booster during the festivities. Hollywood's animation genius made ample use of the "whisky-on-wheels" vehicle, having every reason to celebrate that day—and celebrate he did! Taking a respite from his carefully cultivated image, secure among the friends, he had himself a well-earned, richly deserved blast!

Disneyland was a tangible tribute to his genius, with a childlike enthusiasm, he tasted the "chocolate cake" he'd baked, relishing every mouthful of it.

Could Walt Disney, with all his brilliance, hard work, talent, ambition and ego, have anticipated the phenomenal impact he would have throughout the world?

The answer, a resounding, Y*es!*

Citadel of Constraints

In September of 1952, GQK decided her son had enough of the home life—or, she'd had enough of him. His uniform put in moth balls, he would return to civilian life as a ninth grade student at the Cate School.

South of Santa Barbara in Carpinteria, Cate is the equivalent of any top Eastern prep school. It wasn't co-ed at that time, and very San Francisco oriented. The Malcolm Gordon School looked West with skepticism, Cate looked upon the South with a kind of affirmative-action tolerance, although located in the Southern half of the state, its allegiance belonged to the Northern half.

Most were decent chaps, but a few faculty members went to the head of the class in pomposity, taking themselves seriously enough to be comedic. Several went a step further into the realm of mean-spirited hostility. When it came to preppy, we made *Brooks Brothers* look like *the Gap*.

What caught my interest during Parent-Day weekends, was the attention GQK received from a number of the father's of San Francisco classmates. The fuss made by admirers of the former Gladys Quarre in past years was a revelation. I was surprised the father of a particular classmate had been such good friends with my Mom in the old days. When we talked about it, the classmate didn't seem the least surprised. He told me, his dad had been in love with Mother many years ago, and asked her to marry him. Feeling excluded again, I asked his son, how he knew about it?

"My dad told me, when he saw your Mom here. Everyone knew about it at the time."

"It?"

"You're jumping to conclusions," he assuaged.

"What conclusion would *you* draw?"

A Lily in the Valley

"The same, I guess," he grinned.

I never felt completely comfortable at neither Cate, nor it with me. Our thought processes not really in sync, which my grades reflected—25th in a class of twenty-eight. Paradoxically, when class elections came around I was the front-runner for class president. An upperclassman under-cover faculty envoy, covertly advised some of the freshman class that another student should be elected class president. When someone asked if they had someone specific in mind, the upper-classman replied, "No, just so long as it isn't Knapp."

Being Elsewhere

A lesson GQK passed along was an ability to entertain myself without outside assistance. On the move a good part of the time, it was hard to establish ties with other kids my age, I learned how to be alone, having only me for company was never a problem, and I relished it.

Gladys imparted a piece of personal insight, logically and succinctly, "No one has more in common with me, than *me*. I and me enjoy each other's company, we agree on most issues, have identical taste, virtues, flaws and mood changes, as well as talents and interests. I respect "me's" privacy; we give each other all the space we need."

When verbally interacting, self-absorption can be a life-saver. Thoughts meander, your banter becomes redundant and less coherent, often lacking continuity, and one spends more time on digressions than on the subject at hand. Knowing full-well what you find fascinating is boring everyone. Your waxing-idiotic about trivia you've accumulated over the years, or your concept of the universe, is of no interest – it doesn't matter. Self-involvement affords you the latitude to continue the tirade, heedless of others.

You are listening to what *you* have to say and find it profound.

Romping with Royalty

Cobina Wright, Sr.'s daughter, Cobina, Jr. had been a good friend of H.R.H. Prince Philip, not long before his marriage to H.R.M. Elizabeth II. The Prince consort had remained good friends with Cobina, Sr. during the intervening years. In 1954, he was hosting the British Empire Games in Vancouver, Canada. Cobina was invited up as a house guest of the F. Ronald Grahams, the C.E.O. of the Bank of Nova Scotia. He and his wife, Helen, had an enormous house on Marine Drive on Vancouver Sound, with an Olympic sized indoor swimming pool. Cobina asked GQK if she'd like to join her, and bring me along too, as the Grahams also had a young son and plenty of room.

Ronny and Helen had ten children by previous marriages, all out the nest, except their son, who at thirteen was still at home, and whose roommate I would be during our stay. The Grahams huge house was well staffed, including an excellent cook, who rarely had to perform his duties. The Grahams liked to dine late, their staff liked to go to bed early, the result, the Grahams and their guests, including; Cobina, Gladys; the soon-to-be hotel magnate, Hyatt von Dehn, who'd have been voted "The Least Likely" to build a multi-billion dollar hotel chain, based on his drinking habits, playboy behavior and his being too nice and easy-going a guy to climb the cut-throat corporate ladder— he must have been *"The Scarlet Pimpernel"* of the Board Room, jockey, Johnny Longden, and his wife, a foot taller than he; had to fend for themselves in the cavernous kitchen at dinner time. No one was traumatized by the staff's absence, however, GQK thought it odd, paying a professional cook a large salary to retire at nine p.m., when

you rarely eat before ten p.m.. Jovial Ronnie looked and
acted like Santa Claus *sans* beard, Helen was big handsome
woman, both loved to entertain until the late hours. One
evening we went to the local amphitheater to see an
excellent touring company production of *Oklahoma,* and
Ronnie and Helen were impressed enough to, on the spur of
the moment, invite the entire large company of actors and
crew, back to their house for drinks, supper, and a swim!

The staff retired, the Grahams and their house-guests
hosted the forty-plus exuberant, hard-drinking, hard-playing
members of the company. Assigned to work behind the pool
bar, two years before I was of legal drinking age, put me in
the hub of the festivities. In a one-to-ten for looks, there
were several "elevens," the lowest mark you could give any
of the group was eight and a half. Many hadn't thought to
bring bathing attire, no matter, as the party progressed, off
came their outer clothing, and into the pool they went.

At the gracious invitation of three company members, I
took a recess from my bar duties. Being a relative novice in
the ways of the world, I didn't really know what I was
doing, in lieu of technique, all I could offer was
enthusiasm—but the two young ladies and the other chap
were patient and instructive.

On the third night, after his official duties, Prince
Philip, his chief aide, Michael Parker, and several equerries
arrived, escorted by police cars and various local officials.
His Royal Highness was as physically impressive in person
as appears in the documentaries currently aired virtually
every week on American TV. The two nights he slipped
away from official functions and joined us, he was in
ebullient spirits, additional spirits were readily available.

On those evenings at the Grahams, royalty, His Royal
Highness, and commoners alike, having imbibed, joined
together for a midnight dip. The father to the heir of the
British throne, unaware of GQK's aquatic limitations, burst
out of the water behind her and playfully dunked her head

under the surface. Resurfacing in a sputtering rage, she demanded to know, "Who's the sonuvabitch that did that?" H.R.H. apologized profusely, and upon realizing who her assailant was, GQK extricated herself not-so-delicately, "My God, your Highness, I almost yanked off your bathing suit." Prince Philip thought that was jolly good, with a beguiling smile he offered, "The evening isn't over yet." GQK thought that was jolly good too.

Chapter 10

CHANGE OF COURSES

Touched on earlier, Gladys was going through a show business phase of her own, in the person of, "A man you love to hate," George Sanders, recently divorced from Zsa Zsa Gabor, another pal of GQK's since the Hollywood Canteen days, when she was married to Conrad Hilton, her first husband—in fact, her *second* husband. Whenever Mother waxed nostalgic about those World War II days, Zsa Zsa hastened to qualify, "Gladys darlink, you haf to remember I vas only fourteen!" No point in quibbling over a lousy decade.

The year before GQK met George Sanders he won the Best Supporting Oscar for *All About Eve*, in which George played a acerbic powerhouse drama critic, *Addison De Witte,* in truth, George simply played *George* superbly.

He and Mom spent many evenings in the Palisades living room, George's powerful singing voice echoed through the house, he played the piano beautifully, composed songs and thoroughly enjoyed performing. His musical talent was only utilized in one film briefly, *Call Me Madam.* On quieter evenings, Mom fed him lines for scenes he was shooting the next day. A truly bad picture can be a memorable experience, but a simply innocuously bad film serves no purpose. One of George's films *Jupiter's Darling,* the nadir of MGM musicals, had the vices of all and the virtues of none. There wasn't even enough content to hate. It was the beginning of the end for the careers of Esther Williams, Howard Keel, Marge & Gower Champion, and director, George Sidney. George Sanders weathered the storm. On an historical Hollywood note, the day George took me on the back lot set of *Jupiter's Darling*, I got a ride back to the main building with Esther Williams in her limousine.

She was very detached and quiet during the ten minute drive. I later found out she was going to Dore Schary's office where she was told her contract had terminated and her career at MGM was over.

In person, Sanders's acerbic style was gentler and less blasé, with a subtly self-deprecating humor. His Russian extraction resulted in bouts of melancholia which eventually did him in. He was complex, intelligent, at times intimidating and very big physically. He had no aspirations to be a "great actor," and too admittedly lazy to stretch his repertoire.

During that period, I recall one incident in particular. George invited GQK, I and our house guest, Basil Rathbone, to the premier of *King Richard and the Crusaders,* in which George played the title role. The four of us arrived at the Egyptian Theater in Hollywood amidst the excitement, then walked down the long red-carpeted entranceway into the theater with noisy fans three-deep on either side. Being on public display with celebrities, when you're *not* one, can be excruciating, a graduate course in humility. They didn't faze GQK; she'd smile radiantly and nod graciously, while the fans tried to remember the films they thought she had starred in. Thank God, George Sanders and Basil Rathbone, both certified stars, weren't the kind who elicit mob hysteria.

Inside the theater, it got rougher. GQK showed her metal that evening, sitting through a beyond-bad movie, next to her gentleman-friend, one of the stars of the debacle; flanked by Basil who audibly dozed off repeatedly; her bored-antsy son squirming in his seat; and the film's director, David Butler, a friend since childhood, seated directly behind her, she never flinched, maintaining a frozen smile throughout, resisting the urge to lock herself in the ladies room.

Sanders, our host, walked through the film as if he'd wandered onto the wrong soundstage. Rex Harrison's performance clearly let the audience know he was doing it for it for the money and Laurence Harvey, making his American film debut, gave the impression of wearing lingerie under his armor. Cast opposite these hapless but distinguished actors as the elegant lady-love, Virginia Mayo, was her regal self.

What do you say to those heavily involved in an atrocity? Gladys had a flare dealing with that dilemma, "I'm sure audiences will gobble it up. Well, you've done it again."

The fondness I had for George was cautiously reciprocated, in a gentlemen's agreement sense. Long after he and GQK went their separate ways, he and I remained on very cordial terms.

Coat and Tie Required

In the Spring of 1954, Mom announced we were off to New York for a brief visit. Not having been east for six years, the prospect had definite appeal, but I explained it was mid-term, taking time off wasn't academically feasible. In the meantime, GQK had taken care of the problem in a circuitous manner. On learning the school's library needed expanding and remodeling, she offered the principal substantial monetary assistance. A man of practical priorities, he reconsidered my mid-term absence, on the proviso I take a study outline and adhere to it while I was away. Placing that kind of trust in me, put me in the awkward position of being honor bound to comply.

When the DC-7 touched down in New York, my heart raced, by the time we crossed the Triborough Bridge there were palpitations, and as we reached the River Club, I was in *A New York state of mind.* The first night, I took longer than usual primping, so GQK went down to greet our dinner companions. A few minutes later, a knock on the door, standing there, was a man with a unforgettably unique face who greeted me in the most ingratiating manner, "David how are you? Your Mom asked me to come up and see how you were doing. I don't know if you remember me." Did I remember the piano player—Artur Rubenstein!!

The following ten days, Mom and I attended seven evening performances and two matinees. I'm not absolutely sure about some of the plays we saw that season, I'm positive about the first three; *Anniversary Waltz* starring Kitty Carlisle and Macdonald Carey, a favorite film actor of mine and future friend, Franchot Tone and Gig Young in *Oh Men, Oh Women,* and for a specific reason, *Pajama Game,* that night, one of the leads, Carol Haney, having broken her ankle, was replaced by an unknown, Shirley MacLaine. Everyone in the entertainment business knows the story, but not many were actually present the night it happened. Years later when GQK and I told Miss MacLaine we'd been there for her Broadway debut, the star was skeptical at first, but Mom convinced her with, "Of course, you were nervous that night, but you did a wonderful job."

I think the following year we saw Bernard Shaw's *Major Barbara,* with Charles Laughton. We went backstage after the performance because, although GQK had bought Laughton's house six years before, she'd never met the man—his wife, Elsa Lanchester handled all the negotiations. Backstage we explained our mission to the 'remarkably proficient ham,' delighted, the first thing he asked, "How are *my* camellias?"

On annual visits throughout the remainder of the '50s, we saw so many shows it is difficult to recall the correct order. I believe the following season was, *Happy Hunting*, starring Ethel Mermen and Fernando Lamas, a memorable event, if not with the critics, at least for us. Lamas was married to the equally beautiful Arlene Dahl, they'd produced an equally beautiful son, Lorenzo, whose career acting and directing career fell far short of his good looks, it far exceeded his talent. He was aggressively inept in both categories! Arlene invited us to their eastside apartment where we had a pleasant afternoon. Arlene was as sweet as she was beautiful, and when Fernando turned on the charm, he too was simply "mah-vel-ous."

Miss Merman's a.k.a, *Uncle Ethel* allegedly came about during the preproduction of *Happy Hunting*. On being introduced to her handsome co-star, Miss Merman told Lamas, *"You remind me of my niece,"* a faulty start with a machismo Argentinean, who countered, *"And you look like my uncle."*

Hence, *Uncle Ethel*—but I recommend, not to her face. Lamas further consolidated his position at every performance, a scene in the second act required them to kiss, immediately after, and Fernando would unobtrusively wipe his mouth. The night we saw the production was no exception.

A Princess in the Palisades

On Sunday mornings, driving to Corpus Christi Church in Pacific Palisades, GQK and I sometimes picked up a passenger en route, other Sundays she waved us on, choosing to walk the mile distance. The tall young lady, usually in flat shoes, a simple overcoat, a scarf around her head and dark glasses, had rented a house up the street from ours. Riding in our backseat, she didn't have a great deal to say and not wanting to be intrusive, I'd adjust the rearview mirror so I could at least see her. GQK cautioned me not to ask her stupid questions about her work week. This was frustrating, I wanted to hear the straight poop about her job, and co-workers and fellows like: Clark Gable and Gary Cooper, illicit information about William Holden, James Stewart, or Bing Crosby. Any subtle attempts on my part went for naught, Grace Kelly wasn't about to volunteer any insights—as it turned out, she had plenty.

Self-deprecation Made Easy

The guys at Chaminade knew I didn't come from a deprived background, but I tried to keep a fairly low profile regarding home life advantages. Any chance of maintaining that evaporated one Sunday evening. GQK, the dogs, and I returned to the Palisades from a ranch weekend to discover most of her jewelry had been stolen from a hiding place in her dressing room.

Uniformed officers were the first on the scene, followed by the first team of plainclothes detectives, who asked all the standard questions, took notes, and then were followed by a second team who asked the same questions. They, in turn, exchanged notes with a third team of more seasoned detectives who, after conferring with the first two teams, proceeded to ask us exactly the same questions we'd answered three times before. Mom's jaws tightened as she repeated the answers in an overly-pleasant tone. Then, she asked the senior cops why they wrote it all down three times if none of them knew how to read it?

The list of potential suspects, covering all past household staff, was a police investigator's worst nightmare.

Several seemingly disinterested reporters appeared, asked perfunctory questions, then departed fifteen minutes later.

Between replacements for the last pair fired, the following morning GQK was in the kitchen preparing her son a hearty breakfast before he left for school. She prepared a bowl of *Wheaties* and a glass of milk with flourish, as I collected the morning paper. On the front page of the *L. A. Times,* a banner headline read: *"$60,000 Jewel Theft!"* underneath in slightly small print, *"Prominent Socialite Victim of Thieves."* The article began, *"The Pacific Palisades mansion of millionairess socialite Gladys Quarre Knapp was burglarized over the weekend, while she was at her country estate in Ventura County."*

I handed her the paper, "You've gone from the society columns to the front page." Her first reaction, "Good God, you'd think they'd find something more important for a headline!" As she read the article her frown turned into a glower, "Don't you love how the goddamned liberal press gets their digs in. It's vulgar. They make me sound nouveau-riche, like I discovered oil in the backyard and hired a press agent!" She waved the paper in all directions, "Would you call this a *mansion?"*

"No Mom, but *'a nice big house'* reads funny."

I drove to school riddled with anxiety. I'd assimilated, now this! How would my fellow students react? Up to this point, I was fondly described as, "an arrogant, imperious, spoiled, piss-elegant prick," by my friends—those who *didn't* like me were less kind. However, these rough n' tumble macho jocks elected the aloof president of the Drama Guild—whose athletic prowess wouldn't get him on Vasser's *B* volleyball team—as Senior Class President.

I was slinking to my homeroom, when I was intercepted by Brother David Schuyler, S.M. All he wanted to know was whether Mother and I were okay. I assured him we were. Other than an undercurrent of awareness, no one at school alluded to the morning headline. I wished the newsmen had shown as much class.

Bro. David and I would intercept for many years to come. On the 2002 cover of the Chaminade Quarterly, David Schuyler and David Knapp are pictured together as co-honorees at a Founder's Day celebration, both having served on the Chaminade Board of Directors. After the school's president, James Adams, gave a rousing introduction, I launched into a brief speech which seemed to strike a cord with the fifteen hundred attentive students. I'd like to say it was extemporaneous; however the four minute address took four days to carefully write, revise, and edit. The effort paid off. That day turned out to be a greater thrill than any S.R.O. theatrical audience.

***

Sunday outdoor luncheons at Charles and Muff Brackett's house in Bel Air, were a pleasure as well as an education. After reaching a satisfactory age, I was permitted to escort Mom to some of these functions. Charlie Brackett differed from the stereotypical concept of a Hollywood producer, as do a substantial minority of them. A gentleman of the old school, a graduate of Williams College and Harvard Law School, he'd have looked more at home in the U.S. Senate dining room or as president of an ivy league university. Instead, he served as president of the Motion Picture Academy and was one of the most formidable writer-producers of his period and a recipient of two Oscars.

For an untried teenager to be seated at the Brackett's, between Edna Ferber and Dorothy Parker, at the same table with Aldous Huxley, Christopher Isherwood, or Gavin Lambert, was in a word, awesome. On one occasion, our host had just completed filming *The Girl On The Red Velvet Swing,* the story of a turn of the century scandal, in which an heir to millions, Harry K. Thaw, shot and killed architect

Stanford White, in a public restaurant, as White was having an affair with Thaw's mistress, showgirl Evelyn Nesbitt, later known as "The Girl in the Red Velvet Swing."

The quiet dowdy elderly woman seated next to me at lunch, didn't make much of an impression, I remember thinking, "Why is she here?" She was there because *she* had been the "The Girl in the Red Velvet Swing," Evelyn Nesbitt.

This taught me, never underestimate the innocuous person seated next to you at a party given by powerful movers and shakers, there is usually a reason they were invited! Although, that didn't necessarily apply to me.

***

GQK and I became aware of our fortieth president's interest in politics at a 1956 cocktail reception she gave at Pinecliff for the Belgian ambassador to the U.S. After most of the guests departed, a few remained, among them, Ronald and Nancy Reagan. This was ten years before Mr. Reagan took his first oath of office as California's governor, and twenty-four years before his first inauguration as Commander-in-Chief. We chatted with the former film star, then spokesman for General Electric, for quite awhile. He seemed genuinely interested in the opinions of a precocious high school student. Reagan's celebrity status aside, he had a presence, a quality inspiring confidence and trust. The kind of guy you want as your commanding officer, to run the show, sensing he'd do *the right thing*, regardless.

Mother vigorously supported all his bids for public office, her son went house-to-house on his behalf, as "special guests" we attended his first inauguration in Sacramento and in the nation's capitol. I'm glad a teenager's instincts were on target, most of the free world seems to agree.

A year or so after he left the presidency, while attending a fundraiser-birthday party for Jimmy Stewart, the Reagans arrived to the amazement of our group *and* me, the first thing the former chief executive did was walk directly over, shake my hand, we had a thirty-second exchange, he wished me well and was hustled off. I'd like to think there was a hint of recognition, not just my proximity to the entrance. Reagan was a man who matched mountains.

***

Mom had definite ideas as to where her pride and joy would receive his higher education, persuading me with little difficulty, I should attend an Eastern school. "You'll always be a Californian but you don't want to be *too* 'Californian.'"

Accompanied by a former Yale graduate friend, we drove up to New Haven, a grungy, bleak, unappealing town except for the university and the campus-affiliated areas. It was a chilly overcast day, making even the campus dreary and unappealing. Never mind the fact, my chances of being accepted were slimmer than a spider's web.

Our next stop Washington, D.C., and more specifically Georgetown University with that cozy, unadorned, just-plain-folks aura, synonymous with Jesuit institutions, and the credo, "'Piety and principle over power and profit," permeated the campus.

Then we were off to Charlottesville, Virginia for a look at the University of Virginia campus. On a warm spring day the symmetrical red-brick Jeffersonian buildings, against the lush green flora is an idyllic setting, as were the young attractive students relaxing on the rolling lawns, taking in the sun during class breaks. GQK surveyed the scene commenting, "I don't see you getting much done here."

Minor Birds—Major Problem

My graduation presents, a new '57 Oldsmobile sedan, more practical and appropriate for an Eastern undergraduate, and a third trip to Hawaii.

Steve Royce, an *hotelier par excellence*, another old pal of GQK's, ran the Royal Hawaiian, as he had the Huntington Hotel during our stays there. The Royal was having its pink exterior face lifted, the aroma of fresh paint permeated a good part of the hotel, but when it wafted its way up to Mom's suite it encountered a formidable advisory. She called Royce's office, demanding to know why they were painting the hotel while she was a guest! They explained, it had been planned and was in progress long before her arrival. I don't know exactly what transpired over the phone, but the next day all painting ceased on Mom's side of the hotel for the duration of our stay.

One evening at dinner, Steve recounted a funny story. It seems a colony of minor birds had taken up residence in Banyan trees around the Royal, apparently sensing it was the best hotel in town they chose it as their perching place. The birds were non-stop talkers, vocalizing en masse day and night, driving some guests to distraction, or to other hotels. How to deal with the black feathered non-paying guests was a problem, they wouldn't be *shooed* out, intimidated, or threatened and ornithological genocide was out of the question. The hotel management was convinced the dilemma would be solved by hooking up a wide strap to a powerful pneumatic motor-like devise, wrapping the strap around the trunk of a tree, literally shaking the birds away, if the racket from the motor didn't scare them off first. At great expense, a contraption was designed and the plan implemented. The birds watched with keen interest from the branches as the strap was placed around the base and attached to a motor the size of a car engine.

It performed beyond expectations, vigorously shaking the tree, emitting a deafening noise in the process. The startled birds flew off to adjacent trees and the hotel roof, but remained within view. In minutes, a number of the more intrepid beaked boarders decided to stick it out. After checking out the *rock'n-roll'n* first hand, they reported back to the others favorably. Others returned to the shaking tree, where the loud noise wasn't a problem, and they could take it *and* dish it out. Now they really had something to shout about! They *loved* the vibrating effect. Word went out to all their friends and relatives in the Waikiki area, and within hours the Banyan trees of Royal Hawaiian were host to triple the number of original occupants. Those not having the ride of their life anxiously awaited their turn in nearby trees. Eventually the management found another way. A few tail feathers ruffled, but no one got hurt.

Chapter 11

CLAUSTROPHOBIC IN OPEN SPACES

In the fall of 1957, GQK accompanied her about-to-be-collegiate son to Georgetown, as many parents do the first day or two, to get their sons settled in—but few go to the effort and expense of remaining in the vicinity for almost two weeks—Mom did. Whereas, others were settled in, I was tucked in, figuratively speaking. I arrived the first day of indoctrination, through the university's front gate, not in a station-wagon, surrounded by family, no sir, in a limousine with Mom and a chauffeur, a ticket to popularity. I was the only student with this type of transport; the other freshman arrived by more conventional means.

"Mother, I'll unload and carry my own luggage!" The chauffeur thought that a swell idea, and volunteered to unlock the trunk for me. I began yanking bags out of the limo, when Mom posed, "Shouldn't you find out, *where* you're going to carry them?"

I have no compunction about asking directions, fully aware it challenges manhood. I was about to ask, when Mom pointed in a general direction, "You don't suppose that's the building, do you?"

"Which one?"

"The one they're all going in and out of."

Mom's smug expression left me at the point of no return, had it been a cargo container, I'd have done it alone! My bags piled on the sidewalk, Mom reminded me, she'd be in Washington the rest of the week. Oh, and "Don't forget we're dining with Conchita and Carlota tonight. I'll pick you up right here at six-forty-five sharp." Not in that limo, I'd meet them there.

Typically, I'd over-extended myself, it would take two trips to carry my belongings to the dorm. Not wanting to leave half my stuff sitting there, I asked an all-American-looking fellow with a near-handsome corn-fed face and winning smile, if he'd keep an eye on my stuff. He offered to help me, that way it would only take one trip. I went through the protesting motions unconvincingly, while he gathered my other bags, then, both loaded down, I followed him to the dorm.

"Old North," a brick building, served some function during the Civil War. It must have been an historical landmark, as little if any renovating had taken place since. Judging by the interior it must have housed prisoners of war. When I facetiously asked a priest what *Old North* was North of, his Jesuitical response was, "Everything South of here."

Ted was big, very fit, the climb up three flights of stairs didn't faze him, while I had to take a breather on the landing. He grabbed a bag I was carrying adding it to his load, and by the time I finished telling him "Please, you've already done too much," he was on the third floor. We exchanged names, Ted, was from Pueblo, Colorado. "Hi, Dave, good to meetcha." How do you tell a guy who's just carried your bags up three flights of stairs, "It's David, not Dave!"

We paused long enough for me to find my room assignment. When I told him the number, he shook his head and said, "You're kidding?" No, I never kid about room numbers. Ted led me joyfully down the noisy corridor, guys running in and out of rooms, unpacking, and getting acquainted. He opened the door at the end of the corridor, I froze. The small dreary room the size of a walk-in closet, had bunk beds and some nitwit had mistakenly unpacked their belongings, which now occupied half *my* closet, with other items neatly stacked on a *my* dresser.

"There's been a mistake, I asked for a single room! I couldn't share a room this size with a canary!" This was wholly unacceptable. "Could you imagine living in this rat hole with some slob you've never met before, who reads comic books and girly magazines, chews tobacco, wears dirty underwear, and showers once a week?"

Ted shuffled sheepishly, "What about a guy who showers every day, sometimes twice, doesn't smoke, who's pre-med, doesn't have much time for comic books, only reads *Playboy* for the editorials..." As he trailed off, I added, "Who's neat and organized." He nodded contritely, "I'm sorry, I should have said something sooner. I thought it'd be fun to surprise you. Dumb idea."

He began to collect his belongings, "I'll see what I can do."

I felt as if I'd left a loquacious dog along the roadside. "Put your stuff down, Ted, and gimme a chance to adjust."

"I'll try not to get in your hair, Dave."

I was being manipulated again, I had to reassert myself, "I want the bottom bunk." They're always nice at first, but Ted Vidmar kept it up for two semesters. We did get moved to a larger room and lived happily during our freshman year.

Sisters Sublime

Two relatives GQK adored were Princess Pignatelli's two daughters, *Little* Conchita and Carlota, who lived across the Potomac in Arlington, Virginia. Both had long since married junior naval officers, who by then were senior officers, Captain Frank Raysbrook on the faculty of the

National War College in Washington, and Commander Bob Munroe (later Captain), respectively. Frank and Conchita's eldest, son, Chuck Raysbrook, now a retired naval Commander, is one the heads of the California Game & Wildlife Commission. He and his wife Dodie, are not only family but two trusted and valued friends. Chuck is the brother I wish I'd had. Conchita's daughter, Herlinda and her husband, Doug Ellis, are in part of the family circle as well.

Bob and Carlota Munroe and their two children, lived down the road a piece from the Raysbrooks. Frank and Bob are gone, but their wives remain a testament to sisterhood, a sibling bond letting no one put asunder. During my tenure at Georgetown, I was fortunate enough to be treated as a Raysbrook-Munroe family member.

Conchita, Carlota, and I knew we were related but never quite sure just *how*? Further complicating the connection, our generations didn't match up. They were half a generation older, but we've never spent much time analyzing it.

No matter, Mother appointed Conchita and Frank my legal guardians, as I was about to turn nineteen. It was Mom's way of asking them to keep an eye on me, least I wander too far off the path.

When All is Said and Dumb

Students at Georgetown were required to wear coat and tie to all classes, meals, and functions on campus—the dress code eased a little on weekends. But wearing a coat and tie to dinner in a paneled hall, a room with walls reminiscent of a hospital corridor, Formica-topped tables, and cafeteria style service, doesn't warrant dressing for dinner, and smacks of bourgeois pretentiousness.

General hazing was still in vogue at G.U., under the guise of "orientation." Although fraternities were banned, all incoming freshman were subjected to very short crew cuts, tantamount to having one's head shaven, further humiliation with a beanie which had to be worn the first week. The worst was walking around for a day with pants rolled up to the knee.

A seasoned man of the cloth explained, "You may have been a big man on campus at *'Kokomo High'*, but here, freshmen are little more than excrement." Not having attended Kokomo High aside, it struck me, the word *excrement,* in that syntax was fatuous.

Having given the massive volume of *G.U. Rules and Regulations* a cursory glance, I hadn't noticed the paragraph stipulating, *"Freshmen and Sophomores were not permitted automobiles"*—after GQK had shipped my Oldsmobile East. I decided to slip this in at dinner, her last night in town. My pants rolled down and *sans* beanie, I arrived at the Shoreham Hotel. Mom saw my new look, gasping, "My God, David, where's your hair?" Then, wanting to know why my pants were so wrinkled.

When advised of the car dilemma she took it in cavalier fashion, she had an idea! "Leave the Olds at Conchita's during the week for her use, you drive it on weekends. God knows, she can use it."

Frank subscribed to frugality, the family car was a vintage Nash. They'd stopped manufacturing Nash's years before, which didn't become a factor until parts were no longer available. Conchita referred to it as an "ugly embarrassment," a noisy, hard-to-drive automotive antiquity, feeling no sentimental attachment for its standard transmission, erratic heater, and lack of suspension. The Olds was put to the best possible use.

***

Students then were required to attend 5:00 p.m. daily Mass, to assure our attendance and faith, we turned in an autographed chit at the door. Jesuits know infinitely more about everything than mortals, *however* forcing church attendance, in most instances, causes disaffiliation, rather than devotion. I think many clergy agreed, Mass was usually said in a speedy perfunctory manner. We took bets as to which priest could say Mass in the shortest time. One was timed at nineteen minutes—I doubt it was a record.

R.O.T.C. was the easiest three-credit elective I could find. Thank the Almighty, the officer in charge wasn't commanding in the field. One could see him rising to the rank of "Bell Captain" in a hotel, but lieutenant colonel?! Everything he said in the classroom sounded memorized from the day before, and questions were not encouraged.

I went so far as to volunteer for the drill team, *Spraker Rifles,* thus assuring a decent grade average—Gung Ho, gone awry. Only the drill team was issued uniforms, feeling apart of history donning the same coarse woolen pants and ill-fitting jacket worn by soldiers in the trenches at Verdon and Flanders Field; rifles used by General Sherman's men marching through Georgia; and the same boots carrying the Rough Rider's up San Juan Hill.

The big bonus came with six a.m. drills on Saturday mornings held in the quadrangle surrounded by the windows of half the freshman class. The legal drinking age in the nation's capitol was eighteen, meaning many first year students were hung-over and grumpy on Saturday and Sunday mornings. Being awakened at dawn by terse commands, stomping boots, clanging rifles going through the manual of arms—with the nation in the midst of a twelve year war hiatus—to many, was not purposeful, popular, or patriotic.

Windows were opened just enough to yell expletives, or toss liquids and hurl miscellaneous missiles on or at members of Spraker Rifles. Fortunately, we convinced the command to issue dress parade helmets ahead of schedule. I suspect we were the only college R.O.T.C. unit to earn the *Combat Service Medal* prior to active duty.

All this came to fruition when Spraker Rifles finally utilized their training skills, showing their stuff, by marching proudly at the opening of a shopping mall in Maryland!

***

Mom returned to visit to the campus several months later to see the author on stage. Georgetown's drama group, *The Masque and Bauble,* wasn't as pithy as the name suggests—a fun group in fact. The first production, John Patrick's *Teahouse of the August Moon,* a big hit on Broadway a few seasons back, would be the biggy for the year, performed *on* campus in Gaston Hall, the University's wood-paneled, balconied, principal auditorium-lecture hall-assembly place and theater.

They went all out with an unheard of budget, more than the total cost of six productions at Chaminade. Excellent performances with elaborate sets on rollers, and a live billy-goat made for a fine evening's entertainment.

GQK, along with the senior Raysbrooks and Munroes, attended opening night. The fact that the play's author gave my character a good lead-in so the audience is anticipating his entrance, I assume, is why I received an ovation. It gave me an adrenalin lift, which resulted in a performance that had a little something extra. You sense it while it's happening, as though something else is in control, it is contagious, the other cast members and the audience pickup on it, and everything clicks. The audience's enthusiastic lengthy response at the final curtain, felt like being on the *Great White Way*. Having appeared in two dozen plays in houses ranging from seventy to a thousand seats, those performances of *Teahouse* remain among the most gratifying.

Bob Munroe was about as interested in the theater as I am in physics admitted, "I wasn't looking forward to this evening, but I had a helluva good time, pal. How'd you get that goat to behave?" I couldn't tell him, whatever it was didn't work at most performances. Our goateed cast member liked relieving himself to the smell of the greasepaint and the roar of the crowd.

The car arrangement with Conchita worked well into my sophomore year, she had the use of it all week and on weekends, and I became the class chauffeur. It wasn't unusual for six of us to cram into the Olds for weekend-daytime outings, but more alluring were the adventurous nocturnal explorations into the seamier areas in our nation's capitol, which abound, varied and reasonably available, to personable strapping young students, unencumbered by legal drinking age laws.

It was a miracle the Olds hadn't been detected in all this time, still unknown to the administration, with so much activity. This illusion ended abruptly one morning when one of the good Fathers intercepted me with a paternal hand firmly on my shoulder, and a Jesuitical smile. He thought aloud, "With a student-faculty retreat coming up in a few days, wouldn't it be nice if *I* drove some of the priests to the retreat site in the hills of Virginia, in *my* car."

"The Fathers and I thought, how much pleasanter it would be for us, and more relaxing for your classmates, if we weren't all crammed together in the bus, don't you agree, David?"

"Oh, you bet I agree, Father!" Pleasanter and more relaxing for everyone, except me. The things I knew I thought others *didn't* know, they *did* know—them knowing I didn't *know* they knew what I *didn't* think they knew and then knowing, I was the last to know what everyone else knew—put me in an awkward position.

Into the Breach Again

GQK and I spent the Christmas break in Palm Beach as guests of her current beau, a charming gentleman of the old school. Howard Bell, a widower, inherited an Addison Meisner-esque house on Ocean Avenue. The house had high-ceilings, multiple living rooms connected by archways, large bedrooms, and bathrooms larger than our room at G.U. The Moorish house had a pleasantly dank smell, which bespoke older seasonal homes in a humid sea-front climate. It was perfectly maintained by a staff of live-in servants and extra day-help.

Howard offered little to dislike, urbane, easy going, with a great sense of wry humor. Despite having indirectly acquired an enviable life-style, he wasn't terribly motivated. Howard's step daughters and their husbands shared the holidays with us. An undercurrent of tension existed between one of the step daughters and her husband, and with Howard. Mother sensed some was attributable to resentment over her possibly taking the place of the deceased mother, "When I sat at the opposite head of the table at dinner, I could feel her reaction." GQK didn't believe in the *divide and conquer* philosophy subscribed to by some stepmothers, who try to sever the husband's ties to his previous relationships in order to secure her own position.

GQK gently convinced Howard's step daughter she was not a threat, and parenthetically, had a few bucks of her own. She was there to unify, not further undo the family. The problems between the young woman and her husband, a bit of a stuffed shirt but decent guy, would have to be ironed out by them—I doubt they ever were.

To give Howard's family some time alone, GQK and I spent the New Year holiday at Round Hill, Montego Bay, in Jamaica. Mom rented the former Noel Coward cottage, presumably his Caribbean base prior to Barbados. It stood high on a hill overlooking the bay with a staff of two. In the neighboring cottage were the Alfred Hitchcocks and the Kingman Douglases (Adele Astaire, Fred's sister and partner in his early Broadway musicals).

Mr. Hitchcock stuck to his image, wearing a black suit and tie, morning, noon and night in blazing sun, high humidity and tropical downpours. It seemed as inappropriate as attending a dinner at Buckingham Palace in T-shirt and track shorts, and a lot of trouble to just maintain an image. I politely asked the filmmaker how he managed a suit in this weather. "It's light-weight," he deadpanned, and then asked me, "Does the prospect of seeing me scantily clad appeal to you, dear boy?" He had me there.

***

Back on campus, Ted was helping me in math and science, economics, theology, mechanical matters and all things requiring technical skills, i.e., light switches, radios, and phonographs. I, in turn, guided him in clothing selections and topical subjects for conversation. Ted had innate good manners, but little experience in the areas of debauchery or those ancillaries. He would emulate me, occasionally paraphrasing suavely to a bartender, "Scotch, on the rocks, *no ice*."

Most of my chums were upperclassmen, among who was a caustic lethally-tongued, never dull, future preeminent American playwright, John Guare. Should John deign to read this, I want him to know, I'm genuinely glad at his great success, admire his brilliant prose—half of which I don't understand. Most, some less read than I, appear to grasp the multi-layered text in John's work with little or no difficulty. I'm more comfortable with superficial plays about pretty young rich kids who kiss a lot.

In the early Spring of '58, I received a telegram reading:

"Howard and I married today in Saint Peter's—Love Mother"

I read Ted the message, he thought a second, responding supportively, "Hey, better late than never, right?" A third marriage, divorced, marrying a Protestant, in *Saint Peter's*—good for you, Mom!

GQK's Catholicism wasn't manifested in regular church attendance or receiving the sacraments, her's was a more personal approach, ceramic saints watching over bird baths in the garden, framed pictures of the Blessed Mother and the *Pieta*—unsigned—in her bedroom. Mom wouldn't dip her fingers in holy water, "You don't know who had their fingers in there," but she'd make the sign of the cross whenever an ambulance passed or when driving by a hospital. For air travel, she had an abbreviated 18 karat gold rosary ring she fingered on takeoffs, heavy turbulence, or engine malfunctions. Her bed table drawer held a worn copy of the New Testament (not the *King James* version), lying next to the .32 caliber snub-nose. GQK would donate stained glass windows, as long as they depicted her favorite saints. Her son has a special affinity for Saint Joseph—who had to be the greatest of all step-dads. Mom was heavily into candle-lighting, disbursing funds for church accouterments, Catholic charities and she adored the visceral aspects. "You have to admit, no one does ceremonies better than the Catholic Church and the British." As half Anglo-Catholic, I'd like to think so.

GQK's ecclesiastical devotion came in bursts, and then subsided, reappeared, but she never for an instant lost the faith. She could empathize with an agnostic, someone who didn't believe, didn't know or wasn't convinced—however, she had zero tolerance for avowed atheists who state unequivocally, "There is no God!"

"How the hell do they know something the rest of us don't?"

Conversely, she and I would also get nervous around those who *know* God is on their side.

***

Mr. and Mrs. Howard Bell went to California after their return from Europe, to no one's surprise, Howard wasn't the *ranchy* type, nor equipped to handle people in the entertainment industry. Bless his heart; he had no real interest in anything.

His wife swore, when the subject of (Vladimir) *Lenin* came up in a conversation, Howard responded, "It wrinkles too easily, I prefer cotton."

Howard had a tasteful one-bedroom bachelor *pied-a-terre* in the East 70s with one big bed. GQK believed marriage was no excuse to share a bedroom *or* bathroom, let alone a bed, especially for a couple their age, in their social position. If it should come to *that,* there ought to be enough interest and energy to walk to the next room.

Howard's apartment had a unique second bathroom, a half-bath-powder room, with direct access to the living room—the door to it located at dead center of one wall. One entered and exited the tiny facility in full view of everyone present. Once inside there was no guarantee of privacy, every sound clearly audible in the living room. It was entertaining to observe guests, watching other guests using the facility—hearing them trying desperately not to be heard—and then more fun while listening to futile attempts to drown out awkward moments by turning faucets on full blast, banging and clanging any available surface, even loud humming or singing a chorus from their favorite Broadway musical. Tapping feet while seated isn't for the untrained, cringing at the inevitable flushing noise, and finally emerging to impromptu sporadic applause, or worse, those pretending not to have heard a thing, thus intensifying the discomfort.

In the city Howard had a vintage Bentley with an inherently nasty nature. It was cramped, temperamental and prone to mysterious afflictions. When the driver went over thirty the *ol' girl* would develop a tubercular cough, making strange gurgling noises, and, at forty, belching flatulent sounds. The few occasions the speedometer went above forty, the *ol' girl* quivered, shuddered, a spastic lurch, then stopped; all engine and electrical components simply ceased to function. She then got an easy ride back to the garage aboard a flatbed towing truck. The narrow back seat became an ordeal with three passengers, I was devious enough to ride in front with the driver, and any hapless third person rode in back. During those cramped trips, Howard seemed cheerfully oblivious, his bride stared out the window with a fixed enigmatic expression, and the poor *sonuvabitch* sitting between them looked as if he or she were being transported to Auschwitz.

Turkey Trot

At Georgetown, tradition dictated "those on top of things" spend their Thanksgiving break in New York, meet under the clock at the Biltmore Hotel, at least one lunch at P.J. Clarke's, and most importantly, attend the Gotham Ball held annually the Saturday following Thanksgiving day, in the grand ballroom of the Plaza Hotel. On these gala occasions, the young catholic girls made their social debuts, at least the one's with affluent and/or connected parents, thus being officially introduced to young Catholic men with commiserate backgrounds, who in many cases, the young ladies were already quite familiar. High Episcopalians were acceptable if they agreed to raise the children as Catholics.

The girls having laid waste to Bergdorfs, Bonwits, Bloomies, Lord and Taylors, spending hours at *Mr. Phyllis' Salon* and having depleted their parents' bank account, were ready for bare—looking as lovely as genes, cosmetic technology, and money would allow—then genteelly escorted and introduced at court.

The young men resplendent in white tie and tails, there was no modification or compromising of formal attire in those days. The guys wore black and white, possibly a boutonniere for a dash of color. That was it, as appalling taste wasn't the vogue back then, no cowboy-heeled pumps, ruffled rainbow-colored shirts or improvised haute-couture individuality. *Sending in the clowns* was a no-no, the result, everyone looked great!

New York's archbishop then was Francis Cardinal Spellman, no slouch himself when it came time to dress up. His blending of pinks, reds, purples, with gold accents, put most of the debutantes on a back burner, and did he know how to make an entrance! "Spellman, the Spellbinder." There was a standing prize for the debutante who could get His Eminence on the dance floor—and rumor had it, a grand prize to the guy who did! No harm in asking.

The non-stop music of Lester Lanin or Meyer Davis and all those "pretty young kids who kissed a lot," looking and behaving like ladies and gentlemen, having fun doing it, swept up even the most blasé and jaded among them.

Thursday was Thanksgiving, Saturday the Ball, so, to avoid any lull on Friday, GQK had generously underwritten a dinner party I would host at the River Club. It would be a sit-down for twenty-four in one of the private entertainment suites. I invited several New York friends, the rest were swanky G.U. buddies.

The River Club staff predictably did a flawless job. Each setting on the dining table had a Royal Doulton place plate, flanked by eight pieces of silverware, with two more above the plate, four various sized crystal glasses, tiny silver salt & pepper shakers and a small silver ashtray.

Mom and Howard appeared briefly during dinner to say "Hi" and assure all was moving smoothly. They looked absolutely smashing, every bit the ideal *Town and Country* image of American aristocracy, dressed to understated, subtle perfection, secure in their superiority. The guests, male and female, immediately arose spontaneously, not waiting to see what the others did. Mom with two strands of pearls, Howard's Cartier cufflinks barely visible, I tried not to get too silly about it, but I was proud as hell. They radiated elegance that evening.

After they wished us well and departed, one of the girls wondrously commented, "You can tell they've had a long beautiful marriage." Then asked, "How long have they been together?" I wasn't being glib when I replied, "Almost a year now."

In Palm Beach that Christmas, the ethereal aura around Mr. and Mrs. Howard Bell had evaporated. GQK complained, "Howard doesn't do anything! He doesn't work, has no hobbies, not even a mistress stashed away." She had told me on numerous occasions, "Men were fine after six, but she didn't like them around the house in the daytime." She made the first reference I could remember in years to her former husbands, "At least Fred and Teddy worked. They'd leave in the morning, and come home in the evening. I had the days to myself!"

I knew the pattern, once GQK took a negative stance with someone or something, it festered, mushroomed to point where everything they did was wrong, stupid, malicious or downright evil.

Meantime Howard had given me a new yellow Thunderbird, the original two-seater, with a removable hard top. Whether Howard did it out of pure paternalism or as an attempt to elicit my support, I didn't care, I loved that car.

Mom told me I couldn't accept it, it was mine to drive in Florida, but not in the other forty-nine states, Howard was trying to spoil me—she thought she had the monopoly.

Mom took me aside at every opportunity with, "Howard doesn't play golf, tennis or racquetball—just bridge with old ladies." And continued with, "Howard doesn't have any men friends. Men should do things with other men, fish, hunt, play pool, or watch strippers—something!"

I reminded her, he wasn't hiding anything under a bushel when she married him. "That's typical of you, always taking the other person's side," she said denouncing me.

Howard wore perfectly tailored dark suits north of the Mason-Dixon Line, but in Palm Beach he let it all hang out. His wardrobe was extensive; he never wore the same outfit twice. Jackets, shirts, slacks in every conceivable color and shade, soft pastels to bright blinding colors any rock group would covet—plaids, stripes, patent-leather loafers and pumps, socks didn't exist in Palm Beach.

Howard bought a Masserati, and GQK's reaction, "Men are boys with more expensive toys."

She called me at Georgetown to tell me, Howard had gotten a speeding ticket. "He's so proud of it, he shows it to everybody! I asked him if he wanted to have it framed and hung it in the living room? Do you know what he said?"

"No, Mom, I don't."

"He said, 'Maybe in a guest bathroom.'" Mom continued, "Howard was acting like a damned fool, driving around in that ridiculous car at his age, can you imagine?" The author is now at that age and frankly, he can't.

The *coups de grace* came at the ranch that Spring. Mac, the Irish setter, had inoperable cancer but he wasn't in pain, and Papuli had been blind for over a year, but got around okay, so long as you didn't move the furniture. Howard recommended the two dogs be put to sleep. "They are old, inactive, and totally dependent—of no useful purpose." GQK's response, "If that's the criteria, they wouldn't be the only ones put to sleep."

Howard left that afternoon.

On Impressing Your Peers

Agnes Moorehead came to town with Raymond Massey and Martin Gabel, in Norman Corwin's *The Rivalry,* based on the Lincoln-Douglass debates. I called Aggie at the National Theater to ask her to supper one night after the show. She gave me a date, and I got three seats for that night, wanting to affirm to a couple of skeptical classmates, my friendship with Agnes Moorehead.

On arriving at the theater, I realized it was opening night with Washington's elite mingling in the lobby. Had Aggie gotten the nights confused? So much for dinner afterwards, she would be engaged with opening night festivities. *The Rivalry* was a riveting evening, and she was flawless.

My two classmates accompanied me backstage after the performance, Aggie received me like a prodigal son. My friends impressed, we were about to leave when Aggie announced, "I'll be ready in a minute." We *were* on for supper.

To be on the safe side, I'd made reservations at the Shoreham to see Edith Piaf making a rare appearance this side of the Atlantic. The hotel's night club was packed, even with reservations in all the commotion, the maitre d' glimpsed three college students with an older lady and was about to lead us to a table in never-never land when a customer called out, "We saw you tonight Miss Moorehead, great show!" The maitre d' did a near-imperceptible double-take, then, without missing a beat, led us in a circuitous sweep back to the front of the room. All the tables were occupied. He snapped his fingers, to several waiters, pointed to ringside, where a table was set up on the edge of the stage area.

Seconds after our supper arrived, the lights dimmed, strains of *Le Vie en Rose,* then, center stage, a single pin spot illuminated the "Little Sparrow," a frail diminutive figure in a short black dress and a sweater around her tiny shoulders. Edith Piaf, though in her early forties, gave the impression of having seen a thousand years, as she took absolute command of the room.

The spill from the stage lights partially illuminated our table. Normally I don't like involuntary audience participation, but this night Aggie and I were primarily concerned about being caught in the right light.

Chapter 12

STEPS ALONG THE WAY

During a New York visit with Agnes Moorehead she introduced me to a couple, Albert and Dorothy Strelsin, who lived in a penthouse apartment on the corner of Fifth and 75th Street with an enormous balcony on two sides. The Strelsins hosted Sunday dinners at Luchow's restaurant downtown in the Tribeca area. The German eatery was a madhouse on those nights; you had to shout to the person next to you to be heard. The lady I was seated next to on occasion had no difficulty in communicating. Ethel Merman's voice could fill Yankee Stadium without amplification.

Talented, terse, tough and tenacious, she more than lived up to her reputation and image. It was hard to tell if she liked you or merely tolerated you. In an attempt to deflect her impact, I sought the advice of our hostess. Dorothy—no shrinking violet herself—was a close buddy of Miss Merman's. I asked her if the Broadway mega-star had any soft spots, and the only one that came to her mind was the Republican Party.

I moaned on, "She calls me, kiddo." Dorothy enlightened me, "Oh, for Christ's sake, she doesn't call anyone else that!"

I saw a scarf in thrift shop on Second Avenue, the kind of garish design you'd see on a 1940s Aloha shirt—sailors ogling an over-the-hill hula dancer wearing a straw hat. On impulse I bought it, wrapped it in brown paper, with a card; *"For Panama Hattie. Thanks for the good company,* (signed) *Kiddo."* The next time I saw Merman at Lubach's, I slipped it on her chair before we sat down when she wasn't looking. Pretending not to see her examining the mysterious brown paper package cautiously, I could read her thoughts, "What the fuck is this?" She unwrapped the scarf, looked at the tacky print, not sure how to react, and then read the card. I diverted my attention, finally letting my eyes *unintentionally* glance in her direction. She was looking right at me, a knot in my gut—then she gave me a smile.

Al and Dorothy Strelsin gave entrée to others. When Mom was in town they took us both to a party a block or two from the River Club, given by attorney Arnold Weissberger, and agent-roommate, Milton Goldman.

Those two gentlemen were social meccas of the entertainment world in New York; an invitation to their eclectic soirées became a status symbol, the *"New York Social Register"* of show business. That night GQK was with *me*. Al, Dorothy, and I would introduce *her* to famous personages.

A Rose by Any Other Name

Toward the end of my academic decline, the five Raysbrooks, four Munroes, a couple of school chums, and I went on picnic in the wilds of northern Virginia. When Navy families plan an outing, it is to be done properly—*if you're going to do it, do it right.* Aye-aye, sir. Conchita wasn't the only gourmet cook in the family, Bob Munroe was excellent with cuisine, when and if the occasion presented itself. Commander Munroe and I were both good in the kitchen, but not on a regular basis. Most guys have to be motivated and in the mood.

The vehicle to the campsite phase with picnics involved transporting food baskets, liquid containers, utensils, folding chairs, hibachis, blankets, insect repellent, and first aid gear. In this case, a dozen people attending required organization and stamina. The adults served as pack-mules, while the youngsters ran hither and yon, exploring, examining, exclaiming—having a good time quietly is anathema to children. It had been raining. Everything was damp, and the ground muddy in spots.

During the picnic Captain Frank Raysbrook and I got into heavy conversation as to the state of the world, in general. I was expounding on the merits of military dictatorships, Frank favored the more popular constitutional monarchy concept—maybe the divine right of kings, *off with their heads*, variety. The dedicated, and decorated conservative naval captain reflected a moment, then made one of the most profound and insightful observations I had ever heard, "David, in the final analysis, remember, it's all bullshit."

I quoted the remark to GQK, and she qualified it with, "Well, I suppose it's true—but my God, you can't tell that to a five year old."

Ready for Her Close-up

A memorable stock experience was touring with Gloria Swanson in *Red Letter Day,* a piece of froth by Harold J. Kennedy. Buddy Rogers, Lois Wilson, myself, and four other cast members played to packed houses in Westport, Kennebunkport, Hyannisport, Saratoga Springs, Gilford-Laconia in New Hampshire, and Milburn, New Jersey.

Miss Swanson's triumphant comeback in *Sunset Boulevard* nearly a decade earlier, made her the top draw that Summer. Wherever she appeared sold-out. There were luncheons, and after-performance suppers in her honor. Local hosts vied for an opportunity to entertain her. She had two dressing rooms—one for her, one for her wardrobe.

Her career decline in *Talkies* hadn't been due to aging, she looked fantastic thirty years after the advent of sound movies, her acting was okay if she wasn't allowed to do *too* much of it. It took a few weeks to figure out the real problem. Her voice was in conflict with her persona and belonged to someone else. It was flat, girlish with a Midwestern rural rasp, not all in keeping with an exotically sophisticated image.

Early in the tour Miss Swanson decided the author would be a suitable escort to functions, traveling from venue to venue with her, her secretary and chauffeur-chef, in her Rolls-Royce. It was exciting but taxing. Miss Swanson could be delightful, however one misstep or perceived slight meant banishment to the lowest place in hell. She was unfailingly gracious to me and seemed comfortable, but although I liked her enormously, I was on pins and needles most of the Summer—a forced camaraderie. I knew how her displeasure could be vented, I empathized with the victims.

We'd been doing the play for over a month. One night in Saratoga, I dried up on stage, I'd gone totally blank. Finally, they tossed me a cue. I told the stage manager, "I'd best not take a curtain call," and went to my dressing room and was literally packing my theatrical gear. The curtain came down, a moment later the production stage manager was pounding on the door, "David, get your ass on stage, *fast*, orders from the top!" I rushed to the wings. Except for Miss Swanson, the cast was on stage holding the bow. Buddy waved me on stage, I stepped out not knowing what to do, or where to go. Now I'd also screwed up the curtain call. The audience apparently loved the spontaneity of the debacle I'd created, there was no chance to dwell on it. When Miss Swanson swept on stage from the other side, took her bow, turned and gave an exaggerated wink, the audience loved it even more.

After the curtain, literally shaking, I went to the star's dressing room to apologize. Miss Swanson, with a cocked eyebrow, told me, "You'll have to do better to take your bow after mine." I was hers after that.

***

GQK came east to see the show towards the end of the tour during the Papermill Playhouse engagement. At the party following the show, Gloria and Mom sat conspicuously on a sofa for an hour rehashing the old Hollywood days, versus the new. If I approached the sofa I'd get a, "We-want-to-talk, get-lost" wave off. Every few minutes the two women would break into raucous laughter or naughty giggles, I'd give my soul for a tape of that conversation.

Later Gloria told me, "After chatting with Gladys, I can see dealing with me must have been a piece of cake."

Preparation Period

That fall I was accepted at the Neighborhood Playhouse in New York, still considered one of the foremost acting schools in the country. It's legendary director, Sanford Meisner, was in Hollywood that year with Clifford Odets, working at 20th Century Fox in variety of prestigious positions, with prestigious titles, but not such prestigious films. The only one that comes to mind starred Rita Hayworth, who despite her demeaned position as a "Movie Star," was the only redeeming element in one of the films.

David Pressman, a fine gentleman and director, was running the Playhouse at the time. He invited a few of us to a preview of a play he was directing by Budd Schulberg, *The Disenchanted*, with Jason Robards playing a character named *Manley Halliday* a.k.a., F. Scott Fitzgerald. The play was set in 1940, when Fitzgerald was a failed screenwriter in Hollywood, with flashbacks to the 1920s as a glamorous world-renown novelist. The time transitions were accomplished by lowering the lights to black, Robards turning his back to the audience a beat, then turning back to the audience, lights up again, as the character 20 years younger, or older. I marveled at how Robards achieved these visceral and inner-life transitions in a matter of seconds without benefit of makeup, wardrobe, or set change. He said he would show me the secret. *"Show"* me, surely he meant, *explain* to me? I watched carefully as he spoke the older *Halliday*'s dialogue, cueing a blackout, he gave me a peripheral wink, as he turned and became the younger character. I admitted, "Well, I didn't actually see the transition this time," trying to extricate myself I explained, "When I was sitting in the audience I did—I mean, I *thought* I did." Robards gave me a piece of invaluable advice, "It's more effective if you let the audience do some of the work."

It turned out to be a vintage period at the Neighborhood Playhouse, Brenda Vaccaro, Dabney Coleman, Jessica Walter, Leonard Frey, John Phillip Law, also-starring Louise Sorel, Walter Koenig, Jonathan (Lippe) Goldsmith and Geoffrey Lewis all had careers successful enough to keep up S.A.G. health and welfare benefits. The acting school schedule was eight-to-five, five days a week, often Saturdays. In addition to acting, stage technique, stage logistics, how to talk, sing, fence, dress appropriately, make yourself look pretty—or at least interesting—you were taught movement and modern dance by Martha Graham, and Louis Horst.

Whether you call it, the *Stanislosky-Strasberg-Chekhov* method, sense memory, internalization, finding a character from within or through meditation—essentially, consciously or subconsciously, the actor is acquiring his or her own *technique*.

I was effective in some roles, quite good in a few, but I was essentially a mediocre actor. Some pull it off, making you believe otherwise, and have long successful careers. A successful movie producer told me in the late sixties, "You're too conspicuous to be a steady featured actor, you don't have the motivation or discipline to be a star. You have a lot of the technique, but not the raw energy to be a top-notch character actor."

In a nutshell, I was a Summer-Stock-leading man.

Teaching a Turkey to Tango

Martha Graham's efforts to transform DHK into a lithe and graceful serpentine were tantamount to teaching a turkey to tap dance. The icon of modern dance was a sweetheart with a fire in her belly, in the "mid-November" of her illustrious life, Miss Graham was a perfect blend of lady and delicious broad. In class, I'd be bending at the bar in ballet slippers, leotards and wide support belt, acting as a combination jockstrap-tummy reducer—I wish to God, I could find one now—Miss Graham would step up behind me, "Keep your back straight, dear-thing," tweak my butt, "And stop tucking your tush in. You don't have that much, let 'em see what's there!"

She confided, "Dear-thing, if your career plans include musical theater, let me suggest you concentrate on your *singing*." I don't recall her taking that kind of interest in the others. I felt honored to be singled out.

Easter with Ethel

A classmate at the playhouse I socialized with was the daughter of the best friend of an old *friend* of mine—Ethel Merman. The star of *Panama Hattie*, *Annie Get Your Gun* and *Call Me Madam*, had done it again with *Gypsy*! This circuitously culminated in an Easter Sunday with "Uncle Ethel." If Easter Sunday and Ethel Merman seem incongruous—contrary to any stereotypical impression—she *was* Roman Catholic.

She hosted ten of us, including her two grandchildren, for Easter lunch at the Plaza Hotel. The plan was we would all rendezvous up the street at the Central Park Zoo before lunch so the grandchildren, ages about five and seven, and could have a look around. Miss Merman led the group through the zoo pointing out the various residents for kid's benefit. "Look over there! Those are polar bears!" The little ones nodded unenthusiastically. "Ya' see the tigers lying in that pen?"—minimal response from the youngsters. "Those are seals on those rocks! See the seals!" Yeah, they saw them, so what?

Now, the super-star, followed by an ever-growing group of admiring fans, and getting little reaction from the kids, gave it another try, "Look at those alligators, or crocodiles, or what-ever!"—again an under-whelmed sigh. With that, Miss Merman whirled around to her grand-children in a voice that would bring down any house, and exclaimed, "All right! I've shown you bears, tigers, crocodiles and every other goddam thing here! Now, what the fuck *do* you want?"

The fans fleeing, animals retreating to their lairs, we stomped to the Edwardian Room of the Plaza.

The film *Gypsy*, directed by GQK's good friend, Mervyn Leroy, was a disappointment. Mom pinned down the film's lack of success astutely when she observed, "Roz Russell is a superb actress, but she didn't have the innate coarseness, the part demanded a *broad*. You can put Roz in a funny hat, dress her down and have her talk loud, but it doesn't obscure the fact she's a lady." This was certainly a factor, but the film overall was a lack-lustre production.

Frightening the Horses

GQK was in town on an inspection tour, my upcoming birthday was an excuse to see if I and my "little actor friends," had trashed the apartment. While I was at class, Mom browsed the apartment for telltale signs of misbehavior or communal occupancy. Knowing my lackadaisical housekeeping habits, and noting everything was too blatantly neat—clearly indicating an effort to overcompensate for wrong doing—but with no tangible evidence, she had no qualms about entrapment.

"I must say, *someone* around here is very tidy."

"Some are, some aren't," I shrugged.

GQK hosted my twenty first birthday party, appropriately at '*21.*' She confided to me, her tax people had determined the ranch would have to become a legitimate business enterprise, and make a profit at least one year in the next five to deduct losses for I.R.S. purposes in future years. After eight years of dabbling, tangible losses were no problem, showing a profit would be.

The Hidden Valley Association, Inc. rules prevented many entrepreneurial options, those dependent on public patronage or paid admission, any commercial ventures attracting riffraff—meaning restricted to property owners and invited guests.

A dude ranch, rehab center, or nudist colony implied paying guests and had to be nixed. Gladys Knapp had already made her decision, she would breed horses—the kind that run at Santa Anita and Ascot, thoroughbreds.

21's horsey décor should have been the tip off.

Chapter 13

NO AUTOGRAPHS, PLEASE

Warner Bros. was mounting a film based on Mildred Savage's bestselling novel, *Parrish*. The story was of a young fellow finding his manhood in the cigar-leaf tobacco fields of Connecticut. Actors on both coasts coveted the title role, while those less ambitious would happily settle for several of the juicy support roles. Originally, the project was given to Joshua Logan to direct with Warren Beatty tentatively set in the title role, fresh from his auspicious film debut in *Splendor in the Grass*. When that didn't work out, the studio assigned none other than Delmer Daves to write, produce, and direct it!

A curious combination of elements then evolved—Delmer and Marylou came east to scout Connecticut locations. Mother happened to be in New York at the time, where her son happened to be attending one of the top drama schools in the country. The next thing I knew, Delmer, Marylou, GQK, and myself were dining at Sardi's—*Good golly, Miss Molly*!

With a highly taunted project like this, everyone had opinions as to who should be cast in each role and Warner's had a dozen contractees who could fit the bill. I'd sworn to myself I wouldn't mention the picture—unless, someone else said anything remotely leading into it. GQK took no such oath, by the time drinks arrived she'd lobbed off enough hints to fell an elephant.

By the appetizer, GQK happened to mention, I was studying at *the* best acting school in the country—something which Delmer and Marylou were long since well aware. The main course included GQK's reaction to Troy Donahue being cast in the title role, "Is he someone I should have heard of?"

Delmer graciously feigned an attentive demeanor throughout, while I tried to convey apologetic awkwardness. It was Machiavellian on my part to disassociate myself from GQK's sales pitch, she wasn't looking for ten-percent, and I wasn't a star letting his agent do the dirty work. Yet, it paid off though. Warner's called to set up a screen test the following Thursday. Fantastic! I asked where the New York studio facility was located, and the caller chuckled, "In Burbank."

Playhouse students were not allowed to pursue or accept outside professional acting jobs while enrolled. A dilemma, compounded by the pursuit across country! I had an opportunity to test my acting skills on the instructors who taught me! The following Wednesday, I coughed, wheezed, and gagged myself into an early afternoon dismissal from class, just in time to make my 4:30 p.m. flight to L.A.

GQK's foreman, Jack Dempsey, a saint of a man, picked me up and drove me to the ranch. The Palisades house, as per usual, was rented. The test was scheduled at 1 p.m. the next day, so I could sleep in. GQK regretfully informing, "Not past eight, Dearest, the lawyer is meeting you downtown at the Superior Court Building at ten sharp." She explained, "A little twelve year oversight" on her part required my presence before a judge. The next morning, having shared my bed with two effusive dogs, Mom urged me to "break a leg"—I wasn't sure that applied to movies— but off I went to the studio, via the Los Angeles Superior Court Building.

The legal rendezvous involved my entering the court room legally as, *Robin Howard Peabody*—and less than an hour later emerging as, *David Howard Knapp*. Having been the latter most of my life, it never occurred to me, contracts, passports, legal documents, necessitate a *legal* name. My driver's license read David Knapp. I hadn't really thought about *Robin Peabody* for years. Now, he was gone forever.

Two hours later, I was screen tested on a Burbank sound stage. Three hours later, I was on a flight back to New York. Ten hours after that, fully recovered, I was in class at the Playhouse, none the worse for wear.

Forty years later, driving to the San Fernando Valley is a major ordeal.

Long Shots

Due entirely to Delmer's efforts, I got the role of *Wiley Raike*, the younger antagonistic stepbrother. For most actors worthy of biography, this experience would be summarized in a sentence, in my case, having only made four feature films—two of which, the less said about the better—more time and detail is warranted.

Parrish was the story of a young city boy "Parrish McLean" (Troy Donahue) readjusting to life in the tobacco farming country of Connecticut, where his Mother (Claudette Colbert) is employed as a companion-chaperone for the daughter (Diane McBain) of a successful tobacco farmer, (Dean Jagger), whose nemesis is powerful land-owner, Judd Raike (Karl Malden), and his two thoroughly unpleasant sons (Hampton Fancher and David Knapp). Their innocent younger sister (Sharon Hugueny) is caught in the crossfire. Meantime the younger Raike, "Wiley," marries Post's daughter, who is as big a bitch as Wiley is a jerk. Connie Stevens played a farm girl floozy. Filling out the cast, a New York based contingent, Madeleine

Sherwood, Sylvia Miles, and Bibi Osterwald, as tobacco pickers, a wonderfully incongruous bit of casting, we nicknamed them, *The Tobacco Tarts.*

The Daves' daughter, my surrogate sister Debby, worked on the picture in a variety of capacities, to me the most important of which was her just *being there.* Debby is a daring, delightful, darling, the most fun and healthiest "upper" I could experience.

Observing Delmer in action was a lesson in patience, flexibility, interrelating, while maintaining gentle, but total command. On very rare instances Delmer took off the velvet gloves.

During a big, complicated, three-camera shot involving many actors, extras and a burning barn, a third unit cameraman ran out of film yelling, "Cut!" One person alone is allowed to yell, "Cut", the director. It matters not what's happening on the rest of the planet. Delmer's reprimand was heard throughout the tri-county area. The cast and crew cringed as he concluded, lowering his voice to light thunder, advising the hapless cameraman, "…and don't ever try to shoot a three-minute sequence with *two*-minutes of film in the camera! It can't be done!"

I had no real base of comparison but it seemed a relatively smooth shoot, a few bumps, probably numerous problems those in front of the camera weren't aware of, but Delmer and Harry Stradling, Sr., the cinematographer, never allowed them to surface.

Slam It in Reverse and Floor It

My nemesis came in the form of a red sportscar, a vintage Mercedes convertible. I'd never driven a car with that transmission. I asked could someone show me how before we shot the complicated scene, demanding high speed, and precise *erratic* driving. The A.D. assured me, "They'd get right on it."

They had more important things to worry about than my inability to operate the German import, as a result, I was unprepared, but figured I could wing it. The following day I tried to familiarize myself with the basics while they set up the shot. I couldn't even start the damned thing. Embarrassed, and in desperation I called Debby over, explaining my predicament. Debby's thinking, "He can't be serious," as she pointed to a little button above the ignition switch, slowly explaining, "Turn-the-key-to-the-right, then-push-that-button-and-press-your-foot-down-on-the-accelerator." She was about to continue when I was called into action.

A radiant Diane McBain in the passenger seat, Delmer tells me to follow the flatbed camera truck, also serving as a farm vehicle, with principals sitting at the rear in the foreground of the shot watching Diane and David, following behind them. Delmer explained, "All you have to do is drive it at high speed down a narrow-country road, come up behind the truck, on signal accelerate, swerve out, pull around, then cut back in front of it. Oh, and be attentive to the lady seated next to you who you're madly in love with." Hummmm??? Okay.

Delmer and the others piled on the back of the flatbed, and started off. I'm trying to remember how to apply a horizontal standard shift on a steering column to a vertical four-on-the-floor. Do I use the clutch before and/or during changing gears? Better make sure reverse is upper left—or right?

I shifted tentatively; the response wasn't what I'd hoped for. Diane suggested I put it in first. With clenched teeth I smiled, "I thought I had."

"No, you're in third," she smiled.

"Saves me having to deal with first and second," I quipped.

Meanwhile, the camera truck stops, and all aboard are wondering why the delay. Feeling the pressure, I slammed it in gear, a surge of Teutonic power, and we lurched—but in the wrong direction, managing to stop before our rear end smashed into a stone wall. I knew now where reverse was! Those on camera truck waving us forward, the Nazi-by-product leaps forward, the wide-eyed crew, along with half the state of Connecticut having now gathered, are jubilant when my lightening response prevents us from rear-ending the camera truck.

Minutes later we careened down the relatively straight two lane road, the view ahead hindered only by a sharp-hilly terrain, un-obscured on the crest of hills, and then descending into canyons of uncertainty. Delmer gestured from the truck. "I think he wants you closer," Diane interpreted. I cautiously accelerated, and Delmer kept waving.

"My God, I'm practically on top of them," I tell my movie fiancée.

The movie bride-to-be speculates, "Del probably wants us close enough so they can identify who's in the car." This marriage ain't gonna work!

Practically in close up, Diane looks at me adoringly snuggling as close as bucket seats allow, one hand caressing the back of my neck, then poking a finger in my ear. "Ouch, Diane!" "We're engaged, David, pay attention to me," she hisses with a smile of reckless abandon. Focused on survival, all I can spare her is a not-so-loving lateral punch in the arm.

We get a *pass* signal from Delmer—my white knuckles wrapped around the wheel—we then edge to the left, while noting the sparse space between the truck and the ditch on the opposite side. Someone on the truck shouts something I couldn't have heard right, "Did he tell me to blow it out my ass?"

"No, David" she said. "Now, go on and pass," She soothes.

Abreast of the truck, and Delmer cries, "Cut!" Thank God! The flatbed and our malevolent machine halt parallel. Delmer doesn't look happy.

"We're going to try it again. This time I want to see a guy in love—not a Kamikaze pilot pinpointing a target," he instructed, and explaining my cautiously easing around the truck wouldn't have the visual impact of suddenly swerving out and roaring past it.

"But Delmer, I don't wanna smash into the rear of the truck or sideswipe it," visualizing bodies flying all over the place, decapitating Diane and myself, worst of all, totaling the fuck'n Mercedes.

"You can drive and be in love at the same time," Delmer assured me.

Several takes and no prints later, Delmer gave up the host, and would deal with it in the editing room.

***

Mother joined the company in and around Hartford. I picked her up at train station, and it was nice having her as my guest for a change. On the way to the hotel GQK had a surprise for me, as soon as the film wrapped we would be off for an extended stay in Europe. There was a lot to be attended to over there.

During her Connecticut stay, she and Claudette Colbert found they had more in common than Coco Chanel suits and a preference for separate bedrooms. Mildred Savage, the book's author, remained with us throughout the location shooting, guiding Claudette and GQK on local excursions.

Claudette was entering her fourth decade as a star of the first magnitude, an interesting contrast to the star I had spent the previous summer with on tour. Both were household names, tiny women with large faces the camera adored. Miss Swanson, more theatrically glamorous, but Colbert a far more talented actress whose modulated voice perfectly captured her style and character. She wore her own wardrobe as Parrish's Mother, financially pressed into accepting a domestic position of sorts, arriving her first day on camera in a Chanel suit, which might stretch credibility. In Miss Colbert's case, nobody gave a damn if the struggling lady she portrayed didn't appear to have struggled too hard and wore *haute couture*. Pity any poor soul suggesting gingham and calico might be more appropriate. The former Oscar winner pulled it off beautifully, on stage and screen Claudette Colbert was an impeccable artist and one of the very great light comediennes of the century. When an occasion demanded, she also had a vocabulary rivaling that of Al Pacino, but always used in perfect grammatical context.

After several weeks of Connecticut locations, the company returned to L.A. for studio interiors.

Pinecliff still rented, on days we filmed late and had early calls the following morning, rather than schlep up to the ranch and back, Troy invited me to crash at his apartment in West Hollywood, which he shared with his girlfriend, and actress, Sally Todd. Whatever shortcomings Troy may have had as an actor, he more than overcame as a person, a generous, thoughtful sweetheart of a guy. He, Sally and I, stayed up to the wee hours talking. I'd have had more sleep had I gone to the ranch, but not nearly as much fun. Troy and I remained sporadic friends for three decades, his early death saddened me greatly, and many of us miss him.

Left: Don Juan Bandini, circa 1815

Right: Josefa Bandini Carrillo

Below: Lottie Quarre and her mother
Dolores Carrillo Jackson, 1904

Above: Oswald, Carlotta ['Lottie']
and Gladys Quarre, Larkspur, 1901

Opposite:
Young juror in court.
San Francisco Examiner, **1923**

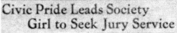

Above: Howard Chandler Christy drawing of Gladys, 1926

Right:
Quarre Family's
Chateau Larraldia,
Brussels, Belgium

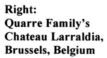

Rathbone party in Los Angeles, 1938. Opposite: l. to r. Douglas Fairbanks, Sr., Gladys, Basil Rathbone, Hedy Lamarr, Richard Tauber and Lesle Howard.

Below: Charles Chaplin and Artur Rubenstein.

Opposite: l. to r. Marlene Dietrich, Gladys, Hedy Lamarr, Mrs. Charles 'Pat' Boyer and Mrs. Douglas Fairbanks, Sr., [Sylvia Ashley Gable]

L. to r. Leo McCarey, Gladys, Charles Boyer and Edward G. Robinson

Below: Gladys and Robin Peabody,
with 'Gerry' and pups. Brentwood, 1939

Above: Robin and 'Dadun'
awakened from a nap. 1940

Below: 'Prelude to C Sharp Minor'
[No pun intended.] 1942

Above: Gladys and Robin,
Malibu, 1941

Left: Cadet Captain David Knapp, Los Angeles, 1952

Above: Standing l. to r. [Unid.], Patrick De Rothchild, [Unid], Atwater Kent, Gladys, Eric De Rothchild, Neil McCarthy.
Seated l. to r. Friedrich Durrenmatt, [Unid.], Bina DeHenckel de Rothchild, Duchess of Rutland, Marcia Davenport, Dolly Green. Los Angeles 1949.

Left: Jean Templeman and Mona McClive, the 'Scotties', with Marilyn, Gloria and Jack. 1955

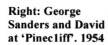

Right: George Sanders and David at 'Pinecliff'. 1954

Above: l. to r. Marylou & Delmer Daves, Charles Brackett, GQK and
Sammy Colt. Premier of 'Titanic', Los Angeles, 1953

Below: l. to r. Belgium Ambassador to U.S., Deborah Kerr,
Nancy Reagan, GQK and Ronald Reagan at 'Pinecliff', 1956

Right: Gladys Knapp marrying
Howard Bell, St. Peter's, Rome, 1958

Below: DHK and GQK with
Gregory Peck, Shepperton Studios,
England, 1960

Below: GQK and
Cary Grant. England,
1960

Above: Peter Lubbock and GQK.
Chapel Street, London. 1972

Right: Steven North, GQK and
DHK. Cannes, 1976

Below: DHK, GQK, Aide H.R.H.
Prince Charles & Monty Hall.
Beverly Hills, 1978

Rancho Gladavida guests:
Upper l. Mary Pickford, 1954
Upper r. Basil Rathbone,
[last photo] 1967

Lower l. Goldie Hawn and
Eve Arden, 1970

Lower r. Zsa Zsa Gabor, 1975

Left: GQK at Kahala house, Honolulu, 1968

Above: Louis & Arlette Quarre, GQK, and Oz Quarre, Brussels, 1970

Left: GQK with 'Feather Ball' and foal. Newmarket, England, 1970

Right: GQK on Bora Bora, 1971

Chapter 14

DAME DYNAMIC

Settling in a new decade, Gladys Knapp-Bell, a hyphenate she used briefly, didn't rest on her laurels. In close touch with her sixtieth year, she experienced a resurgence of energy, gusto, attacking life on many fronts, on diverse levels. Projects of her choosing, which once committed to, would not be abandoned. The breeding of thoroughbreds at rancho Gladavida was annexed to a facility seven thousand miles east, *Hadrien Stud* in Newmarket, England. Colonel Robin Hastings was the man in charge. This level of deluxe horse-breeding farms in England and Ireland are run like four-star hotels, with stalls instead of suites. Airy spacious comfortable surroundings, pristine conditions, prompt service, and great attention to occupant's diet, appearance, and organized to perfection. You don't see bathrooms adjacent to the stalls, but they must be there. Or, they've created an extraordinary breed of animal that drinks and feeds, without having to urinate or defecate—often running at a profit as well.

Mama began with two mares, *Pamfield* and *Feather Ball*, the latter gray with white markings, a "good luck" horse. To prove it, her first colt brought twelve-thousand guineas at sale in 1960, the equivalent of $48,000 in today's market. The first sale didn't set a precedent, however, two

175

more mares, nine fouls, over fifteen years, kept GQK in the breeding business. The financial coups were infrequent and brief, but she thoroughly enjoyed the role of "sportswoman," as well as its secondary function, the overall losses serving as a legitimate tax deduction, while justifying business and travel expenses abroad—but not indefinitely.

Success in skirmishes, could court disaster in battles! The government reiterated its mandate, a business must show a profit at some point to qualify as an entity to deduct taxes from! Paying any kind of taxes on a company consistently losing money, began to grate on GQK, but she was not deterred.

***

Traveling with GQK never afforded me—no pun intended—the opportunity to share adventures with my peers on tight budgets, Eurorail passes, our belongings strapped to our backs, or sleeping in no-frills youth hostels. Eating at quaint out-of-way boites only occurred if they had three or four stars in the guide *Michelin*. Instead of a shuttle bus or taxi at London's Heathrow airport, I was subjected to a Daimler the size of Royal Covent Garden, to be whisked away to Claridges Hotel. GQK's regular trips to Europe over the years were reflected by the hotel staff's attentive deference to her. The manager, in morning coat and pinstripes, ushered us to her suite, where flowers, sweets, a liquor tray and little gifts were waiting. I had never thought of Mama having been away *that* long, or often enough, to receive this kind of service. I would learn better.

After dinner the first night, we took a long leisurely walk, this became a tradition for Mother and son. There were many first night walks in many cities on several continents in the years to come. It was still dusk on that August night over four decades ago, when we strolled down Brook Street into Berkeley Square. Mama pointed to the

Rolls-Royce agency, "That's where we go tomorrow." Jules Stein arranged a special deal for Mama; she bought a Rolls Silver Cloud the previous year, left it in London for use on this trip. At that time, cars purchased and driven in Europe for six months or more prior to entry to the U.S. weren't subject to import duty, hadn't escaped her attention either.

We crossed Curson Street, through Shepherd's Market to Piccadilly. Mama indicated points of interest along the way. Her knowledge and familiarity with London's West End was very impressive. By the time we turned up Bond Street, I was experiencing an acute case of *deja vu*, not just the *feeling* of having been there before, it was somehow *knowing* I had.

When I said, "I've been here before," it was a statement, not an out-of-life phantasm. "I sense it all around me." I tried to sound clinical, no alliterative. There was no hint of incredulity in her reaction, "Didn't someone say something about there being, *things in heaven and earth, not dreamed of in our philosophies?*"

"Yes, Mom, they did, but I don't get the correlation?" She was doing the ol' *musing-enigmatic* bit again.

Mother, referring to the quotation, "Was that Shakespeare?"

"Where?" It was my turn. I looked up and down the street, "If it was, I want to meet him. How was he dressed?"

GQK deadpanned, "I couldn't be sure, he was in a taxi."

Everything in Excess

During the next few weeks I discovered GQK knew as many people in London as in New York and Los Angeles. We were going out with someone for lunch, cocktail hour, dinner, and/or theater and supper, the entire stay.

Rupert Allan, a dean of Hollywood publicists, on his own initiative, hyped me to some London newspapers, implying I was an actor to be reckoned with in the future, a notion I wasn't adverse to promoting, an example of getting more recognition away from home base, while acknowledging, being Gladys Knapp-Bell's son was in no way a hindrance in my ascent to semi-celebrity status.

I'd worked at Warner Bros, but it was the European head of publicity for Columbia Pictures, Halsey Raines, who took charge of press relations. Halsey had much less to work with than he realized, I suppose you're expected to create your own momentum. Halsey treated me like the star of the future, I didn't try to dissuade him. He became a mentor, guide, and an invaluable associate.

He, GQK, and I drove out to Shepperton Studios—well, her *chauffeur* drove us. In her many visits to Great Britain GQK had never driven a car. In a crisis situation she believed she'd automatically react in a manner she'd been accustomed to. If the British chose to drive on the wrong side of the road, so be it. The term *"wrong side"* isn't arrogant, it's accurate. Virtually every civilized nation on earth drives on the right; the only other hold-outs are former members of the Commonwealth. The author inherited that belief. He's driven in almost every country in Europe, but never in his beloved England.

In 1960, the Shepperton Studio complex was one the busiest movie factories in Europe. Columbia Pictures, Disney, United Artists and several independents occupied every bit of space. Halsey took us to an enormous sound stage where two actors were scaling a studio cliff under high winds and pelting rain, also furnished by the studio—an interior of an exterior, so to speak.

The shot finished, one of the actors ambled over extending a welcoming hand, "Hi. How are you? My name is Greg Peck." I almost said, "No shit!" I'm a devout Gregory Peck fan. The integrity, dignity, and skill he brings to his roles gave one a feeling of confidence, and being in safe hands. Many years later Peck turned in one of the most brilliant screen performances in memory, his portrayal of *MacArthur,* would have made the general proud. While maintaining the majestic image of the historical figure, Peck interwove in the character humanity, humor, anxieties, and flaws.

We were having lunch in the studio commissary, my back to the room, when Mama and Halsey looked up, behind me a familiar voice called out, "Gladys darling, how are you?" Mama smiled radiantly, "Cary! Darling!" Cary Grant came around the table, and they hugged the way two people who are really glad to see each other do. He and Mama had been friends since his marriage to Barbara Hutton. He was as charming and amicable as his screen image. After we were introduced he studied me for a moment, "David? Was that your name when I first met you?"

I didn't know Robin Peabody knew Cary Grant. Mother hadn't mentioned it. After lunch, by a sound stage, the socialite and super-star reminisced while appraising one another's Rolls-Royces. I never uttered a word, but I thought Mr. Grant's was more distinct. I took a photo of them side by side, heads pressed together, a lovely picture of two friends.

Independent producer Ivan Foxwell and his wife, Lady Edith were a dynamic duo whose friendship and cama-raderie enhanced our lives abroad for years. The one difficulty was with the proper form of address, Mr. Ivan & Lady Foxwell, Ivan & Edith Foxwell, or Lady Edith & Ivan Foxwell, etc.

Allen and Auriol Palmer were a stunning couple. Their household included three long-haired dachshunds, Grand Mama, Mama, and daughter. Allen, chairman of Huntley-Palmer Biscuits, and Auriol, a beautiful woman in the pure Anglo tradition, were a fun devoted couple with a gambling addiction, in their case, an inoperable decease. When we first met in, they owned a beautiful townhouse in London, a large country estate, both well staffed, an apartment in the South of France, and a Bentley.

Fifteen years later, the Palmers were down to the country place, minus most of the acreage, a part-time housekeeper and a compact car.

Gambling is one of the few vices I haven't succumbed to, not nobly, I've just never had the craving. Another reason was witnessing the decline of this otherwise wonderful couple.

Billy McCann, an Australian, with no title, no power base or appreciable wealth, knew more about what was going on in England, having acquired more influence and connections than most cabinet ministers. Billy could arrange almost anything. GQK mentioned Royal Ascot, it was understood she meant, the *Royal* enclosure. Days later, in a Hardy Amies flower print dress, wide-brimmed hat, she and her heir-apparent in rented morning coat, striped trousers and gray top hat arrived at Ascot in the Rolls, and into the Royal enclosure. In all immodesty, we looked as though we belonged there, people thinking, "She must be the queen of... Somewhere?" I assume they weren't compelled to add, "The one in the dress."

Billy saw to it we viewed the *Trooping the Color* from the third row. H.R.M. Queen Elizabeth II, then in her mid-thirties, arrived on horseback, followed by H.R.H. Prince Philip, her uncle the Duke of Gloucester, and Lord Louis Mountbatten. The Minox served me well; I have several color photographs of her majesty reviewing the troops. A raving anarchist couldn't help but be impressed by the spectacle. The Queen mounted sidesaddle had to be more effective than riding in car.

Billy McCann frosted the cake with seats for the Royal Shakespeare Festival at Stratford-Upon-Avon. The season was sold-out, but Billy tugged a few strings, managing to get "unobtainable" tickets. Again, it was understood, when Gladys said, "tickets," she meant, damned good ones.

The Welcome Inn, in Stratford, was everything its name implied.

The first night we saw *Troilus and Cressida* the following night, *The Taming of the Shrew.* The company was headed by (Dame) Peggy Ashcroft, Paul Rogers, John Neville and a young actor attracting a great deal of attention, Peter O'Toole—before David Lean selected him to portray *T.E. Lawrence*, in *Lawrence of Arabia* (after Albert Finney bowed out). Neither of us had ever seen a production of *Troilus,* nor had we read it, I'm not even sure I knew it existed.

It was gratifying to discover we weren't alone in that regard. I've not met many people familiar with it, if they were, we didn't get around to it.

The *Troilus and Cressida* that night, could have been up there with Shakespeare's blockbusters. O'Toole's *Thersites* may have been a bit over the top for some, but it was theatrically explosive, a dazzling riveting production throughout.

O'Toole blew our socks off the following night as *Petruchio* to Peggy Ashcroft's *Katharine* in *Taming of the Shrew.* Ashcroft and O'Toole went at each other tooth and claw. The fact that off-stage, *Katharine* was twenty-five years older than her *Petruchio*, was a non-issue, on stage, not a second of it showed, their performances and physicality, were ageless and brilliant!

***

London American was a widely read weekly gossip sheet, served to keep Americans visiting London abreast of the comings and goings of other fellow countrymen in town. Many Londoners also found it compulsory reading if they wished to be vis-à-vis on Anglo-American relations—

especially, figuratively speaking. The *London American* wasn't a scandalous tabloid; it was good superficial informative fun. Initially, what was to be a story on Gladys Knapp-Bell, who had decided to drop the *"Bell."* Since David Knapp's name was now getting bandied about, Mother selflessly maneuvered the focus of the article over to me, with a –*"I've done this so often, I don't have much new to say, whereas, David always has something to say, don't you dear."* –wave.

In any event, the article focused on a guy at the threshold of fame and fortune.

The following issue of the *London American,* a large publicity photo of me took center position on the front page. The accompanying two column article was praiseworthy. I was, at once, *"bursting on the horizon, magnetic, charming and cultivated, good looking with a sexy way about me."* –an accurate assessment, but hardly a revelation.

Mama read the piece as an actor would an ambivalent review.

When she finished, I spoke with a hint of self-deprecation in my tone, "Mom, can you believe it?"

"The important thing is, that *you* don't, darling."

Where the Sun Don't Shine

GQK, DHK, and the Rolls took a twin-engine prop Bristol Britannia across the channel to France. They stopped manufacturing the Britannia after World War II, however, if noise, speed and accommodations were indicators, it was an earlier war.

The ugliest flying contraption I'd ever seen, it held two average sized European cars in its belly and eight passengers on metal-framed cross-strap seats in the cabin. The Rolls allowed only enough room for a Moped to share. She was the sole occupant below, and Mama and I the only passengers in the cabin. The Britannia's twin engines must have been audible on both sides of the channel simultaneously, navigation via dead-reckoning was no problem, the pilot merely maintained the plane's normal twenty to thirty feet altitude, then probably followed a cross-channel swimmer to the French coast.

We landed in overcast chilly weather, with intermittent showers.

I was to learn this was not an anomaly in Northwestern France, or Northeastern, or the central sections. I also found out for the very first time, Mama spoke fluent French. I never had an inkling, I was curious to know how she managed to keep it a secret for two decades. It was no secret, I'd heard her speak French on numerous occasions. Silly me, of course I had—*vichyssoise, nouveau riche, bourgeois, merde*! When we got to Spain, I'd show Mama a thing or two.

We drove down the coast a piece to Deauville. Our hotel was the most impressive firetrap I'd ever been privileged to stay in—a French version of that huge hotel on Mackinaw Lake in Michigan. The weather had improved, the showers subsided to a drizzle, now warm enough to take off the extra sweater and a brief flash of sun through a sliver in the clouds. In minutes the hotel beach was alive with people scurrying into itsy-bitsy cabanas, reappearing in varying degrees of undress.

The first priority was getting that beach umbrella opened and firmly imbedded in the wet sand. Until then, I'd been under the impression beach umbrellas were designed as buffers, to protect from the sun. I didn't realize their foul-weather purpose, as shelters from rain, or when angled correctly, wind deflectors. Next, two beach towels at each place, one to lie on, and the other underneath it to absorb the dampness.

The ritual of sunbathing with no sun, swimming in bikinis in water barely tolerable in a wet suit, the redundancy of taking an outdoor shower under cumulus clouds was questionable. I was fascinated by the oblivious attitude to conditions, as though these were normal people behaving in a normal manner, under normal circumstances? Turning on air conditioning in an igloo.

Eternal Eclipse

Standing on the bluffs overlooking the Normandy coast, 'Omaha' and 'Utah' beaches below, still littered with tangled rusting sections of coiled barbed wire, corroded shells of military vehicles near the water's edge, scattered pieces of unidentifiable equipment long since abandoned, all reawakened images of combat photos and newsreels I'd seen as a child. Looking out at deserted hulls of landing craft protruding from the sea, even bits of debris bobbing on the surface, real or imagined, gave me a sense of guilt, "There, but for the grace of God. . ."

Steven Spielberg's *Saving Private Ryan* was a vividly realistic reenactment of that experience.

The U.S. War memorial and cemetery at Eze-Sur-Mere is representative of America in its organized simplicity. The perfect symmetry with row after rows of white crosses and Star of Davids as far as the eye can see were visually impressive, imposing, but impersonal.

The British cemetery has a more bucolic quality, smaller, somehow gentler. The grave marked with more than name, rank, unit and serial number, and most had family thoughts inscribed. We walked slowly through a section of this final resting place for so many valiant warriors who made the supreme sacrifice for God, king, country, countrymen, and humanity. It became impossible not to react emotionally reading the sentiments expressed on the grave stones. One continues to haunt me decades later.

Taking a photograph of the site seemed disrespectful, but I did, *out of respect.* I've never regretted it.

Five of a Kind

Mama never 'drove,' she 'motored.'

For two weeks, GQK motored, while her son **drove**, through Central and Southern France. The Rolls rolled through Charallet country, the Gorge du Tarn, Gargonne, Carcassonne and Rocheforte, down poplar laned roads, winding mountainous passes, past villages not on the map, probably places where no Frenchman has ever been. We saw local women wearing wimples, men in three cornered hats—I'm sure I did. My French is the restaurant-hotel-boulevard variety, but at one out-of-the-way stop I'm certain I overheard locals making treasonous remarks about overthrowing the monarchy.

It's much easier to find your way from one end of France to the other, than it is finding the right freeway on-off ramp ten blocks from your home in Los Angeles. California highway and traffic engineers take great pride in planning roadways comprehensible only to them, and sadistically designing interchanges.

***

We continued South, across the Spanish border to the Costa Brava spending a few nights in Sagaro at a hotel villa owned by writer Robert Ruark, second only to Ernest Hemingway in depicting Spain and Africa. Ruark took us to my first bullfight in San Feliu de Guixols. Loving animals, I had misgivings. Mama reminded me of a picnic long ago in a pasture near the Ojai Valley school, ending abruptly when, out of nowhere, a bull bore down on us for no apparent reason, other than our general proximity. We made it over a fence seconds before the animal crashed into it. I remembered its sheer bulk, and the malevolence in its eyes. Why was he so pissed off? Did our picnic blanket look like a red cape? Mother explained, "Bulls are color-blind, they are just mean-spirited sonsuvbitches."

The pageantry and spectacle get the aficionados worked up for, what Hemingway termed, *Death in the Afternoon.* Catholic countries traditionally carry off these kind of events with more pomp and panache than Protestant, Muslim or other-oriented nations. The picadors are on blindfolded horses, with padding on the sides, hopefully horn-proof meshing in the material. The matadors, flanked by attendants, dressed almost as elaborately—these guys tease or divert the bull if things go the wrong way.

The first fight was a baptism of fire. To me, the matador belonged in a butcher shop not the ring. I knew little about the sport, but, if what I witnessed was the norm, my first fight would be my last. Moments later seasoned spectators loudly affirmed it, the matador exited the ring waving no extremities, the only waves he received were one-fingered. The rest of the afternoon was what it's supposed to be, a riveting and thrilling, as GQK described it, "ballet *noir.*"

A brief visit to Barcelona, decisive insofar as becoming a victim to charm, pace and style. I recall "falling in love" daily. It remains one of the very few places I could live year around.

***

Mama decided enough fun and frolic, time to buckle down to serious vacationing. We motored from Southern France to the South of France. If that's confusing to those not geographically inclined, what is termed "The South of France," a.k.a. the Riviera, Cote d'Azur, is a relatively small section in the Southeastern part of Southern France – if that clarifies it, "You're a better man than I, Gunga Din." In

GQK's words, "Those who refer to the South of France as Southern France, probably haven't been to either."

The Carlton Hotel in Cannes was our base. Her best friend in the area was the Begum Khan, widow of the Aga Khan, whose son by his first marriage, Ali Khan, married Rita Hayworth, which made the Begum Khan Miss Hayworth's step-mother-in-law. In any event, Miss Hayworth divorced Ali Khan, making it a moot point. The Begum Khan, as beautiful as her former step-daughter-in-law, had a villa in the hills above Cannes almost as big as the Carlton Hotel, she was also one of the loveliest women I'd ever meet, a warm elegant mother-earth.

A week later we drove east, zigzagging from the awesome vistas of the *Grand Corniche*, to the more direct and interesting views from the *Moyien Corniche*, then down to the erratic and sporadic *Corniche Inferior*, en route to Monte Carlo. Monte Carlo is a city in the principality of Monaco, which takes up the entire principality. Therefore to live in Monaco is to live in Monte Carlo, as in Manhattan, you must therefore be in New York City. Monte Carlo still abounds with ex-patriots, those with mysterious pasts, and a lot of folks who prefer the tax-free environment.

The casino is a two minute walk from the Hotel de Paris. At the time dress codes were in effect, coat and tie required, ladies wearing pants weren't allowed, black tie after 8 p.m., or at least a dark suit, on most nights.

GQK thought it might be fun to stroll over, she wanted to see any changes in the casino's interior. She hadn't been inside for almost a year. She prowled around and then decided to try her hand at *craps*. I suggested roulette might be a more dignified game for a lady of her statue, less back alley. No way, GQK considered roulette too much of a gamble, as players had no control—unless they got to spin the wheel. I wondered, if by spinning the wheel you do gain control, wouldn't it cause concern angst among the other players? "Craps isn't what you'd call a game of skill," I remarked. "By the way, Mom, what the hell do you know about playing craps?"

"There's not much to know. If your first roll comes up seven or eleven, you win, roll a two, three, or twelve, you lose."

"What about the other six?"

"Why don't you look around for something you might find of interest, and leave your Mother to her own devises."

"Is that a brush-off?"

"Unless you want to be accused of being bad luck if I lose?" I left.

Sadly today, the decline on the French Riviera is evident on arrival, you don't even have to leave the Nice airport. At one time this gateway to sunshine and elegance was a joy—the embodiment of what lay ahead. The four-star restaurant that was on the second level no longer exists. Why should it? There's no one around now to patronize it. There will be more about this in future pages.

***

All roads may lead to Rome, but once there, it's infinitely more complicated. The outskirts have raceway-like thoroughfares, which turn into a labyrinth of narrow meandering traffic-sodden streets, originally designed for chariots. We were looking for the Excellsior Hotel on the Via Veneto. I was at the helm, GQK in the passenger seat, was unable to read maps in a moving car as it meant taking her eyes off the road, normally the driver's responsibility.

We finally had to pull over to stop, no mean feat in Rome, where parking places aren't an issue, as none exist. A Roman simply stops his car and gets out. Attempts to double park are usually thwarted by eruptions of local disapproval, negating any tenure beyond five minutes. Parking on sidewalks is popular, but not without drawbacks, many extend only half a normal car's width, forcing pedestrians into the street to get around them, frequently resulting in expressions of disapproval with sharp and/or blunt objects. Wedging bicycles or Mopeds between parked cars can be problematic, if the car's driver has insufficient space to pull out, he'll have to create space. However, none of this compares to the logistical horrors of driving a Rolls-Royce in Rome.

Mother and I were at odds over map interpretations, we were on a via which we couldn't find on the map! A taxicab happened by, Mama called at the taxi driver, "Hotel Excellsior, perpicheri," with an Italian inflection. He shakes his head, points in a direction. "W*e know*, that's why we stopped you! We need you to lead us to there."

Not wanting to be conned by people in a Rolls, he wants some of our luggage in his cab as collateral. I give him a few pieces, along with a wad of lire, as a deposit, hoping it will cover the trip. He gestures us to follow him.

GQK is curious to know how much I gave him.

"Just what I had in my pocket."

"Dearest, I asked how much, not where you kept it."

"It was a five-something, Mom. I can't remember the exact number of zeros."

I don't have a problem with most foreign currency, but I've never mastered the lire or the Mexican peso. Was it four hundred to the dollar or four-thousand?

A half hour later we were still following the taxi through the maze of chariot routes dissecting the Italian capitol. "You don't suppose he thought we meant the Excellsior in *Florence*?" Gladys wondered.

Eventually we pulled up to the Excellsior in Rome.

There might have been a shorter route to the hotel, but we were too exhausted to negotiate. I'd peel off a bill, hand it to the taxi driver, he would nod, palm out. Another bill, another nod.. A third lire note, his palm remained out. I called the doorman over, and ask him how long would it take me to get to from the hotel to where the cab driver intercepted us? He calculated, "About thirty minutes, signor" I'd accepted that, when he added, "But better you go by car, only ten minutes." The taxi driver was gone by then.

***

Baroness Rene de Becker and Baron Eric de Rothschild lived in a magnificent apartment on the via Monte Giadorno. They weren't 'Baron' and 'Baroness' in the Mr. and Mrs. sense. Their titles were separate and apart. Both had been married, he to Bina de Rothschild, Maximilian's sister. He and Renee shared their lives for two decades. The Baroness de Becker, a Belgian, was the first lady to own a bank, Eric a *grand boulevardier*. They were the most aristocratic, amusing, and gracious couple imaginable.

We left Rome around noon, drove to Ostia for lunch and swim at the beach, then back in the city by four in afternoon—with today's traffic, you'd be lucky to get to Ostia and back in one day!

Keeping in touch with the family was exemplified by Gladys and her seventh cousin—God knows how many times removed—Mario Bandini, the great-great-great-great grandson of Juan Bandini's elder brother, who inherited the family's Italian estate in the 1760s, indirectly responsible for the other's voyage to California. To further confuse, Mario's wife, Marcella, was from Peru, where Juan's younger brother, Jose, set up house. The Rome Bandinis entertained us at their villa in the hills, guided us on nocturnal rounds of the city, which cousin Mario was very familiar, having been quite a lothario in his bachelor days. Mama described him, "One of Italy's top-flight swordsman." After first meeting this short, stocky distant cousin with thinning hair, I asked her what all the fuss was about. "Be patient, you'll see." After some socializing I understood. Mario exuded charm with innate sexuality, you didn't have to be interested in him, but you were cognizant of it, as women are aware of the allure of other women.

Reflections without Mirrors

The drive South to Salzburg, prior to the Autobahn, was spectacular—Wolfgang See, *mad* King Ludwig's castle, a monument to garish opulence, and a walk down the Mozartstrasse in Salzburg in an eighteenth century world. The *Goldner Hirsch* restaurant, with the most insidiously delicious dessert ever served.

On the way back to Munich, GQK pointed ahead, "If you want to see Berchtesgaden, go to the right up ahead." On a steep hill overlooking the town stands Hitler's Bavarian retreat, *Eagle's Crest*. The only access to the summit is an enormous elevator, installed by Der Fuehrer in 1939, which continues to serve visitors sixty years later. At the top, is the impressive schloss where the plans were made which Dachau implemented. In 1960 Hitler's living/planning room was still intact with the original furnishings, now it's a cafeteria for tourists.

***

Several days at the Hotel Grand Bretagne in Athens. The first powerful impact of the history taught at the Malcolm Gordon school came at viewing the Parthenon on the Acropolis, the seat of western civilization. Its architectural perfection a sacrosanct survivor of two thousand years of wars, hostile assaults, Turkish and Nazi occupations, the natural elements, and tourists. In those days visitors were allowed to wander though the acropolis, sit on the steps of the Parthenon, and permitted to absorb the cultural significance and timeless wonder in the footsteps of

Socrates, Plato, and Aristotle. Erosion now necessitates the Acropolis only being viewed from afar.

***

More mundane knowledge acquired during the latter half of the trip. Superbly engineered motor cars that they are, Rolls-Royces, get testy in hot weather—GQK's built in 1959, when air conditioning was relatively new to British automobiles, and an appendage rather than an intricate part of the car. Located in the boot (trunk), the one large duct behind the rear seat, when turned on, could blow off hats and cause hypothermia.

Driving across the Alps, we also discovered a six-cylinder Rolls-Royce is an *under-powered* vehicle. Whatever distress it caused us was compensated by the joy it gave compact car owners driving by a disabled Rolls on the roadside.

My twenty-second birthday was celebrated back in Cannes, at a dinner hosted by Harry D'Arrast, a prominent silent film director and former husband of actress Eleanor Boardman, a life long friend of GQK's.

The Rolls had an easier time of it in the lowlands of Holland and Belgium. Brussels is rarely on most tourists' lists of places to go, which works to its advantage. Our Quarre cousins made our Brussels visit a homecoming. When weather permits, there is no nicer city in Europe. Some are faster paced, with more night-life, attractions, activity, and variety, but Brussels has plenty going for it, and perhaps why Belgium is the number one choice of militaristic powers for occupation.

Mama introduced me to Bruges, a medieval town northwest of Brussels. Bruges isn't as well-known as many less deserving places of interest, but it's a crown jewel. On a clear day under a deep blue sky, dotted with cumulus clouds, this Flemish village is among the most wondrous sights on earth. As a backdrop for Rembrandt, Ruben's, Hals, Vermeer—a first reaction of familiarity, reminiscent of a magnificent reproduction on a film set, it's too perfect to be real. Few cities in Europe equal the impact of Bruges.

Slowing to a Gallop

GQK and I returned the Rolls to England in November, where, the following year, she would exchange it for a newer model with an *eight*-cylinder engine, but there would be one last fling this year. Our English chauffeur was a chap named Tony Purslow. He drove GQK and me up to Hadrian Stud in Newmarket, where Mama had several brood mares, one of whom had produced a filly while we were on the continent. We spent a pleasant day with Colonel Robin Hastings, who advised and oversaw Mama's horse interests in England—her three mares and the newborn. The foal was gray with splashes of white. I'd inherited Mama's affinity for gray horses.

Col. Hastings was going to hitch a ride with us to London's Paddington Station to catch a five o'clock train. It's three-forty-five and an hour and a half drive to the city. GQK and Hastings in back, I ride shotgun in front with Tony Purslow driving. Time is of the essence when you have to be somewhere in less time than you've got to get there—on a busy two-lane road. I leaned across to Tony, "Any chance of making the train?"

"In this car? Oh, yes sir."

"Why in *this* car, Tony?"

"People clear the way for a Rolls-Royce."

I hadn't realized that? Then, with a lorry coming from the opposite direction about a hundred yards away, Tony presses the horn, pulls out, passes two cars and cuts back, missing the lorry by twenty feet, and the car behind us by five feet. Tony performs several more death defying feats with the Rolls, abruptly accelerating, tailgating, swerving in and out of our lane, cutting off other cars to a point where I'm literally afraid to look out the windshield. Throughout Colonel Hastings sits impassively, probably having experienced episodes as harrowing as this during the war.

"Purslow, you don't have a clear view of oncoming traffic from that side!" Mama pointed out. "That's all right ma'am, we'll make it," Tony assured her, missing the point entirely.

I was acutely aware, driving on the *left*, with *left* hand drive, designed to be driven on the *right*, wasn't a safety feature. Exacerbated every time, Tony leaned in front me to see if we could pass and survive. I secretly worried about the heavy 6-cylinder Rolls at some critical point not having enough accelerating power for the course.

"What time is the next train Colonel?" I ask offhandedly, trying to avoid any innuendo or subtext.

The important thing, Hastings made his train. After Purslow left us off at Claridges, I remarked to GQK that it had been quite an experience. She shot over a look with daggers, informing me it was in large part my fault! My fault?

"You got chummy with the chauffeur, you called him, *Tony*. This is England, people like him expect to be called by their last name, or they get familiar. From now on, please refer to him as Purslow."

Anything, if he'll slow down.

Chapter 15

CIRCUMAMBIENCY ON A FLAT TOP

An Absence of Ticker-Tape

GQK flew directly to Los Angeles, and I returned to New York.

I phoned the guys at William Morris to tell them I was back, one didn't know I'd been gone, another wanted to know how the Bardot shoot went, the other was probably scrambling through the files to catch up on who I was. Those guys were on top of things.

I enrolled in Columbia University's School of General Studies, a "Bachelor of Social Sciences" would look impressive on my resume, along with Agnes Moorhead classes, stock productions, equity shows, the Neighborhood Playhouse, and a supporting role in a movie. I rationalized, with all my attributes I'd have to be a star. A career as a featured actor wasn't realistic. What star in his right mind would tolerate a younger, better-looking, more charismatic and talented actor on the same sound stage. He'd have to be nuts! In future years, some were, thank God!

***

195

Gladys Knapp was busy with more erstwhile projects. Frank and Blanche Seaver got her involved with Pepperdine University, then in its adolescence. It has matured into a world renowned institution of higher learning with a reputation in Business Administration well deserved, as those on its mailing list can attest.

Pepperdine's prowess at fund raising far exceeds that of the White House. GQK became an '*associate*' of the school, as would the author at a later date. The University knows how to treat its donors, and beneficiaries, its sprawling campus in the Malibu foothills hosts breakfasts, luncheons, high teas, cocktail parties, dinners, galas—at least seven days and nights a week, honoring more people, awarding more plaques, awards, and certificates, than all the music award shows combined. Its annual newsletters are issued monthly. Pepperdine University also serves as a refuge for those not wishing a *too* liberal education.

On one such, what the administration termed, "bruncheon," GQK was a co-honoree, and seated between her and Blanche Seaver was the 'Duke,' John Wayne. The *Duke* was an enormous man. I was six-one, 185 pounds, but felt like Peter Pan next to him. On that particular morning Wayne towered in size, but not charm. He'd give an occasional terse look, and I'd smile back. I think he took it personally.

The superstar was upstaged when a big helicopter descended from nowhere, landing fifty yards from the tables, the air turbulence could have scrambled the Eggs Benedict. Men in dark suits jumped out surrounding the hatchway. The Duke would not save this day, as he was too busy keeping his hair piece from blowing off. The group rose en masse as President Gerald Ford emerged from the chopper, trotted over, greeted the thirty guests in a personal and gracious manner, then trotted back, to the Presidential chopper and took off—all in fifteen minutes. It was an inauspicious visit, so far as visits from the Commander-in-

Chief go. I asked GQK if she knew Ford was coming, "No, but I think it was sweet of him to do it."

Still with us at this writing, Ford has the unique distinction of being about the only U.S. President that no one has anything really negative to say about. A good decent man caught up in a controversial time in history, and did what he believed to be the right in pardoning Richard Nixon, knowing it would cost him the next election.

***

DHK is ambling through his fifth college semester at Columbia with no Jesuitical intervention, maintaining a proximity to the phone, so he doesn't miss the call from David Lean, begging him to replace Peter O'Toole in *"Lawrence of Arabia."*

What he does get, is a call from Warner Bros., inviting him to a studio screening of *Parrish*, meaning, the film is going to open at selected theaters soon, where he'll be seen and thus, inundated with film offers.

Back in California, GQK accompanied DHK and the three guys from the Morris agency to the studio screening. Delmer and Mary Lou greeted the guests enthusiastically, and they were obviously pleased with the film. I noticed very few other cast members in the audience, when I naively asked Marylou about it she said, "Well, honey, most of them are working." Why hadn't that occurred to me?

The opening credits rolled, with priorities in order, my first concern was a billing upgrade. It seemed like two hours before I appeared on camera. I was trembling with anticipation, what would I look like on the big screen, how would I sound, did wardrobe know what they were doing, most importantly, was the makeup man just pretending he liked me—oh, and if my acting was okay?

How I could have spent so much time working on the film with so little time in it? I gave me a B-minus to a C-plus, I wasn't bad, nor was I particularly good, my opinion was pretty much shared by the studio *and* my agents, two of whom would go on to reasonably successful careers as film producers.

Someone at Warner Bros. called wanting me to read— he meant *interview*—for two back-to-back shows they were doing with ABC. Well, somebody thought I was okay. Don't sound too eager, would they send me the script? No, I'd get some sides when I came in—the shows were *Bronco* and *Hawaiian-Eye*. Not being much of a TV viewer, I knew little about them, but I wanted to do a western, a trip to Hawaii didn't sound bad either. The air let out of my tires when I went in for my "interview," to see ten other actors, my age and type, sitting in the reception area, looking over sides.

***

A return to New York was postponed several years when I picked up a letter informing me my draft number had been "selected." I hadn't even submitted it! In 1961 the draft was in effect as was a vague statute regarding two years of some sort of compulsory military or related service.

Feeling notification was a direct result of the Democrats being elected to power the previous November, GQK still had friends in high places. She'd make a few well-placed phone calls, just in case. As many of the family had been Navy men, it seemed the best way to go. My plan was, to get a commission and serve in the reserves one weekend a month and a month each summer—the least a patriotic American could do for a country that been pretty good to him.

I marched down to the Naval Reserve Center in West Los Angeles and presented my plan to the veteran Chief Petty Officer in charge. Due to my previous military training, it seemed reasonable to skip the rank of Ensign and go in as a Lieutenant (Junior Grade). The CPO agreed it would be nice, inquiring as to my college degree? I explained I was only three semesters short of one, five out of eight isn't bad. I told the CPO I knew more about the military than most guys with a Ph.D.! He had no doubt of that, but felt the Navy department would require more tangible assurance of my prowess. I understood, volunteering to take an oral or written test, if need be. I assumed it was too late for Annapolis, besides, it would take too much time—the CPO agreed.

Alternatives involving officer's candidate school were briefly discussed, but the requirements and ancillary conditions weren't compatible with my situation. The CPO was concerned enough to ask if I was on medication. I hoped for a letter from the Defense Department telling me it had all been a mistake. I sensed a tentative manner in Mama. I'd try to make it easier for her.

"The calls on your behalf."

"About avoiding military service?"

"Not *avoid*, Mama, just circumvent, until I'm prepared. What if we go to war?" More prophetic than I realized then.

"I've been rethinking, a couple of years of military service might be just what the doctor ordered."

Ironically the doctor wasn't in complete accord.

After a battery of tests and an extensive physical the head medical officer examined the results, looked at me several beats and asked, "Do you want in or out?" I had a choice? Not knowing whether to feel happy, relieved, concerned, or rejected, I asked if they'd found an internal malignancy disqualifying me from service?

"No, not in the strict medical sense."

I picked up on his intonation and expression, the inference was clear. I knew responding to the innuendo would be confirming it. Christ, I'm not sitting with my legs crossed! I stood tall, feigning all the naiveté I could muster, "I want in, sir!"

You can announce your proclivities without a problem, but let one person surmise it, it becomes offensive.

I would be serving in the Naval Reserve one evening a week until I was called up some time in future, if at all. Eight weeks later, I received my orders to report to San Diego's Naval Recruit Training Center.

I'd been cautioned by veteran military family members to keep a low profile, assimilate, not to volunteer for anything, to be as innocuous as possible. GQK's reaction had been, "You might as well put him on a high-wire with no net. Dear God, help him.

No Grass on This Ass

I reported in amidst hundreds of apprehensive disorganized young men. We were divided into companies of eighty, told to fill out forms with background information, education, military experience, etc. The four years at a military academy, plus Culver and four semesters of R.O.T.C. at the university, gave me a head start.

The official CPO company commander took me aside, indicating my questionnaire, "How much of this is bullshit?"

"None, sir."

"How'd you like a cushy job? Knapp, I'm gonna appoint you 'RCPO' of the company. Do a good job, you'll have it real good. Fuck up, your ass is grass, and think of me as a lawn mower." He didn't waste time.

"What exactly does that entail, sir?"

The conditions: He would be around the first two weeks, from reveille to 'lights-out,' from then on, I would run the company so as not to necessitate his being on the base after seventeen hundred hours, or before zero seven hundred hours. "I don't wanna have to come in at zero three-thirty hours," he explained.

"Why would you have to come in at *three-thirty in the morning*, sir?"

"That's reveille."

Good Lawdy Miss Maudy! He'd have a ten-hour day, I'd be up at 0400 hours, and in the office until 2300 hours on company business. Rising before the sun, is contrary to natural order and not a normal cycle. Worse, I'd have to wake up the others.

Still in civvies, uniforms yet to be issued, as *Recruit Chief Petty Officer*, I'm standing in front of a motley crew of eighty, here-to-fore independently-minded, high school dropouts, hubcap thieves, court-ordered hooligans, possible skin-heads, as a veteran of two hours. Dear sweet Jesus, why do these things always happen to me?

Eighty pair of eyes accessing me, thirty of whom could probably carve me in one-inch squares with a can-opener. Pray God, it doesn't come to that. Eight hours later, scrubbed up, in uniform, hair chopped off, they looked less formidable – then again, so did I.

Anticipating the potential problem boys, I was crafty enough to appoint some of them to responsible positions, thereby gaining their loyalty and support – theoretically.

Only one was a disappointment, the second in command, a good ol' Texas boy, who turned out to be the worst, undermining behind my back, supportive and steadfast to my face, antagonistic and resentful out of earshot. In years to come, I realized he was just one of a large group. It took four weeks to nail him. The confrontation would put my position on the line.

In addition to four Chevrons on the sleeve, RCPOs wore a black scabbard belt as an identity and authority symbol. One mid-day Tex got a quiet cautionary reprimand. In a voice everyone in the barracks could hear, he let me know, "The day we get out of here, Knapp, I'm gonna be wait'n at th' front gate to kick th' shit outta 'ya!"

Tex now had a full audience waiting to see who was in charge. This was the test, the first time the second-in-command had demonstrated overt hostility, his doing it in such a public manner was not only disloyal and two-faced, but a devious malevolent threat as well. I also was damn sure he was full of 'sound and fury,' he didn't intimidate me. I was bigger, but you can never be absolutely sure. I gambled, "Why wait 'til we get out of here?" Tex hesitated a moment too long before countering, "If you weren't wearing that black belt!"

That extra second told me all I needed to know. I unbuckled the belt and tossed it on the bunk. Tex hesitated another moment too long. I stepped around, "Okay let's go." Now all eyes were on him. "Did I mean, here and now?"

"Hell, yes!" I wasn't bluffing, I knew his ass would be the one kicked, so did he. He backed off. I was in charge. Privately, I was relieved it hadn't been several others in the company, I'm not sure how it might have turned out.

The evening before the only day of liberty, I was summoned to the Catholic chaplain's office. In the Navy, priests in uniforms are referred to as '*Padre.*' The Padre informs me, he and Mama have been in touch regularly. He contacts all Catholic parents to ascertain the status of their sons.

"Status?"

"You're preparing for active duty, anything can happen out there."

"We're not at war, Padre."

"Do you know how many Armed Forces personnel die yearly of non-combat related causes?" The Padre had me there.

"Compared to the number of civilians?" I asked. The Padre ignored my flash of disrespect, informing me I had never been confirmed. I hadn't given that much attention.

"By the way, Mr. Knapp, statistically you're correct, thousands more civilians are killed annually than Armed Forces personnel."

They also outnumber us fifty to one.

"Very few parents bother to respond. I was very impressed with your Mother on the phone, she also wrote a nice letter taking full responsibility for the oversight. She hoped God would forgive her. I assured her He would. When we spoke again she told me all about your cousins in the Navy. You certainly have a big family."

"Not immediate, sir. No siblings."

"She filled me in, no grandparents either. Your mother felt, one of your problems stemmed from her trying to overcompensate, which she felt had spoiled you. Another of your problems was not having a father image. She felt a little of the blame that might rest on her shoulders, two of her husbands were deceased."

There wasn't much point in going into details, "Her marriages didn't go well," I confirmed.

Priest-commander brought me up to date on the arrangements he, Mama, and the military-ecclesiastic powers-that-be, had made on my behalf. Tomorrow, I would be confirmed by the bishop in a ceremony at the local cathedral.

"Tomorrow?"

"I know it's your one day of liberty, but the ceremony doesn't start until seven p.m., so you'll have most of the day for shenanigans. Best make it six, you'll want to go to confession first. Oh, and your mother plans to drive down. Please don't let on that we talked, she wants it to be a surprise."

Mid-morning the next day, figuring I had until six, three company buddies and I headed for the front gate, our spiffy Blue's sleeve insignia clearly identifying our recruit status, guaranteeing to all, we hadn't a clue where we were going, or what to do when we got there, no hair, no money, and in most cases, an inability to hold liquor—the latter two didn't apply to me.

At the base gate we ran into a dozen more of 595 Company, on their way off base after a month. I froze when I saw, GQK's new eight-cylinder '61 Rolls waiting outside the gate. A buddy exclaimed, "Goddam, look at that fuck'n Rolls-Royce!" Oh, Mom, another surprise. I slinked over with clinched teeth, "Mom, what are you doing here, now?" She motored down the night before, was staying in La Jolla and she had my day of liberty all planned. Mama looked at my buddies gawking at us, "Are they your friends?" Well, they *were*. She waved at them wanting to know if we should bring a couple of them with us. I demurred, I went back to the guys, told them lies about a friend of a friend having a local Rolls dealership, etc. "I'll catch up with you later." One of the wise ones commented, "They sure got high class look'n salespeople."

That evening I was confirmed in a San Diego cathedral by the bishop, who didn't know me well enough or long enough to dislike me, nonetheless must have foreseen enmity. The customary pat on the face was delivered with such gusto it might have earned me the *Purple Heart*. GQK and the chaplain watched from the first pew.

***

Mama came down for the graduation parade with Estella and Jim Duffy, CDR, USN [ret.] They sat with the base commanding officer in the reviewing stand. Before the ceremony our official C.O. and I were looking at the reviewing stands, the right half of which was filled with civilian families and relatives, the left side with uniformed personnel and recruits who would graduate in future parades. He asked, "Which side looks better, left or right?" No question, the left. The neat tiers of navy blue and white, made the civilians look like a ragtag mob.

The parade was an impressive spectacle, accompanied by a large military band, two of whom were appropriated from our company early on. All the companies march in review, flags and banners dip, 'Eyes Right,' the RCPO salutes with his saber, sees the proud smiles from the reviewing stand, then saber back to 'right shoulder' he leads his company on.

Afterwards, I asked GQK what she thought, meaning *me*, out there in front. "It was wonderful, dear. Now which one were you?"

***

Working in our hangar office one late morning, I was summoned to the operation gate. GQK, Jean, the housekeeper, and Marilyn in the Rolls, en route to Pebble Beach had decided to pay a surprise visit. How she got in the main gate and two miles onto the Naval Air Station staggered me. As I explained the awkwardness of the situation to her, our operations officer drives up behind the Rolls.

As I wave him sheepishly around Mom's car, he comes abreast and stops. I salute and apprise him of the situation and introduced them, "Mom, this is Lieutenant Commander Salin, our operations officer…"

"Oh, the gentlemen you told me all those wonderful things about," she cut me off with a radiant smile. I don't know if the OPS officer believed a word of it, but he wasn't immune to the beautiful lady in the big car. While he and GQK exchanged waves and greetings, he reminded me, "She's not allowed to see the operations area, but since she came all this way, the least we can do is show her the hangar building and the office spaces." Momma ended up with a brief high-echelon tour of the CO and XO's offices and my anti-office with the LCPO. As she was leaving, she asided to my enthralled commanding officer, "You will keep an eye on him, won't you?"

Later, our LCPO described GQK succinctly—"Wow!"

This is Not a Drill

In October, my squadron, VA-155, on the Coral Sea had the first Naval air fatality of the war, when one of the A4Bs was shot down over North Viet Nam. The following month President John Kennedy was shot in Dallas. My relatively brief sorties in Viet Nam came during our initial involvement; the war hadn't yet escalated into a misdirected and futile bloodbath. The perspective from an aircraft carrier then, as opposed to a soldier on the ground several years later, is an obscene comparison.

Unbeknown to me at the time, as I was getting a taste of Viet Nam, right next door, GQK was touring Angkor Wat in Cambodia with boundless enthusiasm.

In the spring of the following year, when the carrier returned from Westpac I was transferred to Treasure Island Naval Station in San Francisco for processing. A week later, I was a civilian again.

Chapter 16

NO CAUSE TO PAUSE

Farwell to 52nd Street

During my extended absence to keep the free world safe, GQK again decided to divest herself of New York interests. She not only sold the apartment in the River House, she gave up her membership in the River Club! Her not informing me until after the fact didn't cause my ego to soar, but more importantly, this decision, whether made on a capricious whim or a carefully thought out overall plan, was not in anyone's best interest. As would often be the case, she demonstrated excellent judgment in selecting properties, but little acumen when it came time to rid herself of them. GQK and myself, together and apart, would spend a good deal of time in New York in future years The financial appreciation aside, the practicality, convenience, and available facilities no longer at our disposal would be sorely missed – but nobody bats a thousand.

Having returned to the ranch, unpacking my Naval uniforms for the last time, the prospect of being comfortably settled in one place for awhile held great appeal.

"You've almost a week to do nothing but relax," Mama assured me.

"Almost a week! What then, Mama?"

"We leave for New York next Thursday."

The immediate irony of her statement struck me.

"Mama, I just got back. I've been on the move for three years! I don't want to go to New York!" Then a sharply pointed question, "Besides, where would we stay?"

"Darling, don't be unpleasant, we have a nice two-bedroom suite at the St. Regis. We'll only be there a few days, then off to London."

"*London*? I don't want go there either right now!"

"We have to, in order to pick up the car in Gibraltar."

"*Gibraltar*? What car? And what's it doing in Gibraltar?"

"That's where we take the ferry from Algeciras to Tangier."

What's the use? I was packing again, but this time a different wardrobe.

While I'd been chewing my nails in the South China Sea, Gladys Knapp had been on the other side of the globe serving as a founding member of *The American Museum* in Bath, England. *The American Museum was* created and administered by Dr. Dallas Pratt and its director, Ian McCallum, until his death in the '80s. The nineteenth century estate and Calverton Manor was converted into a museum and formal gardens, the *only* museum outside the United States dedicated entirely to America, needless to say, funded largely by Americans.

Her horses in Newmarket were doing what they like doing best, being impregnated regularly. The Italian resort *Il Pellicano* had taken off like wildfire—and Gladys had opened a bank account in Lausanne, Switzerland. Gibraltar entered into it due to GQK's purchase of another Rolls, a '63 Silver Cloud, the same identical color and interior as the '61, sitting in the garage at the ranch. The only difference, the '63 had two double headlights on each side instead of one. She left the newer model in Gibraltar to be used on this trip.

***

Before we left Los Angeles, I bought a new 16 mm movie camera, specially equipped with an eight inch lens. We contacted the host of a popular prime time TV travelogue program, Bill Burrad. I outlined our itinerary and the circumstances. His reaction was cautiously positive, asking for 'first refusal' of the footage on our return. Why would he be entitled to that? Because, *I'd* come to see *him* first.

The last night of our brief stay in London, we had a reunion dinner with Frank and Conchita Raysbrook. Frank had been reassigned to a post near the U.S. Embassy. Conchita made their flat in Lancaster Court into yet another home, with personal touches, including the conversion of a bidet into a goldfish bowl! Mama and I spent a fun evening with them prior to our departure. Mother remarked later, "What a wonderful couple they make."

GQK and son picked up the '63 Rolls in Gibraltar, took the boat ferry across to Tangier for a few nights, then motored south through Morocco to Rabat. The scenery and well maintained roads were beyond our expectations, with no one taking umbrage to our mode of transportation. You didn't see many solitary Rolls on the back roads and alleyways of Morocco in those days.

We drove past peasant farms, robed shepherds tending their flocks, in some cases, a single chicken. Mama watched with amazement as these farmers holding staffs, conscientiously tended one or two scrawny chickens by the roadside. She wondering aloud, "What does he do about them at night?" The possibilities caused us to chuckle a few minutes later, another guy, another chicken, "Wouldn't you think he'd buy a little playpen for it, so he could do other things? What does he think about all day?" she pondered.

GQK was the same age then, as the author is now. Quite frankly, looking back I have to marvel at how a lady in her sixties would tackle her first visit to a third world country in that manner, in those days; on a luxurious air-conditioned bus, in a group with a guide, yes—but on country roads and back streets, in a solitary conspicuous Rolls-Royce, with only her untried son as escort. I know forty years later, I wouldn't attempt it.

We reversed our course on the outskirts of Casablanca, there was no trace of Bogart or Bergman in the romanticized coastal city, no cause to pause. Its mean streets had become a *mean city*, driving through it didn't seem a good idea. On to Marrakech and La Mamoullia Hotel, the image of what Casablanca should be. The rooms with netting over the beds, slow revolving ceiling fans, a balcony overlooking the gardens framed by palm trees. The musky bar with cushioned wicker seats, I *had* the camera, all it needed was Sidney Greenstreet anxiously waiting for Marlene Dietrich.

The flea market offered blinding footage of rolls of brilliantly dye-colored material. The side streets and winding alleys were backdrops for Paramount Pictures in the 1930s. The merchants and traders in the bazaar were as swarmy, sleazy, and sinister, as to be stereotypical.

The drive back through Fez and the Atlas Mountains was a series of Kodak moments.

***

Four decades ago—as everywhere—Spain's Costa del Sol was a different place. Marbella was beginning to blossom. The Marbella Club was about the only first class resort, and pretty much restricted to people its owner, Prince Hohenlohe, knew and liked, Gladys Knapp was one.

She insisted we drive into the hills to see Ronda, a medieval village perched in the mountains divided by a three hundred foot deep ravine with vertical walls. We shot some spectacular film: East to Malaga, North to Granada, the gypsy caves and the Alhambra, the most impressive Moorish architecture in Spain. In Madrid we spent an exciting Sunday afternoon at the bullfights with a couple of American temporarily-expatriate friends, who escorted us to dinner at popular restaurant where *everyone* went after the ring. I asked for bottled water, I would add the Scotch later. The waiter brought a decanter of water, the waiter assured me it was bottled water, and it was the restaurants custom to serve bottled water in a decanter. Our friends nodded, *OK.* Unfortunately, I added the Scotch too late.

A few hours later, back at the Ritz Hotel, I was writing a treatment on my portable typewriter, when I began feeling sick. Ignoring it, thinking it would go away, I kept typing. Finally the acute stomach cramps, sweating, fever and chills, just making it to the bathroom was a near-impossibility. The term, "amebic dysentery," gets bandied about whenever someone goes to the bathroom twice in an hour in a foreign country—Latin particularly. A case of the *"Tourista"* is not dysentery. For two days I prayed for death, a doctor gave me Spanish antibiotics, making me even sicker in a variety of other ways. On day four, I was able to visit one gallery of the Prado, apprehensively and briefly, then back to bed.

GQK thought it was all *a bit much* on my part, "You're not going see much lying in bed." I was very sick! "Then maybe, you need a priest, not a doctor."

***

Barcelona is an enormous sprawling city, approaching from the South and finding your hotel is a grand tour d'force, even with the guide *Michelin.* GQK at the wheel, I was still recovering from Madrid, acting has navigator, as we neared the outskirts at dusk.

GQK and I liked making bets on time-frames, distances, and other nonsense. We bet $100 on whether I could guide us to the hotel without a wrong turn. Reading a small map in a moving car with darkness descending, if you're far-sighted, is no mean feat. I charted a course along the boulevards, through complicated intersections and roundabouts always watching for landmarks. Everything seemed to be going right. "Turn left at the next street, go two blocks, into the plaza, the hotel is on the right," I announced with more confidence than I felt. "All right, dear, left it is." Her inflection was, "But God help you, if you are wrong!" She made the left turn, and for two-anxiety-ridden blocks, I'm biting my lip. We *do* pull into a plaza! I look to the right—no Hotel Ritz. I'm ready to throw in the towel, when mother informs me, "It's over there, dear, on the *left.*"

At the bullfights that Sunday we were seated next to (Sir) John Mills and his wife author Mary Hailey Bell. I'd seen Mills turn in superb screen performances, but none quite as good as his London stage portrayal of T.E. Lawrence in *Ross,* about Lawrence of Arabia, after Arabia.

That afternoon, Sir John told me to keep an eye on a young matador named Manuel Benitez. Benitez made an unspectacular entrance; he looked like a dressed-up farm boy with little of the *élan* we'd seen in others. That changed when the bull burst into the arena. Benitez' raw courageous style was mesmerizing. As "El Cordobes," he would soon be ranked one of the greatest matadors of all time—in a class with Juan Belmonte, Manolete, and Luis Dominguen.

Camelot Considered

Anyone interesting in Monte Carlo could be seen in the bar at the Hotel de Paris, if you weren't particularly interesting, at least you could be around those who were. One evening Mama and I saw Evelyn Sharpe having cocktails with Walter Winchell, the staccato-voiced radio newsman and columnist, *"Good evening Mr. And Mrs. America and all the ships at sea."* Needless to say 'we' were invited to join them, or it wouldn't have been included. Evelyn asked if we'd like to look at a villa she was thinking about buying. The following day we drove to Cap d'Ai, a few kilometers west of Monaco. The relatively small, two-story villa, surrounded by pines and cedars, was French with a California-esque flavor—in the forecourt, a pool, and a pool house. In front, a large terrace overlooking the sea with stone steps leading to the water sixty feet below. Mama mused, "Lovely place, don't you think?" Rhetorical. Now with only the ranch, the timing seemed propitious.

"Mom, I think you ought to at least think about it."

Mama and I returned several times. I watched the deductive mental process. She weighed the pros and cons. The narrow winding road off the *Corniche inferior* down to the villa could be treacherous, the parking minimal.

It was located only a ten minute drive from Monte Carlo, but far enough away not to qualify for the tax benefits. In traffic, an hour drive from the Nice airport, and a half-hour longer to Cannes.

The seasonal factor had to be considered, though many live all-year around on the Riviera, it was essentially mid-April through mid-October on a good year. The rest of the year could be dreary, bleak and wet.

Mama finally passed.

***

GQK and DHK drove down to *'Il Pellicano'*, which was thriving having added several additional guest cottages. The resort was getting an international reputation, becoming a getaway for celebrities and movers & shakers in general.

We rendezvoused with Marylou Daves in Florence, from there we'd drive North to Lago Garda where Delmer was filming on location.

Few traveled light then, certainly no one we knew. Now, with the three of us there wasn't room in the car for the entire luggage. The author, single-handedly, in Florence, on a Saturday afternoon, found a place that would install a baggage rack on the top of the Rolls in a matter of hours. The pride taken in little achievements. I'll wager, a feat no other person can lay claim to.

The next day the bellmen loaded the extra luggage onto the new baggage rack, Mama deadpanned, "Dear, that little extra touch makes all the difference, *'Ma and Pa Kettle at the Ponte Vecchio.'*"

The trio stopped for lunch en route to the lake country at a rustic taverna. A narrow door oddly placed next to our corner table caught Marylou's attention throughout the meal. GQK and I could see her eyeing it, she had to know what was beyond, finally GQK suggested she open the damn door and find out. When Marylou did, brooms, mops and pales cascaded out onto our table, knocking over dishes and glasses. Waiters rushed over as Marylou quickly regained her composure, smiling, "Well, now we know."

Leaving, we passed an Italian family seated at a table with several beautiful children chattering away in their native tongue. Marylou paused, turning to GQK, "Isn't it amazing children that age can speak such good Italian?" I loved the story, repeating it at the Daves' dinner parties, and with gracious resignation Marylou would add, "You realize I was kidding." I've no doubt she was, but it's funnier my way.

In the Northern Italian lake district, Delmer was filming *The Battle of the Villa Fiorita* with Rossano Brazzi, Maureen O'Hara, and a sweet young creature making her film debut, Olivia Hussey. The mountain-lake scenery was idyllic and Delmer was taking full advantage of it with the aide of a superb British cameraman, Oswald Morris, who won an Oscar years later for *Fiddler on the Roof*. Ossie had a delicious sense of humor, the baggage rack on the Rolls caused him to remark, "Nice touch. Ya' think they'll make them standard?" I was ready, "Only on convertibles." Ossie continued surveying the Rolls, shaking his head, "That really is very naughty."

I explained it was temporary and detachable. "Of course, but in the meantime people will see it," bemoaned the cinematographer.

Delmer again was wearing multiple hats, working fourteen-hour days with his typical professionalism, but he was exhausted. The interiors were to be shot at B.P.C. Studios Borehamwood, near London. The location work made more difficult with a largely Italian crew, not that proficient with live soundtracks, most Italian pictures then were filmed M.O.S. (without sound), and the dialogue looped after principal photography was completed.

Marylou confided to Mama, Delmer was so drained he needed help taking off his shoes. The contemptuous English first assistant director was more of a liability than a source of support. His kind of attitude would virtually destroy the British film industry by the end of the decade. I was covertly urged to act as an unofficial 'associate producer,' during our stay, in an effort to relieve Delmer of some of the small details and problems that otherwise wasted his time and energy. My first assignment was tricky. Maureen O'Hara, an upfront woman of talent, beauty and integrity, had little eccentricities, one involved washing her own underwear then hanging it out to dry on her balcony. The hotel management felt, Miss O'Hara's balcony, overlooking the hotel terrace, was an inappropriate backdrop for fluttering lingerie. How does one broach that to an established film star?

I told Mama my predicament, she'd handle it for me, it was a 'girly' issue. She reported back to me, Maureen had been a wonderful about it, they got along splendidly, "Maureen, poor darling, can't help it if she's Irish," adding with a salacious smile. "When we get back, Maureen wants you to meet her daughter."

Delmer and Marylou hosted an informal dinner at the hotel, for the Brazzis. Rossano Brazzi exuded charisma off camera as well as on.

When Marylou remarked on how charming he was, GQK agreed, but sensed he could be *not*-so-charming under different circumstances. His wife, Lydia, was a glorious lady from an aristocratic Italian family. A warm intelligent woman, you knew had been a knockout in her "salad days." Still a handsome lady, but she succumbed to Italian cuisine, didn't bother much with cosmetics, allowing nature to take its course. She appeared somewhat older than her glamorous husband.

The company returned to England, Mama and I had to motor back with the Rolls. We took a side trip to Baden Baden, the resort spa in the West of Germany. The captivating atmosphere transposes one to a bygone era; it retained its traditional elegance and style. Baden had one of the largest and finest *pitch 'n putt* courses in the world, no structures, just greens. The nine holes averaged about fifty feet apart at par twenty for the course.

We had a go at it, one of those few days when you can do no wrong. GQK made a hole-in-one on the second hole. I did the same on the third. Some hotel guests were more attentive when she made a birdie on the sixth hole, then we both sunk another ball with one stroke on the eighth. We heard, "*vas ees das?, mein goot!,*" from the gallery.

Mama made three holes-in-one; I came in two under par. I remarked on how lucky we were, and GQK responded, "*You* were lucky. *I* was in good form."

In Paris we had lunch with Olivia de Havilland and her husband Pierre Galante, editor of *Paris Match,* with them was novelist, John O'Hara, author of *Appointment in Samara, Ten North Frederick,* and *Pal Joey.* O'Hara looked like the alpha guy I'd envisioned with a reputation for being *tres formidable* with a few drinks. That afternoon he was warm and easy to be with, and he asked if I'd like to go book hunting with him.

I thought of Arnold Palmer asking, if you'd like to play a few holes with him! Wandering around Paris with a great American writer was as close to being there with the literati in the 1920s and 1930s as I could aspire to.

We went to several antique book stores on both sides of the Seine, ending up at *Shakespeare's Book Shoppe.* By chance, I found a book he was looking for. Back home, I received a note from Mr. O'Hara, thanking *me* for fun afternoon in Paris, and for finding the book.

We returned to London. I'd been working on my first screenplay, based on a novel about a rodeo clown, the one I was working on in Spain when dysentery struck. As if Delmer hadn't enough to do, I gave it to him to read during his "off hours." I thought the contemporary Western drama might be to his liking. Wonderman that he was, he immediately read it and gave me four pages typewritten single space notes, covering it in detail.

To say he didn't care for my screenplay would be the understatement of the millennium, worse, he was absolutely right. I reread it ten years later and felt embarrassment, a classic example of how *not* to write a screenplay. I've kept Delmer's notes as a reminder. I still believe the story could make an excellent film, in the right hands.

***

Finally, a trip to Bath and visit to The American Museum—a two hour train trip west of London, near the Welsh border. Bath has the pastoral quality of a John Constable landscape, founded by the Romans, abounding Georgian architecture and crescents. Splendid Calverton Manor cottages displayed exact reproductions of rooms typifying various periods and places in American history from an eighteenth-century colonial drawing room to a one-room New Mexico frontier cabin, as well as displays of authentic clothing, paintings, artifacts and literary work, pertaining to the U.S.

***

When we returned to Los Angeles, I took the Morocco-Spain footage to Bill Burrud's office. He concluded, "I assume you haven't edited it." I lied. I'd taken out fifteen minutes of flat-out-lousy footage, judiciously leaving only snippets of Mama and me—down to fifty-five minutes of air-quality film. I made a print for myself, gave Burrud the original. Burrud said he'd get back to me. I got a phone call weeks later telling me they would air it. I suggested I'd do an *on camera* narration at no extra cost. I got a less than tepid response.

On the night it aired, with a dozen Hidden Valley denizens, including the Alan Ladds, Eve Arden and Brooks West. We gathered around the TV to see my one-hour filmed odyssey of Morocco and Spain. Mama and I didn't watch the show on a regular basis, not realizing, the travelogue's 7-8 p.m. time slot, had been reduced to a half-hour. Okay, we'd get all the major highlights. The show was in two segments, we would share the half-hour time with penguins on an island off Chile. Well, fifteen minutes was better than no minutes. After Burrud did an unusually long introduction, and conclusion, with a commercial break for three sponsors, we viewed eleven minutes of my fifty-five-minute masterpiece.

***

Frank McCarthy and Rupert Allan hosted many memorable luncheons and small dinners at their cozy home in the Hills of Beverly. Rupert was arguably the most respected and best-liked publicists in the business. I must divulge on one evening to which Frank invited me, "Just a few of us, very casual," he said on the phone. When I arrived I noticed the dining table was set for twelve, seated around the living room were Kirk and Anne Douglas, Jennifer Jones, Natalie Wood, George Peppard, and Sandra Dee.

Minutes later, Deborah Kerr and husband, Peter Viertel, arrived with another lady. I was focusing on Deborah, who I hadn't seen for at least ten years. Then, I threw a cursory glance at the lady with them. Extending my hand, "Good evening, my name's David Knapp."—clearly requesting her identity with my inflection.

The lady gave me a lovely smile, "Hi, my name's Rita Hayworth." My mouth went dry, my stomach tightened. Incomprehensibly, I didn't connect immediately with my favorite movie star, a woman I idolized, who's pictures I'd gone to see three or four times. The only explanation I have, she was dressed simply with virtually no makeup, her hair was brown, not auburn; she was much smaller than I had envisioned. Her face, once ravishing, had 'matured' into one of an extraordinarily handsome middle-aged woman—but always the glorious *Rita Hayworth*!

Fred Astaire was asked 'who his favorite leading lady was?' He replied, 'A gentleman doesn't answer that kind of question.' The interviewer persevered, finally Astaire hedged, "One lady, not necessarily the *most* talented, but who overall, seemed to bring everything together better than anyone was Rita Hayworth." Amen.

The first time at their home, after Frank's Oscar win for *Patton*, I prowled around his house looking for the statuette, and while making a piss-run I discovered it standing inconspicuously on his bed table. Frank made the supreme gesture of friendship when, with a packed house of industry luminaries, he held up the first screening of *Patton* for fifteen minutes so I could extricate myself from a fender-bender and rush to the studio. A sweetheart of a man and fine gentleman, I miss him.

An Angel in Fur

Years before Golden Retrievers became all the rage, the popular favorite, there were relatively few around. This doesn't imply we discovered them, but GQK sure helped put them on the map. I met one as a kid, and I have never forgotten her. This was the opportunity. I combed around for a Golden, ending up driving to somewhere in Orange County. A lady had one a year old she'd sold, then had returned when the owners relocated. The lady and the golden were seated in a breakfast nook, it was love at first sight. Her name was Honey Bee—sweet as honey and busy as a bee. I thought it too sweet, renaming her, Marilyn. Driving back to the ranch I stopped at a park to let her pee. She refused to get out of the car. She had been shuttled around too much, and was scared I'd leave her.

Mama told me to keep Marilyn down in my quarters when at the ranch. She didn't want the dog in the main part of the house. It puzzled me. Marilyn took it very personally, making a nest in my closet and refusing to go in the main house even if GQK asked her!

Fate stepped in, I had to go somewhere for a week, thinking it would traumatize the animal if I uprooted her after barely settling in. I asked the "ranch matriarch" if she could possibly take care of Marilyn during my absence, and she reluctantly agreed. A week later, when I returned to collect my dog, Mama's chin started to quiver. Marilyn was standing cautiously behind her, eyes saying, "Please, I love it here, don't make me leave." Marilyn left *us* fourteen years later. I flew out from New York for one day to help mother bury her outside the bedroom window.

Chapter 17

HULA DAYS, HAPPY LEIS

With 1965 around the corner, GQK sold the Pinecliff house. With only the ranch, a second home was on the agenda. She decided on one in Honolulu. Situated on an acre at 4585 Kahala Avenue, the not particularly distinguished one-story house, had 60 feet of beach frontage, stretching back about five hundred feet to Kahala Avenue. In addition to the nine room main house, a small guest house, servant's cottage and garage. A large thick hedge buffered the property from the street.

Mom had a number of friends from previous visits living there, and would accumulate many more very quickly. One was a great asset in the in renovating, Phyllis Spalding, her husband Phil, came from a distinguished and affluent Hawaiian family. Hawaii, Honolulu in particular, despite its multiracial population, is socially *cliquey*. The Anglo-Hawaiian descendants of the original land barons, sugarcane and pineapple moguls, and import-export czars— the ones *firstest* with the *mostest*—were socially circumspect. And, with the influx of tourists, businesses and new residents, who can blame them.

Encounters and episodes in Hawaii from '65 to '70 were many and diverse. The first and most welcome came with hearing the sound of a car idling on the street one morning while I was puttering in the garage. After several minutes, I stalked out to see what the problem was. The two men sitting in a car polluting the environment were Bill Croarkin and Bro. David Schuyler. After seven years, these two symbols of my days at Chaminade were a welcome sight. The first thing I noticed was Brother David's *Roman* collar, now, *Father* David, vice chancellor of the Honolulu Archdiocese and barely thirty—obviously having spent his time more productively than his former student. Bill Croarkin was teaching English and Drama at Chaminade University in Honolulu. We had an animated reunion. GQK was thrilled to see them, and they'd prove to be a Godsend during her tenure at Kahala.

Also from further past, Richard Smart, owner of the Parker Ranch on the Big Island of Hawaii, his oldest son, Tony, a class ahead of me at Cate, and his younger son, Gil, and his wife, had a house across from ours on Kahala. We'd known each other since the Brentwood and New York days in the 1940s.

Dick Smart's ranch house on the Big Island, *was* a ranch house, but beautifully appointed. Gil Smart, his then-wife, Trixie [not the author's idea!] saw a lot of each other, as we were about the only people in our age range in the Kahala area.

Gladys made another friend-for-life, our new neighbor, playwright, politician, Clare Boothe Luce. The two ladies opted for friendship rather than rivalry*, pool the ol' resources* as it were, between them. They knew every interesting person coming to Honolulu, who in turn, was interested in seeing them.

General William Westmoreland, then, Supreme Allied Commander in the Pacific – Viet Nam in particular—played tennis next door. If his command on the court was reflected in Southeast Asia, it might explain a few things.

GQK and Clare gave a cocktail party for William F. Buckley, with whom I shared a political philosophy,

Catholicism, and a penchant for laconic prose and button-down shirts. Mr. Buckley is intellectually intimidating to those intelligent enough to be conscious of it. His appearing to look down on people is partially attributable to having no choice; he's literally bigger than they are. Any man three inches taller and thirty pounds heavier than the author is someone to be physically reckoned with.

Not wishing to seem smarmy, but wanting to establish my political allegiance, I reminded him of the old bromide, *"Not be a liberal at twenty, is to have no soul; to be one at forty, is to have no mind."* Mr. Buckley accessed me, "Is that to say *you* have no soul?"

For Christ's sake, of course I do, I'm Catholic! Instead, I thanked him, admitting, "I'm closer to thirty."

"Which might, conceivably, leave you without a soul or a mind," he proffered. I had to digest that.

The existing guest cottage was uninhabitable, rotted, termite ridden, so, I designed and helped construct a new one comprised of a sitting room, bedroom, kitchenette, and bathroom with a dream shower – resulting in my being clean as a whistle throughout the tenure in the cottage.

GQK occasionally rented the main house for short periods, in one instance the real estate agent was sworn to secrecy as to the identity of a potential tenant. Mom wouldn't rent the house unless she knew *who* was renting it, the agent claimed she couldn't violate the agreement, the person involved was too important, the owner stuck to her guns, no name, no house. The intrigue continued several days, the client was getting anxious, wouldn't the name be revealed on the rental agreement? Not necessarily, if handled through a corporation. Finally the agent made a desperate call to the client and was given an okay to reveal the identity, but only to Mrs. Knapp, if anyone else found out, the deal was off.

It became academic, the minute GQK heard it was Senator Robert F. Kennedy, and family, the deal *was* off!

Claiming, she didn't want, *"a litter of Kennedys destroying the house!"* The true reason for Mom's refusal went far beyond the kids, back to their grand-father, along with a deep-seated political animosity.

Fools Rush In

After Frank Raysbrook's retirement from the Navy, his long marriage to Conchita began to unravel. Their stay at the home of his Mother-in-law, Princess Pignatelli, evolved into a nightmare. His mounting eccentricities, contempt for those who disagreed with his right-of-right political philosophy, and steadfast refusal to move to other quarters, resulted in a domestic horror show. The Raysbrooks finally rented a house, but the conflict exacerbated. Living under the same roof, in immediate proximity with someone you're unable to communicate with on any level, when love deteriorates into loathing, the emotional and physical effects were devastating and scaring their children. Conchita had strength, incredible capability, along with enormous character, but the aggressive combative edge was foreign to her nature. Conchita's cousin, Gladys, had the lion's share of the family market in self-reliant resiliency. Conchita had been an exemplary daughter, sister, wife, mother, and friend. She didn't deserve this.

With anxiety and trepidation, I invited Frank Raysbrook to lunch. My senior and superior in virtually every respect, a man I greatly admired, a mentor and a role model, I suggested to him the disintegration of his marriage to my cousin was creating an untenable atmosphere, tearing not only his immediate family apart, but reeking havoc with a larger extended family and their friends as well. It was as agonizing as it was intrusive. To Frank's everlasting credit, he didn't assume an indignant or defensive posture. He listened silently, then nodded, and resigned to the only reasonable option he had. I don't know to what effect our conversation actually had, but Frank moved out shortly after. However, he scored some solid, if below-the-belt, punches in the final round by moving to Mexico, to avoid paying his wife of thirty years, a cent of alimony.

The whole experience took a mighty toll on Conchita, eventually leaving her near death in a San Diego Naval Hospital. Had it not been for the skill and sensitivity of her son Chuck, who took control of the situation, while nobly trying to reason with his father across the border, the outcome might have been disastrous. Without the loving support of the rest of her family and her faith, we would have lost her. Forty years of Easters, Thanksgivings, birthdays and visits back and forth to her, and sister Carlota's homes in La Jolla, Conchita and Carlota, remained two of the most special people on earth to me.

***

By 1966, commuting from Rancho Gladavida to Los Angeles became risky. After an evening of imbibing there would be delays. Suddenly, out of nowhere, flashing red lights appeared in my rearview mirror. I'd either feign unawareness or pull to a right lane, waving them on. They wouldn't go away. One even turned on his siren to affirm his presence. Citation is a misnomer, since you receive a citation for a heroic act, or after twenty years of devoted service, not for going seventy in a fifty-five mph zone.

I sensed, although GQK found me more amusing in my twenties than she had in my teens, was wearing thin on her. We were very compatible most of the time, but at logger-heads other times. The ranch was hers, so, I rented a one bedroom apartment in Westwood with a big terrace. By a happy coincidence, a college buddy from the Georgetown days, John Anthony "Tony" Hayes, rented an apartment across the street. Tony was an F. Scott Fitzgerald figure in college, two classes ahead of me, dashing good looks with flare and style, drove a Jaguar sportscar, and was a helluva nice guy to boot.

After introducing GQK to Tony, her maternal instincts came to bare, "Watch your step with him. He's better looking than you are."

Tony and I shared many fun times on both coasts. He was a girl magnate, colorful and subtly gregarious, yet always a gentleman. He was pursuing an acting career, but not diligently—a career having a zenith and nadir simultaneously as a young romantic lead in a Joan Crawford horror film. His first marriage was another horror, derailing after a few years, he married again and moved to Florida and hasn't been heard from since, at least by me.

Aegis on the Aegean

In 1966, not sufficiently occupied with the ranch, Honolulu, *Il Pellicano*, the American Museum in Bath, Pepperdine, and Scripps, GQK chartered a 120 foot sailing yacht, the *Alexandra Lisa*, and organized one memorable odyssey.

We rendezvoused in Athens with Delmer and Marylou Daves, Tony & Beegle Duquette, Brian & Eleanor Aherne, then embarked on a three week voyage through the Aegean Sea, with extended stops at Delos, Serifos, Kos, Santorini, Mikonos, Rhodes, Naxos, and Spetsai.

The nine of us with a crew of nine had an idyllic adventure, GQK also arranged for a chef from the French Embassy in Ankara to handle the culinary chores. Watching this big man prepare gourmet meals in a 6'x 8' galley, at interior temperatures of ninety to one hundred and ten degrees, was nothing short of miraculous.

I had the 16 millimeter camera aboard with the specially designed zoom lens. Ashore, Delmer would act as a one man crew, a ludicrous juxtaposition but fun, and help with the minimal equipment. When I'd set up a shot, picked a position, Delmer would wonder aloud, "Are you *sure* you want to photograph from there?"

Rethinking fast "Not really."

He points to a spot a few yards away, "It might be interesting from over there?"

I moved the tri-pod.

Later, while setting up an *artsy-fartsy* shot, Delmer wants to know, "What are you planning behind those bushes?"

"I'm framing the shot."

"Foregrounds are useful, if they establish a point of view," Delmer agrees conditionally, "But, dead branches in the foreground, with the children playing outside the church in the background. I dunno?"

"You think it might be mixing visual metaphors?" I ask.

"Mixing metaphors is risky," the writer-producer-director smiled—without gagging.

I had an alternative solution, "How about if I pan, then zoom in."

"The ol' zoom lens again."

"It was specially designed for the camera, Delmer."

"I understand, you want to get as much use out of it as possible. Right?"

"Well, I don't want to overkill either."

"For what it's worth, David, sometimes a devise or gimmick is more effective when used sparingly; over-use tends to lessen the impact. A steady positioned shot from several angles can be effective, rather than the camera jumping about. Easier on the audience too," the maker of thirty features suggested.

I draw an analogy, "Like saying '*fuck*' once in a script, is more effective than using it throughout?"

Delmer, after cursory consideration, nods, "In the words of the poet."

Anyway, we got some excellent footage. Oddly, some of the best were candid stills taken by a third person, of Delmer and I, setting up shots.

Interesting times came at sunset, our group gathered in the main salon over drinks to talk of *ships and shoes and sealing wax, of cabbages and kings.* Brian Aherne's stage and screen career spanned thirty years, giving him fascinating yarns to spin.

Eleanor, his wife, was an ebullient lady who'd seen and done it all. Tony Duquette, an ephemeral and prolific artist, with a very engaging personality, humorous perspective and an astute promoter of his work and himself. He'd buy a piece in a Hong Kong flea market for $10, give it a few creative touches, then sell it for $500, and upwards. Tony had a beguiling charm and a lust for life which made him absolutely unique. Beegle Duquette was the diametric opposite of her husband, a quiet unassuming darling, the little gray hen with a *master-of-the-barnyard* rooster. These sessions were an education and a source of insider information. Delmer, Tony, and Brian were raconteurs, whereas, I just talked a lot. I learned to love good conversations more than sex or rich desserts—increasingly so with each passing decade—but a lot harder to come by.

My only contemporary aboard was a crew member, Nick, a couple of years younger than I, with a face and body reminiscent of an ancient Greek statue and a profile worthy of a rare coin. Proper decorum between passengers and crew members on any vessel is a given, so, Nick and I found ways to circumvent, rather than violate, seafaring tradition. When moored off an island, we'd take our snorkeling gear, jump in the zodiak and head for a nearby cove—there always seemed to be one—once out of sight of the yacht, we would *skinny-snorkel.* Nick was delightfully uninhibited, innovative and fun, a vicariously erotic adjunct to the classic surroundings. We knew what was going on but never acknowledging it, just guys being guys. If things felt a little intense, it was time to talk football or in Nick's case, soccer.

The yacht was a people magnet, drawing attention at every island port. GQK going ashore with a scarf over her head or a wide brimmed straw hat, wearing dark glasses, became a spectator sport. Locals and tourists would watch in fascination, not knowing who she was, but knowing she was *someone.*

She told me once, *"class"* is a word used by those who don't have any.

Too bad, because it sure applied to someone who *did* have it.

Scanning Scandinavia

After the voyage, in sharp contrast, GQK & I took a week's tour of Scandinavia—more succinctly, Copenhagen, Oslo, and Stockholm. I don't think it was out of genuine interest as much as saying, "We'd been there." Perhaps, the sunshine and exotic aura of the Greek islands needed to be balanced with the overcast and somber atmosphere Scandinavia offers. Copenhagen was quaint with a tinge of *pizzazz* for a few days, then, a drive up to Elsinore Castle. One can empathize with *Hamlet* and his neurotic colleagues, anyone would get testy in that bleak oppressive environment, with no central heating. The weekend in Stockholm, Sweden, we switched from driving on the left and joined the rest of the continent on the right. The transition took place over two days without a hitch. GQK observed, it bespoke a lot about Sweden, "Had the changeover been in Italy, France, Spain, or any country with fire in its belly, it would have been utter chaos."

Another thing she found puzzling, smorgasbords. Serving a buffet of unappetizing cold food in a frigid Nordic climate seemed contrary to logic and human need. To me, serving pickled herring, anchovies, lingonberries, the tongue of any animal or aquavit, anywhere, should be a felony—in a pinch, the latter could be reduced to a misdemeanor.

No Reason for Modesty

In London we met up with the Duquettes and the Ahernes. While GQK went to Newmarket to visit her horses, Brian, Eleanor, and I saw Noel Coward (Knighthood on the way) in his last play as author and actor, *A Suite in Two Keys* (the title differed in other productions), with Lilli Palmer and Irene Worth. Coward's wit and humor was applied in a more serious and insightful vein, it worked wonderfully, seeing a legend in his final stage production was a privilege.

The Ahernes took me backstage to meet the stars. I was a big fan of Lilli Palmer, who was suffering from a mild stomach flu; Miss Worth had a serious cold, a consummate actress but not a bundle of laughs, so the introductions were brief.

It occurred to me, the first time I'd seen Brian Aherne on stage was with Alfred Lunt and Lyn Fontanne in *Quadrille*, by Noel Coward.

I was in awe of the legendary prolific playwright-author-composer-actor-producer-director-entertainer, who did it all superbly! He wasn't particularly attractive physically, but blessed with extraordinary talent, he took full advantage of what God gave him, no human could learn or acquire that degree of genius solely on their own.

Framed in the doorway of his dressing room, in a silk dressing robe, backlighted by a makeup mirror, Coward looked every inch a god of the theater.

He gave me cursory once-over, while embracing Eleanor, having decided the young American stranger was presentable; he suggested we all have lunch with him the following day.

Being part of the foursome at the Savoy Grill, I realized how very fortunate I was to have the kind of background allowing me to *appreciate* who this man was. I observed and *listened* for a change. The author of *Private Lives* pretty much ignored me throughout lunch, an occasional glance to see if I'd poked my eye out with fork and always catching me gawking at him. Finally, Coward turned to me, "Why are you staring at me like that?"

"Sorry, Mr. Coward, I didn't mean stare, I-I'm just overwhelmed."

"By what?"

"What an honor it is to meet you," with just enough deference.

Staying in character he asked, "Were you aware of my existence prior to last night? You can be truthful."

"I've seen a lot of your work, sir," praying for a chance to elaborate.

"Really?" A challenge in his inflection, "Do you have any favorites, Mister...?"

"Knapp," so as not to be cheeky. "But please, call me David."

Resuming his questioning, "You still haven't told me what you've seen of mine that you like?" He remained dubious about generalities.

"My favorite is *Design for Living.* I think *Cavalcade* and *Blithe Spirit* run a close second." I saw no point in bringing up *Nude with Violin,* which he wrote and starred in while his talent was on hiatus. What's a cake without frosting, "Oddly enough, my two favorites were your films *Brief Encounter* and *In Which We Serve."* A sprinkle of cinnamon on the frosting, "Acting-wise, I thought you were a hoot in *Our Man in Havana."*

Then, knowing Coward had been David Lean's first choice for the Alec Guinness role, "I'm sorry you didn't do *Bridge on the River Kwai*."

"So am I, but I wouldn't have survived in Ceylon." My passing marks were confirmed when he sardonically offered, "Tell me, *David*, did you enjoy my performance in *Bunny Lake is Missing*?" A sort of industry "in" joke, as it was easily one of the ten worst films ever made. A brief chuckle, I answered honestly, "Actually, sir, I thought you were wonderful in it." To that Mr. Coward sat back in his chair and asked, "Do you come to London often?"

It wasn't an invitation to tea, but it sufficed.

***

Sunday, the Ahernes and I took the train to Headcorn in Kent, where we'd been invited for luncheon by GQK's former paramour, George Sanders, now married to Ronald Colman's widow, Benita Hume. George greeted us effusively, then with his wife out of earshot and a trace of awkwardness he asked, "How's your dear Mama?" I told him she was in Newmarket, not knowing whether she'd been invited, or chosen not to come.

At lunch, George and I exchanged fraternal banter, which diminished during the course of the afternoon. The rest of the day was *outdoorsy*, "gent's only" croquet, no-nonsense serious stuff, a far distant cousin of the game I'd played in California. The squat eight-inch-wide metal wickets were replaced by sturdy ceramic wickets, no more than six inches wide, barely enough to accommodate the diameter of the ball. Ours had been about eighteen feet apart; the English version had them twenty five feet apart.

We played, "every man for himself." You hit a wild ball, it was your problem, no one else's. George's group was divided into *two teams*, adding further competitive pressure—you screw up, your team screws up! I try not to take any games too seriously but I invariably get caught up and yell louder than anyone. Being the recipient to George Sanders' glowering is unnerving, he was clever enough to put me on the opposing team, virtually assuring his team's victory.

Chapter 18

WHO LEFT THE GATE OPEN?

Probably the happiest day in Aunt Kate's life came when she and Oz sold their ranch and took a house in San Francisco. They gave a cocktail-dinner for GQK, attended by a number of Northern members of the family. Aunt Ruth had passed away well into her nineties, but her daughters, Harrie Page and Juanita Schurman attended.

Among the other guests, was a senior relative, I'll call, *Harley*, a seasoned man-about-town, who was walking a tightrope between lucidity and senility. Harley didn't permit others to finish sentences, an annoying trait which I acquired to some degree. We were chatting in non sequiturs.

"I understand you live in Santa Barbara," Harley misunderstood.

A little South of there, in. . ."

"Of course, I remember, *Montecito*-ites consider themselves separate and apart from Santa Barbara," Harley knew of life's nuances.

"It's not that," I tried to explain.

I tried to clarify any inconsistency, while Harley searched his brain, which didn't take long, "But you're not *from* Southern California?"

"Actually, I was born in San Diego."

"Oh dear, what did you say your name was?"

"David Knapp."

"Oh? Some damned fool told me you were Gladys Quarre's son!"

Laughter from Above

In 1967, Basil Rathbone completed his one-man tour in Honolulu, returning to New York via Los Angeles, to spend a few relaxing days at the ranch. The man I picked up at the airport, looked ten years older than he had two years earlier. The tour hadn't been a major success, critically or financially, Basil was exhausted and bordering on emaciation. Mom took one look at him, deciding he needed rest and as much nutrition as we could stuff down his throat.

He was pampered for three days, sleeping until late morning. Our housekeepers, Jean and Mona, brought him breakfast in bed, after which, he lounged by the pool for several hours, took a nap, then cocktails, dinner and retired by nine-thirty. I took a wonderful picture of him sitting in the garden with Marilyn, his aquiline profile and her golden muzzle nose-to-nose. I think it was the last photograph taken of him.

I drove Basil back to the airport, he paused before getting out of the car, leaned over and kissed me on the cheek, something he'd never done. "This may be the last time we see each other," he didn't dramatize it, only a sense of weary resignation his voice.

Watching him disappear into the terminal, I felt great sadness on somehow realizing how prophetic his words would be.

Two months later Ouida called to tell us, Basil had passed away.

GQK & Son were on the next available flight to New York. Ouida's niece, Ouida Wagner, Cornelia Otis Skinner, and Mom took charge of the arrangements, as the widow Ouida was barely functioning.

July was hot and muggy the day of Basil's funeral. Mom and I went to the funeral home as Ouida's envoys for a final viewing before sealing the casket. We were informed by a little man in a dark suit, there was a problem, Basil wasn't at the funeral home.

"Where did they take him?"

They weren't sure, it turned out, and he hadn't been checked out either! Of course he hadn't, not until *we* got there to okay it. The mortuary assistant fidgeted, explaining, he'd just returned from his vacation, and wasn't quite caught up, and asked if we had we checked the city morgue?

GQK took umbrage to the idiotic question, "People don't go from a funeral home to the morgue, it's the other way around! Now, find out where Mr. Rathbone is."

The attendant scurried out, returning with the funeral director, who officiously offered to call the church. After a brief phone conversation, we weren't privy to, he relayed, the priest told him Basil wasn't there and they didn't have a funeral scheduled that day. "The *priest*?" GQK was incredulous. "They don't have priests at *Episcopal* churches!"

"*Episcopal*?" It was his turn to be incredulous.

"*Saint Edwards,* where the funeral's going to be!" Mom exploded, "He's been taken to the wrong church!"

He then called the right church and was told, "Mr. Rathbone hadn't arrived, but was expected."

"Not if he's been taken to the wrong church!" Her inflection adding, "You miserable damned fool!"

We grabbed a taxi on Madison Avenue, for the five minute ride to Saint Edwards. Mr. Rathbone still hadn't arrived! The church then got a call from the funeral home, there *had* been a mistake, "Mr. Rathbone *had* been checked out over an hour ago, to the correct designation."

They would check with the police, to find out if there'd been an accident involving a hearse—no reports of one.

When Mom and I stepped outside for a breath of hot muggy air, she looked skyward, chortling to herself. I asked, what was so amusing? A rueful smile, "Basil must be looking down on us, having one hell of a good laugh."

The hearse arrived minutes later, the driver had stopped for a leisurely lunch, on the assumption his passenger wouldn't care.

Cornelia Otis Skinner delivered the eulogy to a full house. After the service concluded, we stepped outside, a sizable crowd had gathered on both sides of the street. Four police motorcycles waited to escort the flower-laden hearse and limousines for the hour drive to Basil's burial site in Hartsdale, Westchester County.

Mom and I were riding in the lead limousine with Ouida, Cynthia, and Miss Skinner, when we turned east off Madison Ave. toward East River Drive. I looked out the rear window; following the other limos, a line of cars with funeral stickers rounded the corner behind us. I watched as more cars continued to make the turn, the procession soon stretched back for two city blocks. The police had to request additional motorcycle officers to escort the number of vehicles following the hearse.

By then, I don't believe Basil was laughing from above, certainly no one down there was. He had to be gratified, seeing so many people paying homage to his long and distinguished career, and more importantly, to him as a person. Basil Rathbone's legacy is assured.

Curiously enough, his name is recognized by more people throughout the world, than many past and present "superstars."

How was it For You?

The Kahala house and the new guest cottage, became popular layovers (again, no pun intended) for friends en route to and from, the Orient, along with those from the mainland—as well as some last minute over-night guests. Moonlight skinny-dipping, on a balmy night in the placid waters off Kahala beach, with palm branches swaying in a gentle breeze, a couple of Mai Tais under your belt, is a pleasant experience. More so, if you share it with someone.

I was showing my cottage to an acquaintance one evening, who remarked on seeing the shower facility, "You could get four people in there."

I knew it held three comfortably, but four?

I learned exchanging addresses with people from Cincinnati or Cedar Rapids, exchanging addresses, with a "Whenever you're in town please let me know," is safe for *them*, the chances of you ever being in their home town are practically zilch, *not* the case if you live in New York, Los Angeles, or Honolulu! You can bet your first-born, you'll get calls, "Arriving on such and such a date, can't wait to see you." Not wanting to fall into the trap, you ask pointedly, "What *hotel* will you be at?"

"Well, we don't have any reservations."

A more dramatic situation arose when, Michael Boyer, the only child of the Charles Boyer's, ostensibly took his own life. Michael was several classes behind me at Chaminade, a student of Bill Croarkin and David Schuyler's. His "suicide" was generally believed to be a cover-up to protect the reputations of several prominent young people present at the time of his death. Charles and his wife, Pat, were decimated by the loss. Michael, born well into their marriage, was the center of their lives.

GQK invited Pat Boyer to Hawaii, hoping it might help her though the recuperation process. Bill Croarkin and

Father David were there for her too, unflaggingly lending
their support, both had known the Boyer family better than
GQK. It was a difficult period. Pat Boyer was emotionally
overwhelmed, and at a certain point GQK simply didn't
know how to console her.

GQK tried to put herself in Pat's place, had it been me
instead of Michael—a difficult comparison. Pat was a sweet,
softly-dependent lady, devoted to her husband and son.
Gladys Knapp was the other end of the spectrum, gentle and
compassionate, but not soft and never dependent. She
wouldn't allow herself to put all her *emotional eggs* in one
basket. GQK would suffer, but survive. Pat and Charles
never fully recovered from their son's death.

Home on the Plains

The following year, I bought my first home at 135
South Bowling Green Way in Brentwood—a mile from the
old Cliffwood house, but South of Sunset Boulevard, and
not quite the same. The house could be better described as a
large cottage, a charmer, surrounded by lush greenery, with
most of the backyard taken up by a lagoon-like swimming
pool and a small thatch-roofed mini-cottage, *sans* plumbing.
GQK found it "simply adorable," promptly making it her in-
town headquarters.

One thing bothered her about my bedroom, "The bed, it
faces North."

I hadn't thought about that superstition, but it was the
only placement the room allowed, other walls had
obstructions.

I shared the space with Marilyn's daughter, Gloria, and
a super mutt we'd adopted, *Leo*. Gladys Knapp never
acknowledged having mix-bred mutts, they were ordained,
"a rare breed." She decided Leo was a Dandie Dinmont
Terrier, since he resembled one and most people had no idea

what they looked like anyway. His credentials were never challenged. Many years in the past GQK rescued a large stray who was pure mutt, but after a week of solid meals, a bath and grooming, he turned out to be a handsome dog. She anointed him, a *"Mendocino Elk Hound,"* and pulled it off. People would nod thoughtfully, "I think a friend of my father had a Mendocino Elk Hound."

Bowling Green was an ideal cozy setting for small dinners. There was a lot of that kind of entertaining back then, few do it now. My generation slowed down or got lazy, this generation, wouldn't know how.

Having been logistically isolated at the ranch and relatively quiet at the Westwood apartment, I realized many of the people I knew in town were really GQK's friends.

Tony Hayes helped me get into the swing of things. His former roommate, Christopher George, and his wife Linda Day George, both with major careers in TV—Chris starred in *Rat Patrol*, a successful series; Gary Collins and his wife Mary Ann Mobley, I met through Bill and Debby (Daves) Richards, and I was introduced to Stewart Moss, and his exquisite wife, Marianne McAndrew, two extremely talented busy actors at the time. We would work together on many projects in the years to come. Stewart was brought to Hollywood by Otto Preminger to do *In Harm's Way,* the World War II Naval film, with John Wayne, Kirk Douglas, and Patricia Neal. Another star of the Preminger film, Tom Tryon, became a friend. When his acting career faltered, Tom became a highly acclaimed author, critically and commercially.

***

Eleanore Phillips, the West Coast Editor of *Vogue* magazine and a dearly missed friend, did a photo layout at the house with Lesley Ann Warren and myself, the latter in the background, in flared-plaid pants, trying to look lustfully dashing as he ogled Ms. Warren in a billowing skirt. In future years, Ms. Warren went on to receive an Oscar nomination, a height she never achieved in personal popularity. The framed layout hangs over the toilet in my guest bathroom.

I went through a period when I had virtually *everything* I deemed significant framed, the walls covered with photos, letters, articles, posters, etcetera, the only prerequisite was my direct or indirect involvement—then again, who displays personal memorabilia having nothing to do with them? On the other hand, I know several people who hang portraits of individuals with whom they have absolutely no connection. Seeing an eighteenth or nineteenth century painting of a distinguished or ferocious-looking individual, asking the owner who it is and they haven't a clue, "It just looks nice." If it's an ancestor, or a Rembrandt, Gainsborough, or Goya, fine, but who wants a total stranger looking down on you from the wall?

I was fortunate to be a frequent guest at the homes of other show-biz heavyweights, Lawrence Kasha, Douglas Cramer, Ross Hunter and Jacque Mapes, Irving Rapper, Tony Charmoli, choreographer *extraordinaire,* and the legendary George Cukor. It was always a pleasant surprise when a mega-power-house in the entertainment industry, Barry Diller, accepted invitations, then went on to be a delightfully gregarious guest. These led to friendships with Los Angeles' Broadway community, Robert Fryer, Jerry Herman, Joseph Hardy, Jerome Lawrence, and Richard Barr. One of the aforementioned gentlemen was a top Broadway producer; his many successful productions were world renowned. For whatever reasons, his career took a down turn and he was compelled to move from his lovely home in the hills, on Thrasher Way, to a small apartment in a modest section of Hollywood. His decline was as depressing to his friends as it must have been for him.

Last, but foremost, Jon Epstein, a top TV producer at Universal, a social magnet, a sweetheart of man, with a cracker-jack sense of humor, but never at anyone's expense. I'd kid him about his Leftist politics, calling him, a "screaming liberal." Jon would feign indigence, "Only to you members of royal court." The easy and lively parties at his Coldwater Canyon home were conduits to all strata of the Hollywood community, super-stars, mingling with unemployed bit players—all made to feel equally welcome.

I'm eternally grateful for the times spent in the company of men like that. In those days, I took it for granted to some degree. I don't know.

I felt relief knowing the household-names I met, who were genuinely nice, wholly unpretentious and not "preoccupied," were the norm, not the exceptions.

The Point Being?

In April of 1970 GQK and DHK were back in London. The horses at Hadrian Stud, the American Museum in England, Il Pellicano in Italy, and investments in the Bank du Lausanne in Switzerland were on her agenda. Her son had a possible British-financed film project to promote.

The Golden Youth of Lee Prince by Aubrey Goodman, was a controversial novel set in New York in the Fifties. Seeking British backing for an American film was feasible at the time. With the interest of Carter DeHaven, an American producer living in London, meetings were set up with several British film consortiums, Joe Shaftel and John Daly among them. Things seemed to be promising, except some felt the story could be effectively adapted to London; another wanted a composite of the two principle characters, thus eliminating the core conflict; one suggested 'Lee Prince' become 'Leah Prince.' Despite very much wanting to see the project happen, what was the point of making a film if you abandon the essential elements that peak your interest? After the deal-making, compromise, multiple script adaptations, budgetary demands, and ten executive producer's opinions, a convoluted and *re-concepted*, totally different project evolves, with only its title intact. No one remembers the original concept that brought everyone to the table in the first place.

By the third day meetings had to be put in abeyance. The direct flight from Los Angeles caused such a monumental case of jet-lag, I was disoriented and shorter tempered than usual. Peter Lubbock took me to Charing Cross Hospital. After the doctors gave me a shot, Peter took me back to Claridges, where I was carried up to my room. I woke up the following morning rested and readjusted. Needless to say, Mom experienced absolutely no ill-effects; she was out and about, chipper throughout my ordeal. Jet-lag only affects me flying West to East as the years accumulate. Even the trip East to New York leaves me bed-ridden until noon the first two days.

Lubbock and Brian Desmond Hurst, a film director of stature, became my London chums. Brian was a devilishly dirty old man, right out of a Hogarth print. He reminded me of the character *Sir* Albert Finney played so brilliantly in *The Dresser*. Brian had a tiny house on Kennerton Street, a short distance from Lord Louis Mountbatten's pied-à-terre.

***

Mom and I then flew to Rome, spending time with Renee De Becker and Eric De Rothschild. Back then, we could drive to Ostia for a swim and lunch, and then be back in town by 4 p.m. for a night on the town with our cousins, Mario and Marcella Bandini. Mario had been quite the man about town in his bachelor years. During the U.S. film boom in Italy in the '60s, he hosted as many American leading ladies as Cinecitta—Kim Novak, among them. Mario finally married Marcella, a Peruvian, twenty years his junior, and promptly produced three beautiful children, which had a substantially settling effect on him.

Next we were off to Porto Ercole for a few days. Il Pellicano had become a celebrity magnet, attracting people from all over. On the third night of our stay, with every table on the dining terrace filled, the chef and most of the kitchen staff walked out in a labor dispute! Not unusual in Italy, but a potential catastrophe on this night!

Patty Graham was a superb cook, but not prepared for varied entrees for fifty guests in a chaotic situation. GQK volunteered me as Patty's *sous chef*, reassuring all, I was quite a good cook. Like I could whip up S*ole Bonne Famme, Tortellini Milanese,* and S*ouffle Apricot*? Fortunately, a few other guests versed in the culinary arts, readily offered their services. "In a crisis, it's fun to do things you avoid doing on a regular basis," the wife of the Spanish Prime Minister confided while she seasoned a sauce. Seeing French actress Michele Morgan, the epitome of elegance and beauty, wearing an apron over *haute couture,* while efficiently slicing vegetables and fruit was a Kodak moment—nor was having dinner served by Yul Brynner, Richard Greene, and Sascha Diestel, a common-place occurrence.

Despite an abruptly limited menu, erratic service, and confusion, all agreed, the evening was a triumph. A contributing factor for rave responses may have been the temperament of the "temporary staff," and the ever-present possibility of *wearing* a plate of pasta, rather than consuming it. There's a way of asking a guest, "Did you enjoy your dinner," which leaves no doubt they did!

Many guests were having drinks in the salon, after the sumptuous meal, when they were treated to an impromptu *bump'n grind.* David Rose's album, *The Stripper,* blaring from the stereo, Michael Graham, Sascha Diestel and myself, inhibitions numbed by a rainbow of bottle labels, began salaciously removing our clothing. What began as a frivolous display, evolved into a serious striptease. The three of us spontaneously choreographed a slipshod routine, falling into unison. Down to our briefs, the audience got a glimpse above and below the tan line—a fortunate few, even a flash of pubes. Lire notes were stuffed in our waistbands by easily excitable fans, shouts of "Take it off, take it all off!" and "Come on fellas, let's see what you've got!"— unnerving from one's Mother!

We gave them as good a show as any airport hotel lounge. Sascha looked a lot better than most strippers of either gender, collecting many thousand lire notes; he had enough to buy Michael and me a drink! Sascha and I agreed later, it was fun wiggling your butt in a *comedic* manner, but it's unsettling if someone starts taking you seriously. Instead of smiling and laughter, you get an intensely suggestive leer and perspiration.

Pasadena Playhouse

Al McCleery tried to realize a dream. Many criticized him, some with just cause, but many admired and respected him as did I. The bottom line, people returned his calls. One was William Inge, the author of *Picnic, Come Back Little Sheba, Bus Stop, Dark at the Top of The Stairs,* and the original screenplay for *Splendor in The Grass.* Bill Inge was arguably one of the greatest American playwrights, winner of the Pulitzer Prize, N.Y. Drama Critics Award, a Tony, and an Oscar.

Only Bill Inge had demons, and wasn't buying any of it. His last play, *The Subject Was Roses,* wasn't a major hit, but it did okay, making a star of Warren Beatty. Even at that, it would have been the peak of many writers' careers.

Inge considered it a death knell, firmly believing, he'd lost his touch and would never taste success again. He set-about to make it a reality.

After a few drinks Inge became predictably maudlin, so, in cavalier fashion I offered, "Would it matter if you never wrote another word? You have an incredible legacy. Most writers would give their souls to have just one of your successes? God man, you're known all over the world!" Inge shrugged, "Tennessee is better known."

So is Shakespeare, so what? You wanted to smack him. Bill was fatally addicted to success. Now in withdrawal, he desperately needed help, a task I was ill-prepared for. Spending an hour with him became an ordeal, being enormously fond of him wasn't enough. Trying to be supportive and reason with him, rattling off names of other known playwrights and authors, who owed their fame, essentially, to a single work, whereas, he'd written a half dozen! "You've been spoiled rotten by the success you've earned!" The tough-love technique was of no help.

Self-pity is unappealing in anyone, more so, when unwarranted. He should have savored his triumphs, he chose otherwise. Inge gave me his original typewritten version of four one-act plays. "Keep them, they're yours to do with what you want. Light a fire with them, I don't give a damn anymore."

"Jesus, Bill, I'm overwhelmed, I don't know what to say."

"Better read them first, let me know what you think—unless you don't like them."

After reading them several times, I couldn't bring myself to get back to him. I took a coward's way out, avoiding the subject by avoiding him. The silence was more eloquent than a volume of criticism. He was sinking and I had no rope to throw him.

Less than a year later Bill Inge committed suicide. Although I was an incidental in his life, still, the finality of knowing you can never go back or make things right, was a source of regret.

Aloha

By the beginning of the new decade, Honolulu surpassed many cities on the mainland in non-stop construction, congestion and commercialism, but with warmer, if not necessarily better, weather.

After five years and as many unsolved burglaries, GQK had enough of Hawaii, she sold the Kahala house. Several years passed before she returned to the Paradise Islands.

Between Hawaii and the mainland, I was having overlapping romantic problems. I alluded to them at the ranch, in non-specifics, GQK sighed ruefully, "Ah, for the peace and quiet of the bed, after the hurly-burly of the chaise lounge." My problem was *not* getting any peace and quiet in bed.

"One day you'll look back on all the huffing and puffing and wonder what it was all about, but until then, you have to struggle though and make the best of it."

Sensing my expectation of more profound counseling, she went on to theorize, "I suspect, love and sex were designed as diversions, to keep our minds and bodies occupied, give us something to do. When you think about it, ethereal notions aside, most lives are about filling time between birth and death, not much else. You're born, you ingest, defecate, copulate, procreate, and survive, so you can leave behind more of the same to carry on the tradition."

"Do you really believe that's what it is all about?"

"The point is, to make certain you don't fall into that category, a *bon mot* on a nautical note. Better to cause ripples, than lie dead in the water," in GQK's case, *tsunamis*.

***

In New York, some weeks later, Hermione Gingold and I attended a Brentano's Bookstore opening on Fifth Avenue. We didn't recognize the lady walking directly towards us, but there was a vague sense of familiarity. She extended her gloved hand, "Hermione, I don't know if you remember me, I'm Joan Crawford." Hermione regrouped instantly, "Joan, how could I possibly forget you. How are you?"

I hate it when someone you don't know all that well, who *isn't* a celebrity challenges you to remember their name. If they thought you could, they wouldn't ask such a dumb-ass question! Having said that, the first words out my mouth, "I doubt if you'll remember me, Miss Crawford." Miss Crawford's expression left no doubt. My cloak of anonymity in place, I gave her a hint, "We were neighbors at one time."

The former superstar tried her damnedest to be civil, asking, "And where was that?"

"In Brentwood." Lowering my cloak slightly, "I came to your house several times to play with your daughter, Christina." Possibly, Miss Crawford misconstrued what I said.

The film icon assumed a lady-like stance, legs apart, shoulders back, "I sold that house twenty years ago!"

Dropping the cloak, "My name then was *Robin*, my Mother was. . ."

The lady who made *Mildred Pierce* a household name, cut me off, "Janet Gaynor! I remember, your father, he designed my clothes at MGM!"

"I think you're confusing me with Robin *Adrian,* Miss Crawford*.* "

"If you're not that Robin, then, who the fu-- ?"

Indicating the literary surroundings, Hermione jumped in, "Joan, have you read any good books lately?"

Later, Hermione, reflected, "I should have realized who she was the moment I saw those shoes!"

She referred to the superstar's legendary spike-heeled, ankle-strapped footwear, known as, "Crawford-come-fuck-me-pumps."

***

Alvin Epstein, was heading the *Yale Repertory Company* and teaching at the drama school, when I went to visit him in New Haven. Alvin was one of the few successful stage actors who rarely succumbed to the lure of the camera, though had ample opportunities. It wasn't due to artistic snobbery; he simply needed the continuity of live theatre. We had dinner at a just-off-campus bar/restaurant. The place was alive and noisy, packed with college-aged guys and girls. I mentioned to Alvin, what an attractive crowd it was. As we were leaving, he smiled, "You might want to hang around here, you may find it even more interesting in an hour or so." He didn't elaborate. A half hour later, it quieted down a little with the guys outnumbering the girls. I sat at the bar, engaging in conversation with an extremely nice-looking young couple.

The girl glanced about, deciding, "Looks like it's time for me to go." Said she "enjoyed meeting me," and gave her boyfriend a peck on the cheek and then left. Puzzled by her abrupt departure, I noticed all the girls had apparently done the same. In a matter of minutes the bar had acquired a frat-house atmosphere. I naively remarked to the boyfriend, "Where did all the girls go?"

***

I ran into George Sanders at the Beverly Hills Hotel, his wife Benita passed away the year after our 1966 World Cup croquet match. His film career subsiding and having made poor investments, he was living in Spain. He may have been at loose ends when he asked, "Would it be all right if I gave your Mom a jingle?" After ten years, I thought she'd like to hear from him. That weekend, George went up to the ranch. As GQK related it, with Jean confirming, not long after his arrival, he proposed to Mom! She mulled it over several seconds, then declined, explaining gently to George, "I've made three men miserable, I'm much too fond of you to make you the fourth."

George left the ranch Monday, drove to Palm Springs, and married Magda Gabor, his former sister-in-law, that Friday. They separated the following week, George returned to Spain, where, a year later, he wrote a brief note, then took his own life.

***

Mom and I ended the year with another all expense paid trip to Las Vegas, hosted by Tommy Douglas to promote the Riviera Hotel. Doris Stein, George Freylinghuysen, Alfredo de la Vega, John and Louise Good, and a dozen others, including a nasty fat-fairy Universal producer were part of the group. We never picked up a tab, it was tacitly understood we'd make up for it with gambling losses. Gladys Knapp had other ideas. One evening in a casino anti-room, I was stunned to see her and George Freylinghuysen in a high-stakes poker game with a group of high-rollers, piles of twenty and fifty dollar chips in front of them. GQK played more conservatively than her partner, George was betting a diminishing pile of chips with each hand, while GQK meticulously bet four or five, increasing her steadily growing pile. Mom left the table with more than when she arrived. In a typically wry manner, George claimed victory in having lost *twelve* thousand dollars!

Alfredo de la Vega was on everyone's social list, immensely popular and liked by everyone who knew him—and he knew *everyone*. He always referred to me as *Junior* well into my forties, unacceptable coming from most, but from him, a term of endearment. His tragic death at the hands of a repressed malcontent shocked and saddened a large community of friends. As testimony to the esteem in which he was held and the influence of his influential friends, the police report of his death never saw the light of day, nor was the incident ever publicized in the newspapers or by the media.

That year, along with others, ended at an annual New Year's Eve party given by Carlton and Augusta Alsop at Chasens. Their galas lived up to New Year's expectations, the kind of evening you hope to be apart of, but rarely are.

Equally auspicious were Jean Howard's annual January 1st luncheons at her Coldwater Canyon home. Jean was a beautiful woman with a worldly mystique. As an aspiring actress, she turned down a proposal of marriage from Louis B. Mayer—an unusual career move. She then married Charles Feldman, a top agent and major power broker.

Jean was gifted amateur photographer, her "at home" pictures represented Hollywood at its most glamorous. Several books of her photos and commentaries were big sellers. Probably the most memorable example was a photo taken at a New Year's Eve party, she and her husband hosted at Romanoff's. Four men, in white tie, standing at the bar having an uproarious time.

It was unique, in that the four men Jean photographed were, Clark Gable, Gary Cooper, Jimmy Stewart, and Van Heflin! Another, taken of a bemused Lauren Bacall looking at her husband, Humphrey Bogart, sitting on Clifton Webb's lap at a pool party, was not only a juxtaposition but a paradox; Bogart seemed to be having a rollicking fun time, while Webb looked a bit uncomfortable.

A non sequitur came on a spur-of-the-moment flight GQK made to New York with Clifton Webb. She'd been planning to go East on business, when Webb proposed she rearrange her plans and join him on a promotional trip to the *Big Apple*, at the bequest of Twentieth Century Fox, to attend the premiere of one of his films, she spontaneously accepted.

On the flight, Webb, GQK, and the others seated in first class were continually harassed by a wretched little girl running up and down the aisle, screaming, knocking drinks into people's laps, and mauling them with dirty hands. The child's mother remained totally oblivious to the havoc wrought by her unruly brat. Finally, someone in their party grabbed the little monster as she swept by and waltzed her back to her seat. GQK watched as he thrust the child at her mother, then, leaned over and said something which kept her silent the remainder of the flight. "If you don't control your daughter, I'm going to fuck her."

Chapter 19

PARAMETERS OBSCURED

In March of 1971, GQK, at seventy, embarked on a fifteen-thousand-mile trek to places, neither she, nor I, had ever been. First stop, Tahiti. Bora Bora more than lived up to expectations, Moorea exceeded them, for reasons the author won't detail. Papeete was a disappointment, the "Gauguin-Somerset Maugham" quality eluded us; the decadence was there, but not the seductive charm. I'd been in a few rough 'n tumble bars, but the patrons in the one I briefly visited, made *Long John Silver's* pirate crew look like delegates at a Republican convention. The beaches brought to mind, marshes after the water recedes from a hurricane. I asked a local why everyone wore protective footwear in Tahitian waters, "If you step on a blowfish, you die," he explained.

From there, we were on to American Samoa, where Pago Pago is pronounced, *Pango Pango,* and then to Western Samoa. We stayed in Apia, where both of the island's hotels are located. We only had one day there and wanted to see as much as possible. We hired a guide who took us for a short walk up a hill to Robert Louis Stevenson's burial site, after which, he was eager to know, "Had we enjoyed the *tour*?"

The isolated resort in Fiji was spectacular; the only unpleasant part was the journey to and from it to the airport.

Next, a week in New Zealand on the North and South Islands. They drive on the wrong side too, so, we hired a car and driver in Auckland for a trip to Hamilton and Rotarua. After visiting both, GQK wondered aloud, "Why do you suppose they encourage visitors to come to these places? We don't send foreigners to Oxnard or Modesto."

South Island's spectacular scenery is not unlike California, it duplicates many other parts of the world.

Landing in a single-engine Cessna on one of Mount Cook's glaciers is a must, just make certain the aircraft's wheels have been replaced with large skis. Many years later, New Zealand serves as a popular location site for filming. Filmmakers have seen fit to fly actors and crews seven thousand miles to shoot scenes that could have been done twenty miles from Los Angeles?

GQK and I flew from Christ Church to Melbourne, then on to Canberra. Tourists rarely go to Australia's capitol, it may be dull living there, but it's a fine pristine city to visit. The military museum is one of the best anywhere and the structures on Embassy Row architecturally reflect the nations they represent. Billy McCann, from the London days, met us in Sydney, introducing us to a wonderfully eclectic range of Australians. The chairman of *David Jones' Department Stores*, Charles Lloyd-Jones, became a special friend and a gracious host, subsequent visits in Los Angeles, New York, and London were always excessive and fun. Charles had a farm in Woolahra, a two hour drive from Sydney, nestled in its own little valley. Years later, he allowed me to bring a large group I was traveling with for a day at the farm. He entertained fifty strangers by staging a mock Aboriginal attack, with painted locals in loin cloths rushing out of the surrounding forest shrieking and brandishing spears.

James Fairfax, the owner-publisher of Sydney's biggest newspaper empire, became a social mentor on several later visits, as well. GQK and I were regally wined and dined, together and separately, her social forays tended toward the chic Elizabeth Bay crowd, mine were more in the King's Cross area, then in its halcyon, raucous, and seedy days— today, only the latter applies.

Mom and I parted in Sydney, she returned to California for business reasons—or so she said. I think perhaps the rigors of extensive long range travel may have been a factor? However, there was no evidence of stress or weariness on her part, during the trip. She was an energized, enthusiastic and flexible traveling companion the entire time, ready for any challenge. Everyone along the way thoroughly enjoyed her company.

I continued on alone to Bali and Djakarta in Indonesia, Singapore, Malaysia, Thailand, Burma (now Myanmar), Hong Kong, a brief stop over on Guam, then to Honolulu and home.

Stairs Leading Somewhere

After returning from Asia, I took a project to *Bedford Productions.* Alan Jay Factor, was the core of the small company, CEO, executive producer, producer and head bottle washer. The meeting lasted an hour and I stayed around for four years. There were never more than three to five of us at any one time actively involved in the company's operation. Nomads, we went wherever the project demanded, at various times we had offices in Beverly Hills, on the Sunset Strip, as well as at *CBS Studio Center, Twentieth Century Fox, Four-Star,* and *Columbia.* The legendary Sam Marx joined the company on a couple of projects. Sam was a big man, in every conceivable way. I'm a (slightly) better person for having known him, a "chocolate fudge sundae with all the trimmings" education. He'd been head of MGM's lower-budget movie division in the glory days. His weren't "B-Pictures," in the conventional sense, they were just made for less money—but they made plenty. Sam was a supreme raconteur with a fascinating litany of nonfiction anecdotes about motion picture royalty. He wasn't a gossip, the tales he told weren't exposés or ugly hearsay, Sam had known them all. My idea of heaven is sitting in a comfortable chair, with a drink, listening to Sam Marx.

Bedford (later, *Factor-Newland* Productions) made three movies-for-television, while I was aboard. Close involvement with a project, from its inception, through the development period, negotiations, pre-production, casting, principal photography, post production, to fruition, can be as exhilarating as it is exhausting. Seeing it breathe a life of its own on the air, or on a screen, is a commitment rewarded, whether good, bad, or mediocre. The gestation process is never the same, there may be similar steps along the way, but no hard-and-fast formula, and each project creates its own identity.

Being "above-the-line" in a production also affords the opportunity to be cast in a role you might not otherwise be considered for. None of mine were the least noteworthy, but I didn't have to compete to get them!

Alan Factor and I hit it off from day one, he was a man of appreciable independent means, but he worked as tenaciously as a person trying to survive. He always had several pokers in the fire simultaneously and truly believed in ninety percent of them. Alan was a comfortable, compassionate and loyal friend. He preferred *his* projects, rarely getting involved in outside ones. I share his sentiments, doing *your* thing, *your* way, you take credit for its success, if it fails, you have only yourself to blame. No one else destroyed it for you—in theory. Unfortunately, or fortunately, this precludes the practical reality of team effort required in an interdependent industry. This concept is available to only a handful of individuals and usually not over an extended period.

Another associate of Alan's subscribed to the philosophy, "Throw enough shit against the wall, and some of it is bound to stick." I'm not sure it's sticking, makes it more palatable?

Something Evil was the first TV film we produced for CBS, it starred Sandy Dennis, Darren McGavin, Ralph Bellamy, and John Rubinstein, son of Mom's old friend, Artur. The director was a very young man on a rocket to immortality just lifting off the ground. Steven Spielberg's only other principal credit at the time was a remarkable TV movie, literally starring a truck, *Duel*. Steven rarely lists *Something Evil* among his credits. I don't know why, if not a great film, it was nothing to be ashamed of. He did some excitingly innovative work, had solid ratings, good reviews, and did well in syndication. Spielberg's resume includes a few other films which weren't exactly earth-shattering— damn few, but still.

Other TV movies with Bedford, were pedestrian entertainment, but exciting to work on.

One required a week's location in Pismo Beach and Morro Bay, midway up the California coast. Originally titled, *Siege*, the network opted for a more commercial title, *Terror on the Beach*; the story of a gang of sadistic thugs on dune buggies, harassing a vacationing family in their van— most of which took place on sand. The shooting schedule failed to take into consideration, working on sandy terrain, slows everything down, driving vehicles, hauling equipment, and movement in general. The dozens of recreational vehicles already parked on our *deserted beach,* with all their camping gear set up, hadn't been anticipated either. The associate producer had to ask all the campers to repack their gear and move out of camera range for several days, and adding to my ordeal, our a budget didn't allow for financial remuneration. Then, adding to *everyone*'s ordeal, was the cold overcast weather the entire time—in mid-August! All this, while being constantly surrounded by campers and tourists, day and night, made for a more action packed adventure, than the film itself. The spectators were generally quiet and well behaved, not always the case with some members of the company.

A number of young attractive females were playing gang members, as a result, the corridors and walkways of the beachside hotel, where we were quartered, were alive with activity—the pitter-patter of footsteps, bedroom doors opening and closing throughout the night.

One of the young male leads enjoyed chatting with visitors, while standing in the open doorway of his trailer dressing room, naked. I suggested to our veteran assistant director, it might not be good P.R. having an actor dangling his three-piece set in front of tourists. "So long as it's just dangling, we're okay," the A.D. responded.

***

The Bowling Green house became a minor watering hole for show biz friends and acquaintances; Allan Carr, pre-muumuu; from S.A.G., Rock Hudson, George Nader, Tab Hunter, George Maharis; representing the D.G.A., Joseph Hardy, Jim Bridges, along with British imports, Anthony Harvey and Anthony Page, who, collectively were responsible for *The Paper Chase, Urban Cowboy, A Lion In Winter,* and *Inadmissible Evidence,* not chopped liver, as we say in the deli business.

Those in attendance from the musical world were Rod McKuen, Peter Allen, Bob Crewe (a special kinda' guy), and Van Cliburn. Van maintained an endearing shit-kicker Texas-boy quality. Peter Allen was a dichotomy, a dynamic performer on stage, ebullient and effervescing as a newly-opened bottle of champagne—off stage, Peter was more like a cyanide cocktail.

***

GQK and I flew to Hawaii for Christmas and New Years, her first visit since selling the Kahala house. We settled in at the Colony Surf, between Waikiki and Diamond Head, it would become Honolulu headquarters. The hotel, owned by Rainie Barkhorn, a lady/broad, was the "in" place to stay in Honolulu in the 70s and 80s, housing one of the best restaurants on the island, certainly the most expensive, *Michels*. Why the Colony Surf became *the* place to stay is hard to pin-down. The building wasn't imposing; the beach was nothing to write home about and a twenty minute to walk to Waikiki. On the plus side, all the rooms were studio suites with ocean views, three to four can sleep together in reasonable comfort—although, the probability of that many being there to sleep is remote.

GQK and Clare Boothe Luce spent a good deal of time together, their social calendar was crammed to the bursting point. Sargent and Anna Kahanamoku, George Freling-huysen, now living in Honolulu, and most of our former neighbors, extended the welcome mat. Father Schuyler and Bill Croarkin came by for visits. Bill seemed well, his heart condition hadn't dissuaded him from conducting student tours each summer to Europe—primarily Italy.

That visit would be the last time I'd see Bill. He died the following summer, while introducing his students to the wonders of Rome. Father Schuyler made the sixteen thousand mile round-trip from Honolulu to bring Bill home. We all need friends like that.

Haven't I Seen You in Something?

With a fair amount of TV work—regardless of what others thought and all the evidence to the contrary—I began to think of myself as a star of sorts. It can honestly be said by most, I certainly behaved like one.

Turning down parts if they didn't have a proper name attached. One producer said, "Okay, we'll call the man in the flowered shirt, *Gus*, how's that?"

My agent, Fernando, called to tell me I was one of three finalists for the title role in a new Fox series, *Custer*. Not realizing GQK was listening on the extension, I told him, "They can narrow it down to two, I'm not interested."

After reviving, he pointed out, "Ju'are en no position to turn down a lead in a prime-time series!"

"I'm not turning it down Fernando. I'm just not going to pursue it."

"Ju can't do thees, ju've auditioned three times! Explain to me, why ju do thees!"

"I never liked Custer, because he was an arrogant vainglorious egomaniac."

GQK was thinking, "Who better equipped to play it."

"Okay, if I get it, demand three-times what they offer."

Fernando said something unintelligible in Spanish and hung up.

GQK, driven to distraction, appeared, "Have you lost your mind?"

"If the show is as bad as I think it'll be, it could do me more harm than good."

"You don't have enough of a career to do serious harm to," she responded, supportively adding, "God help you if the show's a hit!"

God intervened, on my side. After a few episodes, *Custer* bit the dust. The series ended with barely a whimper. Wayne Maunder got the role, if his name doesn't ring a bell, the fact remains, I know his name, it's doubtful he knows mine.

***

My minimal career fell short of some expectations, for most, it probably exceeded them. Somewhere along the line,

I must have done a few things right, during the 70s through the late 80s I did pilots, mini-series, soap operas, TV movies, and episodic shows, appearing to varying degrees in well over a hundred. Although not the principal, or *a* principal, in most, there were a few good turns. However, the majority, even I didn't watch.

When working, with no increase in salary or billing, I'd voluntarily rewrite my dialogue, supervise my own wardrobe, suggest ways to improve my role, and how scenes could be more effectively played—offering directors and cinematographers helpful tips. These gratis services gave my reputation a boost. I had an identity, my name meant something, *"Sure, I know David Knapp, and he's a pain in the ass."*

Other breadcrumbs along the way indicated the hard truth, I wasn't igniting the screen. The infrequent occasions I did appear in a good show, I alerted friends.

One friend conceded, in an incredulous tone, "I was surprised, you were really quite good." Right, buddy! Another wanted to know if the suit I wore was mine, or from the wardrobe department.

"Why?" I asked.

"I dunno, I just thought it was kind of…" The inference was clear.

"It was from wardrobe," I lied.

TV fatherhood is a more painful age reflector than mirrors. One year, you're the parent of a toddler, and then before you know it, you're packing some kid off to college. Another reminder, the actresses I was cast with, kept getting older, from *Little Mary Two-Shoes*, a few seasons later, *Cinderella's Stepmother.*

Wind Pudding and Air Sauce

The commute to the ranch was becoming a bit much, even for GQK. She needed a pied-a-terre in town. I suggested a large apartment, but she opted for a large house on Bellagio Road in Bel Air, with a large rolling lawn down to a large pool and a bathhouse. Marilyn and her progeny would have ample room to cavort, on over an acre.

For reasons I never quite understood, Mom never put any real effort or energy into this very respectable property, it had the aura of a temporary rental. She took her good furniture out of storage, which had already been shuttled from the New York apartment to the Palisades house, to Honolulu and back, then, simply plopped it down in Bel Air. Despite the familiar furnishings, Jean and Mona buzzing about, and the dogs, the house never looked complete or finished. It was a logistical convenience for GQK, but never a home. Within a month Mom was complaining about the traffic on Bellagio Road.

Buffered by a high wall and a hedge, cars were sometimes audible if you listened hard enough, and an occasional a whiff of carbon monoxide might be detected by an alert Bloodhound.

GQK camped there for less than four years, then sold it to actor, man-about-town, George Hamilton, who in turn, sold it less than a year later for almost three times what he'd paid for it. What made Hamilton's coups more irritating, I'd met him a few times in the past and didn't much like him. His mother, Anne Hamilton Spaulding, a guest of mine several times, I thought much nicer.

***

In the South of the border mode, GQK and the Duquettes were invited to Cuernavaca by world renowned artist, Tamara de Kuffner. Her life inspired the unique play *Tamara,* during which the audience walks through various rooms where different scenes are played depicting episodes in her life. Baroness de Kuffner had plenty of room, so I was asked to join them.

The two-hour bus ride from Mexico City to Cuernavaca would be a good chance to see the countryside in a commodious manner. Wrong!

Stepping tentatively down the aisle, over and around boxes, baskets, baubles, scrutinized by dozens of pairs of beady eyes, looking for the smallest animal to displace for a seat without jeopardizing U.S.-Mexico relations, I was rescued by a gentleman of the old school, kind enough to offer me the seat formerly occupied by his traveling companion, a large rooster. The big bird however, less magnanimously, left a token of its displeasure on the vacated seat. Throughout the trip the bird reminded me of its sacrifice with severe pecks to whatever part of my body was in reach. *"Su pollo es muy aggresivo,"* I kidded his owner.

"Emileiano no es un pollo, esta un gallo," the gentleman corrected.

Your buddy, *Emileiano,* chicken or *rooster,* was one mean sonuvabitch.

Tamara was a grand hostess, seeing to it Mom, the Duquettes, and I were never at a loss for things to do and see. Her villa was located in a tightly-knit enclave, referred to as *"Gringo Gap,"* dominated by Americans, Europeans, and non-Mexicans, who only socialized with each other and their respective houseguests. Cuernavaca, like many chic smallish resort communities, tends to get a little cliquish. GQK briefed me, "Every night we'll be invited to dinner by different hosts, to different casas, but be prepared to see the same guests, and have the same conversations, at all of them." Neither of us realized it would be a ritual initiation to prepare her for life in a future home in Montecito.

Tamara was a fascinating, vital and talented artist, it seemed to be the last kind of environment she'd want.

On a Wing and a Prayer

GQK turned ashen when informed I was taking flying lessons. I reasoned, after years in Naval air, but never having actually flown a plane, didn't it seem right somehow? It was time to make amends. "The time you did fly, you nearly got killed," She snorted.

"Someone else was flying the plane!"

"You were involved somehow."

"Are you doing this just to upset me? You can't see well enough to drive without glasses, you don't have the temperament. Oh, dear God."

Too late, I was in my second week at Santa Monica Flier's School and doing splendidly according to Steve, my flight instructor. I could already pre-flight, take-off and fly a single-engine Cessna, go into a stall, recover, make it to Catalina Island or Oxnard and back, without a hitch. In another week or two I'd be ready to solo. To prove this to Mama, I told her the date and time to be out on the patio when I made a low pass fly-over the ranch. I'd wave to her.

Two days later we cleared the mountain ridge and began our descent into Hidden Valley. "Keep her at one thousand feet," Steve instructed. "Give or take five hundred" I winked—we had become buddies, so it was cool. I had to show off a little when I saw GQK, Jean and Marilyn—tails wagging—staring up at our approach from the patio. I roared over, made an unauthorized circle and another pass, which created a flurry of activity below. Mama was waving frantically, Marilyn scurried off, the horses and visible barnyard inhabitants running helter-skelter and Steve was pissed off.

Back at the Santa Monica airport, Steve at the controls—another realization—the daring flight student still couldn't land the plane. That took an additional eight hours of flight time!

Chapter 20

RITES & WRONGS OF PASSAGE

In the spring of 1973, I was back in New York at the old Gotham Hotel off Fifth, managed by Billy Roohan, trying to make a publishing deal with Scott Meredith, and tweak the interest of *New Line Cinema*, in a film project, and to catch up with old friends and see a few plays. The only ones that made an impression were, *A Little Night Music* and *The Changing Room*. The latter's plot frequently required full-nudity on the part of the male cast. Fleeting moments of nudity can be diverting, but watching guys standing around in the buff, off and on, throughout two acts becomes the law of diminishing returns, it's a distraction—doubtful that many remember the plot.

Tony Hayes, now married and living in Connecticut, invited me out for the weekend. We had a great rapport, but he and his wife didn't. She spent a good part of the time taking me aside to tell me what a "rotter" Tony was, or sitting on the floor in tears. She'd done this several times in Los Angeles, so it didn't incite much sympathy. Tony wasn't a rotter, just a gregarious bachelor for too long, not accustomed to spending every minute of every day focused on her emotional needs. Finally, I suggested a solution to their martial dilemma—a divorce. Tony called several months later, "We took your advice."

Dick Kallman had moved back to New York, so we shared some time. His energy and enthusiasm wore me down, but he was a solid and entertaining friend.

***

That year, Paul Woodville introduced me to a graduate film student at U.S.C. looking for additional financing of a short subject he'd written and would direct. The film entitled *Peege,* was the master's thesis for Randal Kleiser. The family story was a bit sentimental for my taste, but GQK thought it a very touching and moving piece, offering to match any investment I made as Randal's co-producer.

Peege was shot in sixteen millimeter in about ten days with an outstanding cast headed by Barbara Rush, William Shallert, Bruce Davison, and Jeanette Nolan in the title role as a grandmother in dementia. Randal used friend's homes, Scott Glenn, was particularly generous in allowing us to use his rustic house. Scott's usually villainous on-camera persona, ends with "Cut."

I hope this doesn't jeopardize his status, but he's a kind, gentle man.

We finagled hospital and convalescent home space for the interiors, borrowed cars and utilized anything we could lay our hands on for free. In one scene the camera was mounted on the family stationwagon (loaned by Alan Factor). Barbara Rush, a superb actress, super lady, accustomed to big-budget films and 35 mil. coverage, looked at the smaller 16 mil. version mounted on the car, remarking, "What a darling little camera."

Randal spent weeks editing *Peege* in the room off my pool, but when we viewed the first cut, something didn't quite work, Randal agreed and reedited the film, on the next viewing, everything came together. After the screening at Fox Studios, the industry audience raved. Gloating with delight, GQK remarked, "Looks like your ol' Mom was right again."

Randal's little gem went on to be an mini-blockbuster, an NBC Christmas regular and its distribution through Phoenix Films earned its initial cost back the first month. Three decades later, its profit return in percentage is in the three digits. *Peege* became one of the highest grossing short subjects on record.

While on his ascent to feature films, Randal directed several TV shows, my appearance in an episode of *Starsky and Hutch* and a TV movie he did for Doug Cramer, *Dawn, The Story of a Teenage Runaway* turned out well, causing no embarrassment. Randal went on to make the record-grossing features, *Grease* and *Blue Lagoon.* Others, including *Summer Lovers, Grandview U.S.A.*, and *Getting It Right*, also turned out very well.

GQK addressed an opposite element of human nature in my friendship with Randal, a questioning way; "It's odd, you have a row with a close loyal friend, who's treated you like a prince for years—he becomes a son of a bitch! While someone whose treated like a son of a bitch for years, says one nice thing—now, becomes 'a pretty good guy after all.'"

Is He, or Isn't He?

GQK came down to see the show *Boys in the Band,* on my birthday. As the play was peppered with expletives and graphic dialogue, I assumed she'd bring hip relatives or friends. I didn't have a chance to see her before curtain, but always knew when she was in the audience, by her clanging bracelet every time she applauded or moved her hand. I didn't hear a single clang that night. After the show I opened the dressing room door, there was Mom, cousin Helen Young, a devout Catholic from Orange County, Mother of four, a right-wing Republican and doer of good deeds; a seventeen year old grand-nephew; Robbie; and Mom's omnipresent Scottish lady-in-waiting, Jean. They looked as if they'd caught me in bed with a baboon. Jean, half-deaf, wasn't sure of what she had, or hadn't heard. What do you say to a cousin with four immaculately-conceived children? With a frozen smile, Mom alerted me to the fact, "Did you know your cousin Robbie is planning to enter the seminary? He's going to *study for the priesthood.*" No, I didn't know that, or *that you'd bring him.*

GQK patted Robbie's shoulder, assuaging, "I told him to think of it as preparation for the confessional. Didn't I dear?"

"Yes, Aunt Gladys, you sure did."

Robbie didn't last very long in the seminary, for which, I take no responsibility.

Later, I asked Mom why she brought them to this kind of play. She admitted ruefully, "I thought, *The Boys In The Band* was a musical, a sequel to, *The Music Man?*"

The birthday party, at the sublet apartment, turned out to be a winner, the cast, crew, producers, and Mom, with the dazed trio. The play following ours starred Van Johnson, who I'd gone to say 'hi' to at his rehearsal space, with a couple of cast members, hoping to God, he'd remember me after ten years. He did, with a big hug. His all-American presence at the celebration lent legitimacy to what Mom had just seen on stage. When she deemed it proper, GQK could play the prude with the best of them.

I asked Van what he thought about Alan's sexual proclivities.

With an exaggerate shrug and a wink, he responded, "How would I know? Would it have made any difference in your performance?"

Just wondering.

By the time I returned home after the play closed, GQK was long gone. She, brother Oz, Aunt Kate, and Cousin Helen Young were having a reunion with family members in

France and Belgium. To some, the photos of Uncle Oz wearing a beret at a jaunty angle, surrounded by his wife, sister, and cousin, may have looked a little bourgeois, but they had a marvelous time.

***

Reluctantly, I sold the Brentwood house in '73, to Pat Riley, former player, then manager, of the L.A. Lakers, and his wife, Chris. And took residence in a nineteen hundred square foot house on Sunset Vale, with a backyard the size of a window box, was nestled behind Sierra Towers, a twelve story condo. Space was an issue, so the patio was converted into an all-weather atrium with great success.

We met a young man at a party, who told us he was working on a condo overlooking the house, his name, John Laurent, a superb master craftsman, and as it happened, I had some work for him. When John finished the condo, he spruced up the Vale house appreciably, turning a Formica galley into a country-French kitchen. He would apply his skills to two subsequent homes, but on a much vaster scale.

***

Mom and I had our Christmas dinner at George Frelinghuysen's. George, from old Eastern money, took a little knowing. His size alone was intimidating, his unamused glower-like countenance and dismissive manner could be offsetting—caustic but not cruel. He adored Gladys Knapp, and I believe he would have done anything for her. It's hard not to like someone who feels that way about your Mom—especially reassuring, if he has more money than she does. Getting a smile and chuckle out of George was more gratifying than a roomful of hysterical laughter. He gave GQK a beautiful oil painting of red geraniums by Janet Gaynor, which hangs in my living room today. I never look at it without thinking of George in his imperceptible suit of protective armor.

***

Uncle Oz passed away in August of '74. At his funeral in Laguna Niguel, where he and Aunt Kate had moved, GQK and I sat across the aisle from his widow, their four sons and daughter. Seeing Aunt Kate, my first cousins, George, Charlie, Phillip, Peter, and Ann together in the first pew, was an emotional experience. Through all the years, ups and downs, they essentially remained a cohesive family unit.

As of this writing, only Peter and Ann remain, however, Oz and Kate's thirteen grandchildren, and their children, will aggressively continue the Quarre name.

Gladys and Oz's relationship was a dichotomy of sorts. Despite Mom's affluence and urbane lifestyle, she would wistfully reflect on the solidity of her brother and sister-in-law's fifty-two year marriage and their devotion to one another. She envied their relationship and elements of their lifestyle, but in the abstract. Mom was wise enough to realize and accept the fact her mental and emotional makeup would never allow her that. It's highly unlikely she ever seriously considered it for herself.

***

I met Lady Sylvia Ashley in London. We hit it off remarkably well, making the West End social rounds. Lady Ashley was Clark Gable's fourth wife. Sylvia bore an uncanny resemblance to his third wife, Carole Lombard, who was reputed to be the great love of Gable's life. Others credibly suspected he consumed more than his fair share of the "noble man's failing." He's been painted in an overly sympathetic light, wholly justifiably in lieu of his film legacy.

An incongruous foursome developed in the mid-seventies; when Lady Sylvia moved back to Pacific Palisades. My Sunset Vale neighbors a block away, Norma Shearer, and her husband, Monte Arrouge, frequently joined the dogs and I on our daily walks. Miss Shearer referred to the three canines, as *The Troops,* the term stuck to this day, despite cast replacements. Norma was the reigning queen at MGM in the '30s, having starred in several movies with Sylvia's former husband. Norma, Monte, Sylvia and I regularly went to films in Hollywood, followed by dinner at *Don the Beachcombers, Musso & Frank's* or the *Brown Derby,* sometimes a sinful stopover at *C. C. Brown's* for dessert. Seated at a wooden booth with Norma Shearer attacking a hot fudge sundae, Lady Sylvia laying waste to a banana split, their lipstick splattered with whipped cream, was a treat in itself. The double vanilla and chocolate medley, covered in butterscotch syrup and nuts, in front of me, was there for appearance's sake. A guy's got to go with the flow.

On occasion, Norma and Monte had us, George Cukor and others, never more than six, for dinner (which we usually brought), followed by a 16 millimeter print of a movie, i.e. *Marie Antoinette, Strange Interlude, Romeo and Juliet, The Women* and *Idiot's Delight* the top-billed female star was always *Norma Shearer.* I remarked to our hostess, "Norma, you're the only person I recall billed above Clark Gable *and* Joan Crawford." With genteel humility, she replied, "Above *everyone*, Luv."

Being married to the head of the studio didn't hurt her negotiation leverage either.

Rolls on the Range

GQK was back on the ranch a good part of the time during the 1970s.
Jack Dempsey deservedly moved on to becoming head of a major thoroughbred ranch in the Santa Inez Valley. GQK had several more foremen, but none quite compared to Jack's work-ethic and dedication. One subsequent foreman did make a strong impression. While GQK was abroad, I was "titular head" of the spread, according to the police report, when our foreman raped a girl in the ranch pickup truck—with *Rancho Gladavida* emblazoned on the doors. To everyone's amazement, mine in particular, I managed to be a genuine rancher, that's to say, none of the animals died of thirst or starvation, no gates left open, before we found a replacement for our incarcerated foremen four days later.

Mom wasn't appraised of the situation, until after she returned. Anticipating a "well done," and a hearty pat on the back, I settled for a wary, "How much are *we* paying the new foreman?"

***

GQK wasn't going into town as much, the Bel Air house held little attraction for her anymore, so she had her social life come to her. People found time to drive up for weekends, luncheons, swimming, tennis, and cozy times around the fire. She created a pine forest behind the house, from seedlings she planted less than twenty years before. Greta Garbo made a guest appearance with Gaylord Hauser, and then disappeared after lunch. She wandered back an hour later, reporting to Gladys, "You have fifty-three pine trees growing behind your house. If you don't mind, I *vood* like to borrow a large pillow case."

While the rest of us were trying to figure out the correlation, Jean asked Miss Garbo if she wanted to lie down. No, she wanted to collect pine needles. We offered to have someone collect them for her. Again, a *no*, she preferred to collect them herself. She knew exactly what she wanted. I was relieved, knowing I'd pick all the wrong ones. What Miss Garbo was planning to do with a pillow case full of pine needles, is anyone's guess.

Neighbors, Richard Widmark, Dean Martin, Eve Arden, and Brooks West often visited. The Ladd family didn't come up to their ranch often after Alan's death in the mid-sixties. Over the years, GQK hosted her old buddy, Mary Pickford and her husband, Buddy Rogers; Randolph Scott came over to swim every day for a week after he finished location shooting on the French ranch next door next. Another broad-brimmed hat came on the head of Dale Robertson, who arrived with his entire family—Mom having forgotten she'd invited them up. In those emergency situations she had Jean and Mona whip up a pot of her "*special* pork and beans" with brown-bread.

She justifiably kept her *secret recipe* well-guarded, as it involved emptying several cans of *Dinty Moore's Pork 'n Beans* into a pot and heating them up—same procedure with the brown-bread.

William Conrad and Joan Fontaine came up for a few days to shoot an episode of his TV series, *Cannon,* and spent the nights in *separate* guest rooms rather than drive back to town each night. The problem, at different times, for Anne Baxter, MacDonald Carey, Fay Bainter, and Anthony Quinn were my lousy directions. I'd told them to turn left, instead of right, assuming they were coming north from L.A.—not South from Santa Barbara!

Bob Cummings got knocked off a horse, Van Heflin was bitten badly enough by a neighbor's dog to require stitches, and Tony Randall got side-swiped on his approach to the driveway. The curse was lifted for Jimmy and Gloria

Stewart, Joel and Frances McCrea, and longtime family friends, Bob and Rosemarie Stack—GQK felt their staunch Republicanism kept them out of harm's way. There were exceptions, Goldie Hawn arrived and departed safely, as did a goodly number of other dues-paying S.A.G. members. Bill and Debby (Daves) Richards brought Gary Collins and his beautiful wife, the former Miss America, Mary Ann Mobley, to the ranch a number of times. They became good friends, as did Mary Ann's equally beautiful sister, Sandra Williams. On several occasions, I served as a quasi-baby sitter for the Collins' daughter—for as long as ten minutes!

I regret not having taken more pictures, but many guests came up to get away from that. Amusing to note how people with major careers in front of a studio camera, become awkward and shy at the prospect of a snapshot from a pocket-camera. This is especially true when they're showering.

Roy Rogers and Dale Evans bought the ranch across the way, and then sold it a few years later, but not before I got to hear Roy use a cuss-word. He once complained, "My *damned* back is killing me!" I pretended not to hear it. Boyhood heroes, Roy and Gene Autry were fellows to be reckoned with—they maintained their images in their off-screen lives with phenomenal success. Rogers was an exemplary man, but not a bundle of personality, he seemed a little shy and uncomfortable off camera, come to think of it, *on*-camera as well.

When I met Autry working on a presidential campaign, he looked like a retired Valley car dealer, short, pot-bellied, with thinning orange hair and a wallet so thick. Gene Autry had the warmth, humor, all-around ability and business acumen; a cowboy star, singer, composer, owner of vast acreages, radio and TV stations, a major league baseball team and museum founder, he had no reason to be humble, but he was. The most immodest thing he said was, "I wasn't much of an actor, other fellas sing and look a lot better—but I must've done something right."

The onetime Oklahoma telegraph operator had a folksy *good ol' boy* way of chopping someone down to a stump before they knew they'd lost a branch. Referring to a leading member of the opposition party, professing his honesty and integrity at a banquet, Autry muttered, *"Being a straight-shooter doesn't mean much if your gun's not loaded."*

Those comments, coming from most people, might sound mean-spirited, but from Gene Autry, they shined with insightfulness.

***

The *Los Angeles Times* did a two-page Sunday magazine spread at the ranch, entitled, *"GLADYS KNAPP – Country Gentlewoman."* The photo-article, by Bea Miller, was comprised of a half dozen not-too-informally taken pictures of GQK, one, which caught the mood, was of her sitting on the front lawn, surrounded by her Golden Retrievers, Marilyn, Jack, and Gloria, with the pastures and mountains as a backdrop. The bucolic effect was somewhat diffused by a smaller photo of the two Rolls-Royces parked in the garage.

Steven North decided the next logical move was to take our diversified projects to the Cannes Film Festival—something our budget didn't allow for. No matter, he spoke French, had European connections, and friends he could stay with. I wasn't certain about anything.

GQK brought up an ancillary point, the festival started in a week, where would I find a room. "I suppose, in one of the places where we've stayed, the *Carlton*, *Majestic* or the *Martinez?*"

"With that kind of expense account, the Rainier's might be happy to rent you a guest room at the palace," she quipped, deciding my predicament might best be solved if she joined us in Cannes, thus, insuring that I didn't get too much sand in my shoes.

Chapter 21

CONNECTING ON THE CROSETTE

The Spill of the Spotlight

All the major hotels on the Crosette were booked, the only first class hotel with rooms available was the Grand Hotel Du Cap, in Cap' Antibes, several kilometers east of Cannes, not that convenient, it meant taxis or renting a car, but it sounded nice enough.

After a short side trip to Lisbon, I rendezvoused with GQK at the Hotel Du Cap. I'd grown a short beard for a TV role, thinking it rather becoming, I decided to leave it on. The moment I saw Mama I knew the waters would be turbulent. She let me know she had an exhausting flight from Los Angeles, and the drive from the Nice airport took almost an hour, due to traffic and road construction.

She didn't like her room either, too small, with no sea view. I told her, I'd do everything in my power to get her a larger room with a view. Her skepticism regarding my "power" was apparent. I was thankful her mind wasn't on my facial hair, then as I was about to make my escape, "David, that hair on your face makes you look ten years older. You're at an age where you can't afford that." "Christ Mom, I'm only thirty-four." "Dearest, check your passport, you've been thirty-four for several years now, it's time to move on," Momma delivered the *Coups Degrade,* "And, that beard makes you look every second of it." Within minutes, my face covered with tiny wads of toilet paper to prevent bleeding from lacerations, I was clean-shaven. Mama was entitled to being grouchy, making the trip solo was commendable. Watching her in action, even on a bad day, it didn't seem possible she was in her mid-seventies.

Mama mellowed by the following evening, the festival's opening film was MGM's *That's Entertain-ment,* clips from the studio's past musicals. A contingency of stars from MGM films were staying at the hotel. Mama and I were coming down the stairs to the lobby, where a large group of top celebrities were waiting for their cars, from their midst a voice rang out, "Gladys!" Cary Grant rushed up and escorted GKQ down into the lobby.

The assembled stars were racking their brains trying to remember, who the dazzling lady on Cary Grant's arm was, obviously, someone they should know. The MGM group affirmed it with a chorus of greetings, "How good to see you,"

"How wonderful you look," most not knowing where they'd seen her, or just how wonderful she looked. Mr. Grant turned to me and said, "Robin –sorry, David, how are you?" He'd seen me three times in sixteen years and bothered to remember my name! It was easy to understand his phenomenal success.

Later that evening, at the Palais Du Festival, GQK looked like royalty in an organdy evening gown. Flashbulbs popped en masse, nearly blinding us—again the star treatment. In retrospect, she *was* one, figuratively, stars come from different galaxies.

Outside, the theatre was packed by fans. GQK got as much attention as a major star in front of us. Having been in the spill of the spotlight by then, I was less self conscious when asked for an autograph by a fan wondering where and if they'd seen me. I'd ask their name, and wrote, "To so and so," signed it and thanked them—makes a good impression. Easy for me, my signature is illegible. I'd smiled and moved on. Mama smiled better, a little wave, never above the shoulder, keeping them at a distance. I loved every second of vicarious stardom, without having to deal with it on a day-to-day basis.

Steven North and I were still trying to get "Fataxe and Staggerbush" and "Arachnophobia," an artful horror piece about a spider invasion off the ground. We worked the Plage Ondine and other spots along the Crosette, evoking interest from several independent producers working out of various Balkan Countries. Steven had been involved in a Hungarian film entered at the Festival, which would be screened at a little theater off the Crosette. The film won the "Bronze Twig"—or some award at the San Remo or Sarajevo Film Festival. The others went to *see* it, GQK and I had to endure it.

The film, made by an auteur shrieked, "Look ma, I'm directing!" It was a 3-D movie, in that it was dark, dull, and disconnected. The hand-held camera wobbled so much, Mama wondered if the cameraman had delirium tremens. The sound was out of sync with the action, with subtitles reading, "From the hills at which I go …For you, my yearn to love is there." I'd seen better lighting in amateur porno, which worked to its advantage, preventing scrutiny of the androgynous actors. The young male lead gave the impression he'd fuck a woodpile, if there was a snake in it. The picture went on to commit the most heinous of all sins—it ran two hours and forty minutes!

We were awakened by several sporadic claps when it finally ended. Steven and company were congratulating one another, with some reservations. When it was suggested some judicious trimming here and there wouldn't hurt, GQK muttered under her breath, "How about the last two hours."

Some of the MGM people left the following day, so GQK's room was upgraded. She hosted a luncheon for our group which had climbed to eight, at Eden Roc, the hotel's swimming and outdoor dining facility. The lunch, and a dinner at a tres chic restaurant in the hills, cost us over 10,000 francs—figure five francs to a U.S. dollar! I love the look of weary exasperation the French get when foreigners go into shock at an "addicion incredible."

I'm in awe of those who go everywhere, do the same things, but never spend a centime doing it. They talk of negotiations, deal-making and multi-buck contracts, but never seem to have cab fare.

London Heat

Mother and son then flew back to London for a few days before returning home. Peter Lubbock invited me to stay at his Belgravia house whenever I was in town, the entire third floor was mine for a pittance. The house on Chapel Street became my London base for the next seven years. By British tradition, Peter was a commoner, but an extremely well-connected one. His sister, Lady Margaret 'Peggy' Wakehurst, the widow of Lord Wakehurst, Governor-General of Australia during World War II, she had also been invested by H.R.M., *Dame* Peggy for her own achievements.

A cocktail party Peter gave resulted in a drastic change of plans, my London stay would be lengthened by over a month. A gentleman who'd been looking at me with academic interest stepped over, and introduced himself. After a brief chat, he gave me his card and told me to call him in the morning. His name was Douglas Seale.

The next day in his office at the Thames Studio, I got the poop. They were in pre-production for a Granada Television movie, based on a novella by Friederich Durrenmatt. A reasonably-known American actor had been cast but due to legal difficulties, his work permit had been revoked, no details were forthcoming. After reading for Seale and the producers, they asked if I was a fast study. I lied. Thirty-six hours later I was issued a temporary work permit with volumes of restrictions. I would work with O.W. Fischer, Diana Wynyard, and Edward Underdown.

California Cooling

Things weren't that desperate, GQK was selling the Bel Air house, but escrow didn't close for another month. The buyer, George Hamilton, gave the house a nip 'n' tuck, then sold it eight months later for two and a half times what he paid for it. I was never a fan of his, but that really clinched it.

Mama was also seriously considering the sale of Rancho Gladavida. It had become too much of a burden and responsibility. It was also obvious her son, a dilettante-weekend-cowpoke, would never settle in as head of the spread. It wasn't officially on the market, but she'd consider selling it at a price.

One Sunday afternoon, a big black limousine came up the driveway; all the occupants were the same color—not a daily occurrence in Hidden Valley during the mid-70s. A huge man dressed also in black emerged. GQK's eyes became slits, her trigger finger was itching, thinking the man crossing the patio toward us was an exiled blood-lusting president-for-life of some African republic, looking for a hideaway. "Those people don't buy ranches," GQK hissed. "This one can afford to," I assured her, "I paid a hundred bucks to see him in concert last week." Barry White, with what appeared to be half of his "Love Unlimited" orchestra, was formidable looking. White seemed as big as the venues he played, his voice mellifluous, sounded like an erotic thunderbolt. That afternoon he was gregarious, jovial, and a thoroughly delightful guest.

After an abbreviated tour of the ranch, GQK warmed up enough to him to say, "You must come up and have lunch one day." For a woman whose only other experience in this racial genre was being seated next to Duke Ellington at a dinner thirty years earlier, this was a major breakthrough! After White and his associated departed, GQK observed, "That man has the most erotic voice. You just want to close your eyes and listen to him." "A lot of babies have been conceived by people doing just that." "What kind of music is it," she asked. "We have a term for it," I answered awkwardly. "Tell your ol' Mama, I promise not to be shocked." "We call it, *Fuck Music."* "Catchy on an album cover," GQK reflected.

Another incongruity came in the person of Zsa Zsa Gabor, who was interested in buying the ranch, to the point of negotiations. GQK okayed a big all-day party as a last blast. Zsa Zsa arrived dressed for the occasion in jeans, boots, a Levi jacket and a sun hat. GQK gave her a hug, "You look like Marie Antoinette-gone-Calamity Jane."

Eighty guests showed up for lunch, at least fifty remained through dinner six hours later. An exhausting day, later exacerbated by a number of phone calls, continuing into the following morning from guests, all suffering from the same malady. We traced the problem to a jar of mayonnaise having been on the shelf too long.

I had reservations about Zsa Zsa in an outdoorsy environment, performing chores, or even turning on a lawn sprinkler. She's an amazing woman, a twentieth century courtesan, with humor, honesty, and heart. She was very comfortable financially, however, I was skeptical about her being able to afford the ranch, and knowing Mama's tendency to accept the first offer once she decided to rid herself of a property, especially if a friend was involved. There was no surprise when Zsa Zsa called a few days later; telling us her accountant advised her not to buy the ranch at this time.

I'd seen James Kirkwood's play, *P.S., Your Cat is Dead* in New York and thought it compelling. *P.S.* is essentially a two character play, with a couple who come in for a brief scene in Act II. *Jimmy Zoole,* a thirty-plus year old actor, catches *Vito Antonucci,* a south Bronx-type, burglarizing his apartment. By fluke, Jimmy knocks Vito out, ties him down on a table, naked from the waist down. A relationship eventually develops between the two. It's a good piece that never quite worked, one reason, it was constantly being *re*worked. Keir Dullea, the star of the Broadway production, and his wife Susie—members of Theatre East—suggested I take a crack at the *Jimmy Zoole* role.

We prepared Act II as an in-house project for invited audiences. What made it memorable and the Theatre East actor tied to the table bare-butt is now president and C.E.O. of CBS Corporation, Leslie Moonves. The *P.S.* project went well, but the payoff came some time later.

***

Delmer and Marylou Daves were in their Summer home in La Jolla. Delmer had retired from films on doctor's orders, due to a heart condition, but remained active. He categorized and worked on his stone collection, researching and preparing a cook book, being idle was anathema to him.

One evening in August of '77, Delmer complained of severe chest pains, Marylou rushed him to the hospital, where she was assured her husband would be okay, probably released the following day. "Go home, get some rest," the doctor urged her. By the time Marylou returned to the house, there was an urgent message from the doctor.

Delmer died of cardiac arrest minutes after she left the hospital.

In La Jolla the next day, I joined Marylou, Debby, and Bill Richards, who were in gentle command, along with

Michael and Donna Daves and other family members for Delmer's funeral. The family held up admirably, I was a mess, choking up every time Delmer's name was mentioned.

A memorial service was scheduled at St. Edward's in Westwood several days after the funeral. Marylou asked me to deliver the eulogy. I was overwhelmed, but didn't believe I was worthy in light of the vast number of prominent people he'd worked with—also knew I couldn't get through it without breaking down. I regret that emotional cowardice to this day. Lloyd Nolan's uninspired eulogy made me wish I had at least written it. It would have been brief:

"Delmer Daves was a renaissance gentleman, and a gentle man. He leaves a legacy of professionalism, creativity, master craftsmanship, and personal integrity. Were I just a fraction of the man Delmer Daves was, I would walk tall into heaven."

Give or Take a Million

In town long enough to help mother with the move to Montecito, GQK appeared to be dealing with the transition in the abstract. Nothing had been packed, not a suitcase or a cardboard box in sight, closets, drawers and storage areas remained untouched. She sold many of the ranch furnishings with the house, however, after twenty-five years, a multitude of other items accumulate, warranting considerable attention. When I reminded Jean, the movers would arrive the following morning, her anxiety surfaced, "Whenever I mention it to Mrs. Knapp, she says she doesn't want to deal with it now." There was no more *now*.

I knew from experience, in a major move, the big pieces can be dealt with reasonably fast and efficiently. It's the smallest ones that, "Will only take five minutes to toss in a box," which prove to be your undoing. This is exacerbated when some items are to be taken, others left behind, and nothing to indicate which category. To avoid confrontation, the situation required subtle, but prompt, action, "Aren't you being a little cavalier about this, Mom? Or have you decided to cancel escrow?"

"Why would I do that?" she asked tersely.

Knowing I'd be better off not answering, wasn't a sufficient deterrent, "Well, it isn't exactly the deal of the century from your standpoint." With a lethal glare, GQK demanded to know, "Really? What's wrong with it?"

"You're selling the ranch for less than it is worth."

"You think *four* times what I paid for it isn't enough, dear?"

"Not if it's worth *five* times as much. Plus the fact, you're taking a lot of paper," I goaded. As to a child, Mama counseled, "Nothing is worth more than what someone else is prepared to pay for it."

"The *someone* in this case happens to be the head of a major accountancy firm. Like, lawyers, bankers, real estate brokers, and car dealers. His profession demands he screw you."

"And who gave you that piece of advice?" she asked pointedly.

"You did, Mom."

"Hopefully, you'll keep it in mind with your future dealings. In any event, I'm selling *now*, not in some future market."

GQK was astute when purchasing real estate, but her business acumen went on vacation when it came time to sell. I also knew when she wanted to move on, that was it, she didn't want to quibble over six digit details. I was prepared to leave it at that—but she had other ideas, "Besides, I won't have any grandchildren to enjoy it."

A good punch, if a tad below the belt. Mama readjusted in the chair, "You surprise me, in that you never really liked it up here all that much, did you, dear? You always seemed happier on the drive *back* to town, than you did on the way up."

"I wasn't conscious of it. Perhaps, if my formative years had been spent in a more rural environment..."

"Poor baby, you've had to suffer through the best of both." Mama's delivering caustic remarks more effectively than I had always been a source of irritation; it was beginning to take a toll. "What's this about? If you're threatening to disinherit me, have done with it," I proposed, vainglory superceding stark terror.

Mama took a beat, "What would you do if I did?"

"I dunno, rob a bank? Marry some rich older woman?"

"I don't think you'd be good at either."

"How about a rich old *man*?"

"Fortunately, I've done enough of that for both of us," she concluded.

In all honesty, I was relieved she was unloading the ranch, shifting the burden of responsibility onto someone else's shoulders. I continued to feel that way for over a decade, until I found out what the ranch is worth today!

The movers arrived the following morning, as we were frantically last-minute packing. Hours later, the truck left with most of the larger items, we would take the rest in the cars ourselves, then meet them in Montecito. It turned out an awful lot remained, including three big dogs. Throughout the chaotic departure process, GQK had a series of changes of heart, "No-no, I can't leave that behind—I've decided to keep it, I may want it some day—Better pack it, you never know."

Finally, after several false starts and hopelessly behind schedule, with what amounted to another truck load, our three car motorcade was ready to move out. Mama driving one Rolls, Marilyn in the passenger seat; followed by the other Rolls with the author at the wheel, Jean riding shotgun, with Jack and Gloria crammed in the back among boxes—we departed Rancho Gladavida for the last time. I watched GQK up ahead. She never looked back.

Chapter 22

BETWEEN A ROCK AND A SOFT PLACE

GQK's new home was off San Ysidro Road in Montecito, South of Santa Barbara. There were similarities to the Kahala House, both were undistinguished architecturally, but located on incredible pieces of property. The house sat on three acres, one of which remained pretty much unused other than for dog walks, maintaining a "vacant lot" look. During her twelve year tenure, GQK installed a swimming pool and Jacuzzi, other than that she left it pretty much as it was. My only contribution was having the shingle roof replaced with a tiled one, which gave the house a little more character.

Montecito tends to be sedentary in some regards. Productivity isn't high on the priority list, the fact you're living there is testament to past productivity in many instances, or you're making a bundle elsewhere, and there are those who've never had to do either in the past. Montecito was primarily the second home for prominent Easterners and Mid-Western industrialists. Now, it's also become a getaway for the Los Angeles-based rich and famous in need of pastoral surroundings on weekends— without having to go too far.

People don't go there to discover life, they go there to enjoy it—and in many cases, to wrap up the last few chapters. Not to say, there isn't plenty of social activity— luncheons, cocktail parties and dinners—at least eight nights a week. It's cozy, affable, and insular. Everyone knows what everyone else has to say, having attended the same social events earlier that week. Couples will see each other several evenings in a row, on the next, they'll all have dinner at the Birnhamwood Country Club.

Sunday polo matches are right out of *P.G. Wodehouse,* wide-brimmed hats everywhere, preferably straw. The guys decked out in brightly colored or patchwork-pants; blue, red, pink, yellow or green blazers, plaid jackets (but not with patchwork pants!), and God help any man wearing socks. Flowered print dresses (for the ladies), none of whom give a tinker's damn about polo, most of the husbands don't either, but tradition and sportsmanship demand cries of encouragement, loud groans of disapproval and shouts to players on how the game should be played.

The half dozen socially acknowledged couples under forty usually follow a formula. The wives have the real money, their husbands aren't particularly motivated or they wouldn't be living in Montecito, which doesn't abound in serious job opportunities. These fellows are usually fairly attractive in a non-threatening way, try to keep a 34" waist, attended good schools, proficient in small talk, from nice, to once-affluent families, or distanced from still-affluent families, with enough intelligence to marry someone with six to seven digit income, and whom, all and all aren't a bad lot—*and* with whom, the author shares a number of things in common.

The ones I feel real empathy for are those whose grandfathers or great-grandfathers made a conspicuous fortune, which subsequent generations mishandled or dissipated—resulting in their generation not quite having the means to live in the style to which they were accustomed, but being expected to. The income from a trust is just enough to keep them for *having* to work nine to five. In one instance, a parent specified to the executors of her will, should her heir ever take a job, he was to be disinherited! In his case, the inheritance was more than enough to discourage any attempt at productivity on his part–or mine, had I been in his position!

GQK had long since acquired her Santa Barbara social credentials; her one-time father-in-law built the Peabody Estate, a local landmark, in her case, gratis. Be it noted, Gladys Knapp didn't need any outside influence to find her place in any social environment.

Dorothy Laughlin, Francoise and Brooks Barton, Eleanor D'Arrast were expatriate friends from other places, while the Gordon Douglas', Lulu (van Allen) and Sandy Saunderson, Dame Judith Anderson, along with Jane and Pat Patterson were neighbors who became among the best friends GQK had throughout her life. Beverly Jackson, columnist with *Santa Barbara New Press*, was especially gracious and hospitable, both socially and in print.

One of the advantages of visiting from Los Angeles via Route 101, once having cleared the San Fernando Valley, it's a fairly pleasant drive and once north of Oxnard, the trip up the coast is scenic and open—perhaps, too open. GQK considered the section from Ventura to Carpinteria to be the Nevada-Utah salt flats, an opportunity to give the two ol' girls (Rolls '61 and '63) a good run.

Silver Clouds were heavy and gripped the road in a manner one isn't conscious of speed—a characteristic common to most cars today, but not necessarily, four decades ago.

GQK behind the wheel, and it seemed to her son in the passenger seat, the scenery was passing by very quickly, and we were overtaking cars moving at a fast clip themselves. He looked at the speedometer, did a double take, "Mom, you're going *over a hundred miles an hour!*"

"Oh, don't be silly," she responded with annoyance.

"Look at the speedometer!"

"I can't while I'm driving! I have to keep my eyes on the road."

"Trust me, Mom, you're going too fast!"

"It cleans out the engine," she explained.

"They're gonna be *cleaning us up*, if you don't slow down!"

She lightened her foot on the accelerator a fraction, "There! Is that better? Honestly, you can be such an old man."

"You're still going over ninety," I cautioned.

"Well, you'd never know it, would you?"

I delivered a low-blow, "You shouldn't drive faster than your age."

"If I did that, we'd never get there," she grinned triumphantly—still, at *seventy-six* MPH, we'd get there eventually.

***

Gladys came East for the holidays, staying with Dorothy Hammerstein at her apartment on Park Avenue. The widow of Oscar Hammerstein II was the quintessential Australian export, a beautiful lady with a ribald sense of humor and real flare for life. She and Gladys were totally in sync.

Dick Kallman hosted a gala Christmas Eve party at his new townhouse at 77 East 77th Street. It seems a paradox, why our Jewish brethren invariably celebrate the Christmas holidays in a more festive and giving manner than most gentiles? Dick was awesomely energetic with a lot of talent and an ebullient personality, who thought GQK a social icon and treated her as "Empress of all the Russia."

Niels Haynes' Christmas party for GQK was not only cozy and festive, it also served to broaden her horizons. One of the guests had presented Niels with box of those "special" brownies, the ones you can't buy at *Mrs. Fields.* Mother claimed she'd never tried pot, there was no evidence disputing that until that merry afternoon. It was holiday time, GQK was a sport in the safest of hands, so, after a bit of gentle coaxing she took a ladylike nibble of a *buzz brownie.* The after-meal treat had everyone caught up in a more-than-happy mood. Secure in the knowledge, the chocolaty enhancer had no effect on her, Mama took another nibble. Then, thoroughly enjoying herself, finding humor in everything, she took a third bite, while wondering what all the hype was about. As we were preparing to leave and after receiving an "Okay" nod from our host, Mama took out a hanky, neatly wrapped the remainder of the brownie, and placed it in her purse.

Christmas temperatures being mild that year, Gladys and son decided to forgo a taxi and hoof it to Saint Vincent Ferrer church. The "no effect" effect, nonetheless swept us north on Lexington Avenue at a spirited gait. With Christmas attendance packing the church, mass having already begun, we wedged ourselves into the last pew. Mama's eyes swept the interior of the church, reminiscent of a small cathedral, and reacted with awe. Her past visits there were eclipsed by a new spiritual awakening, the mundane sermon, jabbing me repeatedly with her elbow, in response to every minuscule point made by the innocuous priest. When he asked, "Who among us, would cast the first stone," I had to restrain her from applauding. Walking down the steps after mass Mama paused, with an expansive gesture proclaiming, "I feel spiritually renovated." I doubt she ever finished the brownie she tucked away, had she, there might have been the first woman ever appointed to the College of Cardinals.

***

Stephen Joyce, from the series, and his wife Billie became family during the course of the show, neither Stephen nor I figured out why, we were total opposites in background, manner, emotion, and philosophy.

Billie was a wonder, incredibly capable, and a Mother-Earth darling. In addition to which, she was one of the best liked and highly respected women in the Broadway theater business. As head box office treasurer of the Shubert Organization, Billie Joyce had clout at every box office in the city, and her name alone meant good seats for any sold-out hit on Broadway. Stephen and Billie enriched my life.

One great regret years later, in a moment of anxiety and frustration, I said something typically me, fallacious and stupid, which ended our relationship. Inexcusable on my part—but I believe, at some point, forgivable.

We Can do Business

GQK flew to New York in the spring for an inspection tour, with an extra agenda. She and I would have a "test-the-waters" lunch meeting with two gentlemen who had been referred to her by valued Santa Barbara friends. Lawrence Bukzin and Norman Volk were then with the *Bessemer Trust Company*, but would soon establish their own independent investment management firm, *Chamberlain & Steward*.

Atypically, Mama was contemplating turning over a substantial part of her portfolio to them to manage—under her supervision. Norman and Larry were low-keyed with excellent credentials, GQK was cautious, waiting for the fast talking pressure-play or an impassioned sales pitch—which never came.

In fact I got the impression they were doing just fine with their other clients, most of whom, had thicker portfolios that GQK's. Each with a marvelous sense of humor, Norman is a chuckler, a Neil Simon man; Larry was a laugher, he struck me as a Woody Allen fan. I enjoyed their company.

Following lunch, GQK and I had one of our productive leisurely strolls along Madison Avenue. Perhaps Norman and Larry were parallel on Park Avenue doing the same.

Mom paused at a window, then offhandedly asked, "So, what did you think?"

"I liked them."

"Good, you may have to deal with them a lot longer than me," adding pointedly, "Thank God they have a sense of humor."

Little did I realize at the time, what significant roles these guys would play in my future.

***

Larry Bukzin and his new client made the first of several business trips together to familiarize me with the new-gotten investments. We felt it was safe to speculate with not more than ten to fifteen percent of your holdings. Larry is a pure city boy, his heart and soul belong to concrete and steel, outdoorsy rural activities and locales are anathema. The suburbs of San Antonio, Texas, and the far outskirts of Atlanta were not his milieu. The blue-collar apartment complex outside of town was okay, but, instead of staying at one of the innocuous modern high rise hotels along the river bank, I convinced Larry we should stay at the old landmark, St. Anthony Hotel, where I'd stayed with mother thirty years before, it had tradition and character— and that turned out to be about it! Dating back to the late '40s, the only things changed were sheets and towels, at the irregular maid's discretion. You had the impression rooms were available at an hourly rate.

Larry's urban background caused him to be wary in a room full of good ol' boys, he wasn't accustomed to men wearing big hats indoors and the sound of spurs jingling were an anomaly. After a manly no-nonsense steak dinner, with all the fix'ns, under the ominous scrutiny of locals unaccustomed to ties and blazers, I insisted Larry see the Alamo, knowing his aversion to weaponry and bloodshed.

Illuminated at night, the Alamo looks awfully small, as it does in broad day light. The size of a tract house in Queens—but its true Americana.

I reflected, "Imagine being stuck in there, with thousands of Mexicans outside ready to tear you apart?" Larry's eyes darted to the group of sightseers surrounding us, wondering if the threat still existed, thankful he didn't live in Southern California. I suggested watching Country & Western line-dancing at a nearby bar, but Larry was just fine with the Rockettes.

Twenty five years later I've had no cause to regret GQK's decision. Larry, his wife, Margie, have been a vital source of wise counsel, compassionate support and unflagging friendship, through meteoric highs and some extreme lows—far beyond the stock market.

***

I met Aaron Copland at the Schirmers. His *Appalachian Spring, Rodeo,* and *Salon de Mexico* made him arguably the premier American classical composer of that century. Mr. Copland affirmed my assessment of his status.

After several Schirmer soirees, Mr. Copland asked me to drive him to a dinner party the following week in Westchester County! He thought I might enjoy the group.

We had a perfunctory chat as we began the drive up to Harrison, in Westchester County. I wanted to be amusing and entertaining during the hour-plus trip. By the time we reached the Parkway, it occurred to me Mr. Copland didn't particularly want to be amused *or* entertained. I thought it best to let him initiate the next round of conversation. An hour later he did with, "Turn right at the next exit."

The host's cavernous home was pretentiously unpretentious, as were most of the two dozen guests. When famous people gather, there's a competitive tendency to see who can be 'Joe Average.' Exchanging cocktail party banter with someone world-renown, but not knowing exactly who, and not daring to ask, is a tactical dilemma. The more you try to extract background information, the more reluctant they are to talk about themselves. So, as fate would have it this evening, the conversation came around to the subject of books. For no particular reason, I confided to this gentleman, "I've recently skimmed through *The Alexandria Quartet,* and found it pretty rough sledding."

"Yes, I suppose it is for some people," he responded with no inflection, excused himself, and resumed mingling with the others. Moments later, Aaron was at my side, anxious to know, "What were you discussing just now with Lawrence Durrell?"

Oh, dear. . .

On the way back in the car, I presumptuously asked Aaron Copeland what he had against writing scores for motion pictures, he'd done so few.

"I have nothing against it, I'm not asked to."

That never occurred to me.

***

GQK was having reoccurring help problems in Montecito. Every time I arrived, a different face greeted me at the door. Infrequent visits weren't the reason; I drove up twice a month! Jean, the only reoccurring face on weekends, was older than Mama. GQK had a knack for finding the Achilles heel in household employees. Some did a good job, but no matter. On their day off, she inspected the kitchen and rummaged through their rooms, in a quest for something amiss. Discovering *yesterday's* laundry in the dryer got one couple axed. Another got the heave-ho by stupidly leaving the broken pieces of a china dish in the wastebasket. Upon finding prescribed *Halcyon*, Tylenol-Codeine, and other tablets in their medicine cabinet, one couple were discharged as "drug fiends." "Why do you suppose they take *Prozac?*" Mama pondered.

One couple prepared every meal meticulously; still, each course was scrutinized to make certain nothing moved on the plate. Frustrated, but not deterred, after an extensive taste inspection during dinner, GQK asked, "Did you taste nutmeg in the spinach?"

"I don't think so, Mom, why?"

"Because I told her I *wanted* nutmeg in the spinach!"

I had a fast fork-full of spinach, "Now that you mention it, I *do* taste it, very subtle though."

Okay this time, but Mama would have her day. The woman must have been a hell'uva good cook, the couple lasted through two more visits.

Gardeners were always GQK's nemesis, the two acres of cultivated property afforded her ample opportunity to vent her displeasure. She had a field day with one nice eager kid. "Eddie" worked hard and conscientiously, but it was fairly obvious, he didn't know a cyclamen from a cyclone, but he was too intimidated to admit it.

Mama didn't like ivy as a ground cover, she wanted *myrtle*. Eddie asked me confidentially, "Who's Myrtle, how do I get a hold of her?" One day, in a panic, he wanted me to show him the prune trees?

"Prune trees?"

"Your Mom wants me to thin them?"

"Eddie, are you sure she didn't say, 'Thin *and* prune' the trees?"

"Maybe, but I still gotta know which ones they are?"

Chapter 23

CARRIAGE TO CONCORDE

After a brief New York stay, GQK and DHK were en route to London, via the Concorde, the first of four trips aboard the marvel of commercial aviation. The author could fill pages with the merits of this supersonic aircraft, the negation of jet-lag is paramount to me. Flying at Mach-two, eleven hundred miles per hour, at fifty-seven thousand feet, seeing the Earth's curvature and experiencing day-into-night, is as pleasurable as the immediate boarding, getting settled-in hassle-free. The vertical take-off, superb service, leisurely cocktails, an excellent four-course meal with coffee and brandy, then hearing, "Ladies and gentlemen, please prepare for landing." Miraculous! I've only flown west to east on the Concorde. Arriving in New York earlier than the London departure holds no appeal.

Twenty years later, the author made his last flight to London on a Concorde, several days *after* the 2000 disaster outside Paris, aboard what was to be their next to last supersonic flight. They were back in service briefly, now, gone forever.

In London, my room at Peter Lubbock's was as warm as I'd left it two years before. Mama, meantime, was at Doris and Jules Stein's flat. The Stein's butler was a character drawn with broad strokes. His dedication to his employers came into play when dealing with the lady of the house. It's no secret Doris Stein wasn't an introvert, prone to social withdrawal, nor was her affinity for the bubbly. When she became a bit shaky and feisty at late hours, the butler handled it all with style and grace.

Story has it, one evening the butler was placating Doris, when she had an abrupt mood-swing, "How do you put up with me?" she asked him contritely. "I'm a demanding, drunk old bitch, aren't I?" With genuine devotion the butler replied, "Yes Ma'am, but you're *my* drunk old bitch."

GQK and I saw Tom Stoppard's *Night and Day* set in South Africa. It was a success in London with Diana Rigg, who I'd only seen in a TV series, not realizing what a dynamic actress she was. The play went on to New York with Maggie Smith, but didn't have nearly the success it deserved. Everyone adores Maggie Smith, I'm no exception, however, on occasion, she can overwhelm the material. *Night and Day* has all the makings of a marvelous film—so, why hasn't it?

We were astounded and enthralled by *Evita*—far too substantial to be a musical in the traditional sense and less ponderous and plodding than most opera. *Evita,* and subsequent productions of that genre by Lloyd-Webber and Schonberg-Boublil, de-polarize audiences, attracting fans with spectacular intelligent entertainment. Even the ones that fail at the box office, do it in a spectacular manner.

GQK saw a good deal of Lord John Brabourne and Lady Brabourne, he was a major force in the British film industry. His shocking death less than a year later, when the small fishing boat he was board was blown to bits by Irish terrorists, also took the life of their primary target, Lord Louis Mountbatten, along with two of Mountbatten's young nephews.

Lord Mountbatten had a pied-á-terre on Kennerton Street off Grovesnor Place, a few doors from my dissolute director chum, Brian Desmond Hurst. What was left of

Brian's health was declining, he thought it might be due to "over-medication"—large doses of *Dewars*, and *Johnnie Walker*. Brian saw to it Mama and I would have a proper "American" Thanksgiving at a friend's house, just South of London in Brighton! When we picked up Brian in our hired car, he emerged with a young protégé. I climbed in front with the driver as Brian and 'protégé huddled in the back seat with GQK, who took it all with amazing grace.

The protégé, according to Brian, was studying to be an anthropologist, they'd met during a seminar at the British Museum. The protégé was apprehensive, having in fact, met Brian at the *Club Napoleon*, a notorious bar off Bond Street catering to an all-male cliental. In a trepid voice, he questioned, "Brian, I don't think that's where we met?" Brian waved off his the boy with, "Well, someplace historical."

Our Thanksgiving host in Brighton was Lord Robin Maugham, a celebrated author, though somewhat eclipsed by the shadow of his more celebrated uncle, W. Somerset Maugham. As Thanksgiving is an anomaly to the rest of the world and turkeys being about the only commodity indigenous to America, unavailable on the Champs Elysee or Tenemen Square, we celebrated our Thanksgiving English style, delighting GQK, with a leg of lamb, her all-time favorite dish. Our host took us to see the seaside residence of King Edward VI, Queen Victoria's son. In the royal bed chamber, Brian alerted us to an historical footnote, as he gave the bed a hearty pat, "This is where King Edward gave Mrs. Fitz-Herbert a good 'what for'—may God protect it and all those who fornicate in it!"

Lord Maugham gave me a copy of his novel, *Knock on Teak*, scribbling a note giving exclusive rights to negotiate a film package. I'd experienced similar spontaneous acts of magnanimity in the past, for the obvious reason, it was a lousy project. Few established writers hand over a property to a virtually untried producer, unless, everyone else has passed—not the case in this instance. He had a solid, if not spectacular, track record, I was flattered. GQK read the novel, as it seemed the kind of story she could visualize.

The business end of the two week London visit was comprised of a luncheon with Ian McCallum, of the American Museum, and a dinner for *Il Pellicano* shareholders, hosted by Michael and Patty Graham.

Mama finished reading Maugham's *Knock on Teak* a week later in Paris, and agreed it was a delight. The story of a seemingly bland, floundering author in search of material in exotic places. GQK asked who do you see playing the lead?"

"Alec Guinness?"

"Not sexy enough," she declared.

"What about the wonderful actor in *Providence,* Dirk Bogarde!"

GQK was on target once again. Guinness was too obvious a choice, Bogarde was subtler and more suited to the romantic implications. Brian Hurst had worked with Bogarde, so I called him.

"What would you think of Dirk Bogarde as 'Teak'?"

"What's *Teak*?" Brian asked.

I just finished "*Knock on Teak.*"

"Knock on *what?*"

"*Robin Maugham's book!*"

"Robin! Do give him my love."

I wrote a forty page treatment for *Knock on Teak* which I sent to Dirk Bogarde's agent in Paris, she liked it enough to send it on, along with a copy of the book to her client in *Saint Paul Du Grasse* in the South of France.

Commuting and Communicating

GQK's Montecito ensemble included Stewart and Katherine Abercrombie and Lisa and Mel Ferrer. Ferrer had a working orchard, selling the produce commercially. I discovered the cultured aristocratic quality he projected on screen wasn't acting, it was him.

GQK's property was in a prime location in an elegant neighborhood, gate posts at the entrance, down an incline into a wide sweeping driveway around an island of trees and flowers. The only problem, after the regal approach, the large sprawling house was an anti-climatic, devoid of style and not representative of the area. How to improve it? Painting it simply meant the same bland innocuous structure—in another color. The shingle roof gave it a *tract* quality. A tiled roof would be more appropriate and safer in case of a fire.

GQK didn't give a hoot about the appropriate aspect. I persevered, finally, she begrudgingly acquiesced. I wanted the roofing to go smoothly, with as little inconvenience to Mama as possible. I told the roofing contractor to keep his crew out of the interior of the house.

After the old roof had been scraped off and the new ceramic tile was being installed, the contractor asked, when his men could get *in* the house. I reiterated I wanted his men *on* the house not *in* it!

Now, he reminds me the house was built to support a shingled roof, tile is heavier, they'll have to reinforce the roof from inside. "We knew that before hand?" I countered.

"My guys have to go in and install extra support beams."

Why did he wait until the job was half finished to tell me? GQK was grousing about the noise, debris and lack of privacy during the process anyway, now I had to hit her with this. I explained the situation, prepared for the worst. GQK listened, rightfully concluding, "You want the roof collapsing on your ol' Mama?"

Marvels in Montecito

GQK was cresting on waves of Montecito social activity as well as hosting house guests from afar. Kahala was an obvious target, but San Ysidro Lane, a two hour drive from the closest international airport would be a deterrent, flights into LAX to Santa Barbara involved changing planes, odd hours, a thirty minute drive to Montecito in heavy traffic. Driving up was quicker and less hassle.

Peter Lubbock, his sister, Lady Wakehurst, Ian McCallum, Charles Lloyd-Jones from Sydney, all house guested within a two month period that year. Fortunately, none were the kind who has to be constantly entertained, that variety is a pain where a pill won't reach. Mama and Montecito saw to it, there were ample social events on their behalf.

My saviors came in the personages of Francoise and Brooks Barton, now divorced, both remarried. At that time, they were about the only contemporaries in the vicinity I could call friends.

As a youth, I sought the company of those older, and as I grow older the company gets correspondingly younger. I now pause in markets to exchange gurgles with infants in perambulators and toddlers. I've assiduously avoided children most of my adult life, now I melt when a grubby sticky little hand reaches out. However, as I do get older, it becomes harder to bend down.

Francoise and Brooks were extremely attractive, intelligent raconteurs and great fun. Francoise had three daughters by a previous marriage, and a fourth by Brooks, a lot of female energy.

Francoise did everything beautifully with grace, never seeming to exert much effort. At the time, a successful realtor, wife, mother of four delightful, well-adjusted, preteen daughters and ran an immaculate house. She prepared gourmet dinners, all the while, being a gracious hostess to her guests, chatting about interesting and worthwhile subjects and she was always superbly dressed. I never saw a dirty plate or a used dish in the kitchen, nor were there any elves with aprons cleaning up magically.

After extolling Francoise's virtues, GQK concluded, "She's an extraordinary young woman—but I adore her, in spite of it."

Comparisons can be odious, so I will decline. Most of the young women I've known with families, are marvelous mothers, so-so wives, slipshod hostesses, and as for scintillating conversation—dream on. They dress in jeans and sweatshirts, most can't cook worth a damn and their kitchens look like the aftermath of a hurricane.

"The better the cook, the cleaner the kitchen," GQK declared.

"If that's true, Mom, yours would be a mess."

"Which is why I avoid it." Her logic was irrefutable.

Southern Sojourns

GQK's seventy-eighth birthday was celebrated at *Ma Maison*, with Jean Howard, Dolly Green, Zsa Zsa, George Frelinhuysen, Alfredo de la Vega, and Maximilian de Henckel. The reason the author specifically lists the guests, had the luncheon been taped it would be in the national archives.

Ma Maison was a very trendy L.A. eatery for years until one of its chefs brutally murdered Dominique Dunne, the daughter of author-journalist, keeper of the public flame, Dominick Dunne.

I've known Nick, not well, but for many years. I'm a great admirer of his documentations, his quiet passion, resiliency and strength under pressure and adversity. When

Nick goes for the jugular, it's with élan, a thorough knowledge of the subject manner, more importantly, he makes it interesting and entertaining.

GQK made a number of trips south, one, to attend Mary Pickford's funeral. "America's Sweetheart" hadn't appeared in a film for forty years, but remained top box office to her friends and fans, which filled the chapel at Forest Lawn to overflowing. Many survivors of time, if not talkies, attended—a stack of their collective memoirs would top Mount Everest. Seated unobtrusively in a rear pew, was her former stepson, Douglas Fairbanks, Jr. Following the service, at the reception held at *Pickfair*, a photograph was taken of the widower, Buddy Rogers, with Lillian Gish, Doug Fairbanks, Jr., and Gladys Knapp—a special memento of a bygone era.

Another of GQK's Southland visits was attributable to a Machiavellian plot hatched by her son. Knowing of her loathing and distrust of anything smacking of communism, the plan involved lunch at the Polo Lounge with George Cukor—the objective, to promote a possible trip to Russia. George had recently completed the first U.S. film made in the U.S.S.R. since the Cold War began, *The Blue Bird*. The demographics, logistics, and tacitly hostile environment the production had to contend with, would test the grit of any man. Cukor, then well into his seventies, also had to deal with an impossible script and a cast headed by Elizabeth Taylor, Ava Gardner, and Jane Fonda, none of whom were considered pussycats to work with.

GQK was a great admirer of Cukor and enormously fond of him—but not the prospect of going to Mother Russia. Knowing my desire to go there, at lunch, George was as positive and supportive of the venture as honesty allowed. Mama, sensing entrapment, peppered him with questions guaranteed to evoke a negative response. Matters of cuisine, availability of Western goods, red tape, and freedom of movement, were tossed out for the director to field. Having gotten the gist, George finally suggested, "Gladys, I have the distinct impression you won't like it there. I don't think you should go, David can do it on his own." Solid advice we both took, GQK stayed home and I went—three years later.

***

I took Mama to a wedding and reception at Patricia and Phil Barry's Brentwood home for their daughter, Stephanie and her groom, Mark. Pat and I shared the *Lovers and Friends* saga, as well as many enjoyable outings on both coasts. It was festive afternoon with Mama on the outdoor dance floor, giving her soul to rhythm, more than holding her own with the best of younger generations. I asked her where she learned to *bop*. She laughed, "I was 'bopping' before you were burped." She also had an opportunity to rekindle her acquaintance with Phil's mother, Ellen Barry, widow of the author of *The Philadelphia Story* and *Holiday*. On that afternoon, Pat Barry introduced me to a dynamic lady, Panda Hoffman, and her beaux, playwright Ron Alexander, with whom I was fortunate to cross-paths often in the future.

Chapter 24

DAYS OF WINE AND DOSES

The Sunset Vale house became a solid rental asset, so, when I was shown a house in a sunnier location with a view at the East end of the Sunset Strip, high above the famed Chateau Marmont, I gave Norma Volk and Larry Bukzin a call. They promptly flew out to have a look. On seeing the fixer-upper house they concealed their dismay, but agreed, it would be a feasible investment, while keeping the Sunset Vale house. They based their judgment on the realtor's credo, "Three primary assets of a property, are location, location, location."

On a quiet Sunday afternoon, less than a month after I took occupancy, Gianni D'Agostino, Fabrizio Mioni, John Laurent, some other friends, and I were sitting around the pool when someone yelled, "My God, look up there!!" The crest of a ridge surrounding the Marmont area was engulfed in flames, it looked like the gates of hell had been flung open, releasing a ground-scorching inferno.

A solid wall of fire rapidly racing from Laurel Canyon, to the north, having scaled the ridge, was now beginning its southern descent into our area.

We heard fire trucks approaching from the bottom of the hill, but with over a mile of narrow winding curves to negotiate before they could reach us, there was no time to wait. We dragged garden hoses on to the roof, spraying the shingles. Up the hill, a half dozen houses stood between us and the blaze, there was no visual activity at any of them, all the neighbors elsewhere on a summer weekend? Realizing, if the houses and hillsides around us were ablaze, no amount of water on the roof would save outhouse. Blasts of orange and red ten feet high were within a hundred yards of the house at the top of the street, and two hundred yards from us. We started up the hill in an attempt to water down the brush area before the fire reached the house at the top, then, it occurred to us we were now in physical danger ourselves, with burning embers raining down on our position, survival became an issue. Wrapped in soaking towels, we prepared to seek the safety of the pool, when, in the nick of time, the cavalry burst on scene in the form of fire engines with flashing lights and sirens blaring. The fire fighters saved the day with only minutes and a few yards to spare.

Sinatra and the Sphinx

Mom and I were on a charter flight to Cairo that September for a very special CBS TV special, "Frank Sinatra in Concert at the Great Pyramid." We were big-time Sinatra fans, front row center for his "final" concert at the Los Angeles Music Center a few years earlier. Mama had flown to New York to see another "farewell" concert not long after that, a third Sinatra *Good-Bye* performance about a year before had begun the cycle.

Aboard the flight, as official guests of Egyptian President Anwar Sadat and Madam Sadat were the Stewart Abercrombies, Sir Richard (now 'Lord') Attenborough, Joe Levine, Cesar Romero, George Lang, owner and driving force behind *Café Des Artistes*, and to make sure the folks knew we were there, Jody Jacobs of the *L.A. Times,* and veteran columnist Jim Bacon. President Sadat had already emerged as one of the great political leaders of that century, and all were thrilled by the opportunity to meet him. Unfortunately, vastly more important affairs prevented that from happening. His beautiful wife assumed the hosting chores magnificently.

The charter flight from New York on an aging Pan Am 707 was not an auspicious beginning. Frayed around the edges, the 707 was designed essentially for intercontinental flights, with little emphasis on long-range overnight sleeping comfort. We made it to Europe, but so did Lindbergh. GQK noted one of the senior flight attendants, remarking, "My God, she's older than I am!"

Passengers ordering drinks from her were brought three or four, when a passenger told her he only wanted one, he was informed, "You'll want 'em all by the time this flight's over, kiddo."

We developed problems affecting the cabin temperature, it was stifling when we made an unscheduled landing in Paris. Egypt and France were having a political spat at the time, and French officials wouldn't permit us to disembark, or even allow us on the tarmac, as we were Cairo bound. It made no difference we were all American or British. The French have subtler ways than the guillotine!

The reception in Cairo compensated, limousines took us the Hilton. The view from our suite looked over a junction of the Nile River and the whole Southern section of Cairo. The following day, I was photographed on a camel, in Arab headdress and robe, a curved dagger sheathed in the sash, with the giant sphinx in the background. Had David Lean seen me, we'd be in pre-production on *Lawrence of Arabia, Part II*—but timing is everything.

The Sinatra concert was a once in a life time event. Several hundred black-tied, evening-gowned international figures seated on carpets, dining on the lawn of the Oberoi Hotel. The breathtaking effect of the great pyramid and giant sphinx illuminated in the background was as impressive as it gets. Frank Sinatra, at his best, backed by sixty musicians from the London Symphony Orchestra, was overwhelming.

Sinatra had a unique command when he stepped on stage, demanding your attention before he opened his mouth. I asked GQK, "What is it Sinatra has?" She wasn't sure, "But whatever it is, he has it."

A Postillion Unsolved

It was old home week in London. Peter and I gave a cocktail party for Mom, which Lady Wakehurst, Ian McCallum, Brian Hurst, Dorothy Hammerstein, and Beverly Jackson from Santa Barbara attended. Several days later, I received a call telling me Dirk Bogarde had read the *Knock on Teak* treatment, and showed considerable interest. I was to contact his agent in Paris.

Days later, I drove up from Nice to Bogarde's house in Provence to meet the international film star I so greatly admired. Several dogs greeted me, a good omen.

Mr. Bogarde, and his friend Tony Forwood, seemed pleased at my rapport with his animals. "I can tell those who communicate with them, and those who tolerate them."

Bogarde was slighter than I realized, slender, bordering on thin and looked most of his fifty-nine years. We talked about dogs, gardens (of which I knew little), and his films (of which I knew a lot).

"I read John Gielgud credits you for turning him into a good film actor."

"Johnny was rather theatrical, terribly serious, humorless—at least in his first twenty or so films. When we began *Providence*, he admitted he'd never really gotten the hang of film acting. I suggested he not act, just think about it."

I asked Tony where I could take them for lunch. He told me we were having lunch at their house, confiding, "He and Dirk had a 'signal system.' If Dirk hadn't liked you, we'd have let you take us to lunch. You be surprised how often we lunch out."

Bogarde recently published two memoirs, a surrealistic-autobiography, *A Postillion Struck by Lightning,* which I found as incomprehensible as its title. Research revealed, a "postillion"' is *one who rides the left horse of a two-horse team, when there's no driver.* That explained it all. His second book, *Snakes and Ladders*—the title again baffled me, but I did comprehend the text and thoroughly enjoyed it.

The *Teak* aroused some interest, but there are always more reasons *not* to make a film, than to give it a green light. I know there were producers who might have made it happen, I couldn't. I'd wager with Robin Williams aboard, *Teak* could get made today.

***

I escorted Mama to Lausanne, Switzerland, to the *La Prairie Clinic* in Vevey for a ten day visit. *La Prairie* is a world renown rejuvenation clinic, without benefit of nip 'n tuck surgery. The patients are put to bed sedated and given only water and prescribed nutrients for days. Sheep placenta is intravenously injected, cleaning out and revitalizing the system. GQK had gone through the *Le Prairie* process on several previous occasions over a thirty-year period. It worked for her, by anyone's standard Gladys Knapp, now in her late seventies, on good days looked, moved, and possessed the mental attitude of a woman in her late fifties. I can attest she never had one iota of cosmetic surgery during her lifetime.

I picked GQK up at LAX when she returned from Switzerland. She looked drawn and pale, older than when she'd entered the clinic. Had something backfired? I drove her to Montecito, but had to return to L.A. immediately for a second episode in a new ill-fated TV sitcom, *The Associates*, with Wilfred Hyde-White and Martin Short.

I was concerned over Mama's pallid appearance, but when I returned to Montecito several days later, Mama looked better than she had in years! It simply took awhile to take effect.

Gladys was of good cheer regarding the *big picture.* Ronald Reagan's victory the previous November affected most of the nation like a shot of Vitamin B.

Mama was elated. Shoes would again be worn in the White House, chitterlings and collard greens put on the back burner in lieu of *medallions de veau* and *petit pois.* She felt the world was a better place with vintage California wines replacing Dr. Pepper at State dinners—and that designer James Galanos took precedence over a back room seamstress.

GQK slept better knowing we had an administration, as she put it, *"For* the people, not *by* the people." Reagan wasn't one of the good ol' boys—he was *The Man.*

Fun and Fluff

Ronald Alexander had several Broadway hits under his belt, having authored *Nobody Loves an Albatross* and *Holiday for Lovers.* He had written a new play, *A Tree in the Middle of the Garden,* and it was decided to present it in a small venue on the West Coast. Broadway production costs had skyrocketed, the trend was away from non-musical romantic comedies and it would be a more feasible way to exploit its movie potential. Ron Alexander's very significant other half, Panda Hoffman would finance the project, but needed an on-line producer. Patricia Barry had put Panda and myself in touch. We clicked in on the same frequency and work began.

We took the main stage at the Cast-at-the-Circle Theatre in Hollywood. Donald May had already agreed to accept the lead in the eight character play, I brought in Stewart Moss to direct and Marianne McAndrew (Moss) to play one of the female leads. Stewart in turn tapped two talented chums, Paul Carr and Jim Peck, to round out the male cast. A beautiful and delightful young actress, Elizabeth Stack, was set for the ingénue. Elizabeth had acquired her initial credentials as the daughter of Rosemarie and Robert Stack. A lovely Lydia Lei in the role of the exotic "dalliance," and the mother would be played to perfection by a late-bloomer find of ours, Lisa Figus.

The author made minor and major revisions daily in the rehearsal period. Without exception, the more successful and tried the playwright, the more involved and flexible they are in working on the script in progress. Whereas, the amateur fledgling writers tend to assume their works are etched in marble, they arrogantly resist any attempt to improve, or in any way alter their material, which they consider to be sacrosanct!

In ninety percent of the latter cases, the results are bitterly disappointing. Without objectivity your own work remains creatively sedentary. The opening night was attended by more celebrities than some Music Center galas.

Mama sparkled that night, happy her son's efforts hadn't raised any more eyebrows. She raved about the opening night party Panda gave at her home in the West Hollywood Hills, adding, "The play was quite amusing too."

It was a fine company. The show went well, and was received very favorably by audiences and critics. However, *"enjoyable* and *entertaining"* don't create lines at the box office.

Everyone involved did a splendid job with Panda generating an after-show social environment worthy of the "Great White Way." No one associated with the show has cause to regret the experience.

Black Tie not Optional

GQK and I were invited to a ball for the International Red Cross, hosted by Her Royal Highness, Princess Grace of Monaco. Marylou Daves had remarried a Texas banker, Sam Young, and they hosted a small cocktail reception in their hotel suite before the ball for Princess Grace. Rupert Allan, the Los Angeles Consul-General for Monaco, escorted Her Serene Highness, who we hadn't seen since those Sunday drives to church in the Palisades. She pretended to remember, which made us feel good.

Downstairs in the ballroom, Mama and I were introduced to the guest of honor, H.R.H. Prince of Wales, Prince Charles. There's royalty and there's *royalty*—dethroned kings in exile, of nations that take ten minutes to find on a map. The ruling family, titular heads of state of Great Britain, Scotland, Ireland, Canada, Australia, New Zealand, South Africa, India, Singapore, Hong Kong, Half the Caribbean, and a dozen others—somehow commands more deference than the Queen of Tonga.

In ninety seconds of one-on-one with Prince Charles, I suggested, if any of his critics worked half as hard and conscientiously as he did, they'd have no time to criticize, and wished him a great reign. His Royal Highness appreciated my assessment. As he was escorted away, he turned, "We must talk more." One of his aides whispered to me, "Well said." Mama beamed, "I thought so too."

The heir to the British throne was seated at an elevated dais, above our table. The chairs on either side of him were momentarily vacated by their occupants, one was California's left-wing governor at the time. It's terribly awkward being center of attention with no one to talk to. Prince Charles glanced across the assembled room, his eyes paused a moment at our table, he nodded haplessly, then focused on his plate. Mama's elbow nearly knocked me off the chair, "He wants you to go up and talk to him!" I looked at her in disbelief. "Get off your behind, David, now is the time to show." She fell silent glowering at the dais; a chair next to the Prince was again occupied. "Well, you can't say you didn't have the opportunity," she lamented. I don't have winged feet of *Mercury*, nor had I brought a business card!

***

May 21, 1981 would mark Gladys Knapp's eightieth birthday. She claimed she wanted a small intimate party, but I knew she'd be livid if it were. Tony and Beegle Duquette and I would co-host a black-tie sit-down gala at Tony's studio for eighty guests. Doris & Jules Stein, Jean Howard, her husband, Tony Santori, Marylou Daves, her husband, Sam Young, Debby & Bill Richards, Dolly Green, Gaylord Hauser, Nancy Cooke de Herrera, Buddy Rogers, Jimmy & Gloria Stewart, Bob & Rosemarie Stack, Frank McCarthy, Dorothy McGuire and Rupert Allan, Peggy and Murray Ward, John & Louise Good, Connie Wald & Peter Pannaker, Brian & Eleanor Aherne. Eleanore Phillips, Luis Estevez, George Freylinhuysen, Jimmy Pendleton, Zsa Zsa, the Bartons and most of her Santa Barbara friends, those of mine I considered acceptable and of course, the obligatory guests no one really wants, but who you dare *not* invite. You can't stop at eighty guests, you're at the level of, *If I invite so-and-so, I'll have to ask so-and-so*, on to *I can't ask them without including...* etc. We stopped at just over one hundred.

The afternoon of the party GQK arrived at my house, asking half-seriously, "Do I have to go through with this?"

Later, "Did you invite *so-and-so*?"

"Yes, of course, Mom."

"Why?"

"I thought she was one of your best friends?"

"You got the tense right."

Conversely, "David, why *didn't* you invite *so-and-so*?"

"I thought we agreed *so-and-so* was a bitch?"

"What does that have to do with it?"

"Mom, let's try to have fun tonight, it's the big *eight-O*."

"The damned fool who coined the term, 'Golden Years,' was colorblind!"

Mama's favorite gift that night was an elegantly embroidered pillow with *"Screw the Golden Years!"* inscribed on it.

Oceania Re-explored

In February of 1982, Ian McCallum organized a tour of Eastern Australia for members of the American Museum in Bath, GQK was more than up to it. It would be her second trip "down under" and my fourth, nor was to be a cursory visit.

After the killer flight to Melbourne, the tour got off to a shaky start. Ian's assistant, well out of the closet, showed up the second morning in a very battered and bruised state. Everyone in the group was sympathetic, feigning acceptance of the "being mugged" explanation—but they all knew better. The embarrassing incident was never mentioned again. I was relieved I hadn't accepted the invitation to "tour" the dock area the night before.

The city of Melbourne compensated for any appearance of inhospitable behavior, when the keys to the city of were presented to us by Sir Robert Law Smith, governor of the Victoria province. Our group of fourteen continued on in a small luxurious chartered bus, then were guided and hosted at the annual *Adelaide Festival* and given the keys to that city as well. Although GQK appreciated the token gesture, she noted, "The keys don't seem to fit anywhere, and they don't let you keep them."

On to Tasmania, where we motored the length of the island from Hobart to Launceston. In Canberra, the American ambassador, Hon. Robert Nessan, held a reception. During the Ranch years, we bought several cars from the Reagan appointee's car dealership in Thousand Oaks. Finally, a final week in Sydney, where a number of my friends also hosted the museum group, making the trip an ideal blend of old and new faces—Sir James Fairfax, owner-publisher of Australia's leading newspaper, his stepmother, Lady Mary Fairfax, Charles-Lloyd Jones, former British film star, Googie Withers, Billy McCann from the old London days, Dickie and Betty Keep, and my oldest Australian friend, harkening back to the first naval visit, Norman Bent, entertained us in the grand tradition. Luncheon at Governor House, a private tour of the as yet uncompleted Sydney Opera House, about which GQK remarked, "At least the interior's an improvement over the exterior."

Mama held up remarkably well throughout the hectic schedule. She was wise enough to pace herself, in some instances not appearing until early evening, but when rested, she would tackle the festivities with vigor and enthusiasm. GQK believed, *Better to sparkle in bursts, than to flicker interminably.*

***

Returning to Los Angeles I had a sad reunion with Alan Jay Factor—I hadn't known he'd been *very* ill. We'd stayed in touch through the *Producer's Guild of America* meetings, and occasional lunches. I'd seen him at an event not long before, he seemed well and energized. When I asked the informant how ill was Alan, the man simply shook his head. Alan Factor, barely in his fifties, was dying of brain cancer. I called his wife, Phyllis, asking if I could visit him. She said of course, but to please do it soon. That evening Phyllis ushered me up to their room where Alan lay propped up in bed. He was weak but totally lucid, I like to think he was genuinely glad to see me. We talked briefly of old times, he then asked to go into his dressing room and look on the counter. In a leather frame was a photograph of he and I, taken years before, sitting on his desk in one of the old offices, looking younger, happier and optimistically at one another. I was deeply touched the picture was where he would see it every day.

I returned to his bedside fighting away tears, then Phyllis nodded, it was time for him to rest. I kissed him on the forehead, and said a final goodbye and left.

I wore a yarmulke as an honorary pallbearer at Alan's funeral held at Hollywood Cemetery. He'd even thought to leave me a residual bequest in his will. I'd been lucky to cross paths with a man like Alan, it's often true, "the good die young."

To Thine Own Self Be True

After dinner one evening in Montecito, I was nursing a scotch, and Mother shook her head, "You drink too much, David." I allowed, as that was a fair assessment—agreeing with the opposition sometimes ends the debate, but not always. "Do you know why you do?" Her inflection implied, she did.

"It could be attributable to a variety of factors," I mused. "Genetics, availability, it's an invaluable assist at social functions and overcoming periods of boredom."

"You find life up here boring, don't you, dear?"

A question not answerable with a simple yes or no. There was plenty of brain-power in Montecito, it just doesn't get enough exercise.

"Is this going to be 'the Summer of our discontent,' Mama?" Paraphrasing Shakespeare puts a sheen on one's credentials—it backfired.

"Odd, you'd say that, I think you drink because you're discontented with yourself," she offered.

"Am I supposed to ask indignantly, why would I be discontented?"

"It would offer a great opportunity if you did. Tell me, what's the longest you've gone without a drink?"

"Let's see, my first twelve years, 'til you guys got me drunk that night before our first trip to Hawaii."

"How long since then?"

"A year," I answered promptly.

"When was that?"

"At Georgetown, you offered me ten thousand dollars if I abstained for a year, knowing there was a one-in-a-million chance you'd have to shell out."

She looked me incredulously, then remembered, "Why was it you never claimed the money?"

"I didn't honor the agreement," I admitted. "I forfeited after ten and a half months."

"David, with just six weeks to go, you broke the agreement? I find that amazing." I had to agree.

She was curious, *why* did I finally succumb?

"It was the end of April in 1958, and I thought, What the hell, I'll toast the bride."

Mama searched her memory, "Oh my God, I married Howard Bell that April!"

"Indeed, you did," I confirmed.

"Were you upset because we didn't include you?"

"You didn't even *let me know* until after the fact!"

She started to explain, I made it easier, interrupting, "It was an excuse, I'd had it with abstinence—and I figured, between you and Howard, I wouldn't be in dire need of the money."

"Your version of financial planning," GQK nodded. "A ten thousand dollar drink."

"Not quite, I had a few more the following weeks. Mom, I've tried to objectively analyze my psyche, to find the deep-seated causes behind my affinity for alcohol, and…"

"*And* it boils down to, *you like the way it makes you feel*," She concluded.

"I'll drink to that."

"Would you be an angel, pour your ol' Mama a brandy?"

Her request surprised me, GQK was a light drinker, going weeks without a drop, and not missing it. When she post-scripted, "Why don't you fix yourself another one too," I was leery—but did as she asked.

After her second sip, from out of the blue, came, "I was hoping for grandchildren."

"Mother, I thought we'd been through all that."

We had "discussed" the subject in the past—circuitously. I told her not to get her hopes up. On one occasion, she responded, "In that case, it might be nice if you became a *Cardinal*."

"If I wanted to play baseball, Mom, it wouldn't be for *St. Louis!*"

"A prince of the Church!"

An option, but a lot of hassle to go through to avoid having children. I pointed out, it meant prayer, studying for the priesthood, climbing up the ecclesiastical order.

"There are ways of expediting that," Mama suggested.

"You don't have that kind of money,' I reminded her.

"There are those who do," she reminded me, having known a few.

"Your super-rich Jewish friends don't select Cardinals."

"Perhaps not," she conceded, "but they donate a lot to Catholic charities."

GQK also offered me the option of being a movie star, "They make lots of money, travel everywhere first class, meet everyone interesting, stay at the finest hotels, get the best tables in restaurants."

"*So do we*, Mom, and I don't have to get up at six a.m. or look my best." This time I had the last word.

"I believe people like you and I, are better off, happier, more productive, when functioning alone. We create our own environment, rather than depend on outside sources."

The Knapps were the antitheses of antisocial behavior, was that a contradiction? "Not at all," she felt. "We just don't have to look elsewhere for things to do. We're both generous to a fault, I'm compassionate, understanding, forgiving—you're fair-minded and overly objective—but essentially, we're both arrogant, selfish, manipulative, and impossible to be around full-time. Love-relationships take a backseat to our most basic survival need."

"We are solitary by nature," elaborating, "No matter how much we love another, it can never be a *one*-person union, and there'll always be *two* individuals."

"Doesn't that encourage promiscuity?" I asked with naiveté.

"Should you ever embrace monogamy, darling, keep in mind the difference between staying warm and suffocating."

"That doesn't paint a rosy picture," I reflected.

"*Now* that you know it, you're better prepared to deal with it!"

"How did *you* deal with it, Mama?"

"I chose not to."

Choices? GQK made a double-edged point, intentionally or not.

I'd chosen not to deal with certain aspects of my life as well. My drinking wasn't as amusing as I tried to make it sound, nor was my growing affinity for the lines of white powder which were so readily available in the mid and late eighties, here and abroad. Cocaine was not simply a

behavioral enhancement, it was the vogue. I recall a cocktail
table at a party in Sydney looking like a miniature furrowed
cotton field. In some cases, people in restaurants didn't
bother to excuse themselves to take a toot in the rest room,
they snorted right at the table.

One friend abandoned the tiny bottle and spoon
technique in lieu of a *Glad* bag in his breast pocket and a
straw. All he had to do was lean forward and inhale!
Cocaine had many advantages over other illegal substances.
When used judiciously, it had little or no visual effect on
one's behavior, your conduct was controlled. There's no
such thing as cocaine-breath or smell, and the other telltale
signs from alcohol or pot permeating the air. It's also easier
to conceal and ingest. All of which makes it even more
insidious. *Psychologically,* it's a killer! It slips quietly and
unobtrusively into your life, then gradually takes over.

People with alcohol and/or cocaine addictions have
almost become the norm. It's accepted as routine, a rite of
passage. Trying to control marijuana is a time-consuming
farce, as anyone can grow it. No one is dependent on a
middle man. When returning from Mexico, a very small
amount of pot was discovered by customs officials in my
toilet article bag. How it got there, I have no idea. I thought
we'd smoked it all up. The gung-ho rookie customs agent
was in a tizzy with excitement. He thought he'd made the
bust of the century, until his superiors fined me $50—on a
Visa or MasterCard! A favorite notice was posted in New
Orleans during Mardi Gras: *"The smoking or use of
marijuana is illegal in public places."*

Now to make too light of it, luck and timing again came
to my aid. My problem didn't develop until midway into my
life. Today I see many very young people, not yet in their
twenties, with hopeless addiction problems which they'll
have to deal with throughout the rest of their lives.
Ostensibly, they'll have to spend decades not doing what

they desperately want to do, or taking cheap imitations more dangerous than the actual drug.

Excessive drinking seems to be au rigueur for me when traveling. Upon returning from one particular trip, I was feeling terrible and decided to go "on the wagon." After the first dry day, I felt much better. The second day, I was sick as a dog, fever, chills, and nausea. Here I was, not a drop in two days, and barely able to function. How could this be? The doctor explained simply, "You're in withdrawal."

"Withdrawal?" I was a heavy social drinker, not a drunk!

I made a fast decision, approaching the mid-century mark, it was time to take control—a rehab program for DHK. My doctor was wholeheartedly in agreement, admitting me to Saint John's Hospital's A & D Unit in Santa Monica the following day, where I languished for four healthy weeks. Early to bed, early to rise, I prayed, played volleyball, attended all matter of meetings, revealing lurid details of our pasts, all dark places illuminated in great detail, and writing autobiographical essays on what a total asshole you are. Being nice, cheerful, and supportive to everyone, day after day, doesn't come naturally to me. Having to listen to other people's woes, when I want to talk about mine, becomes a taxing ordeal. On occasion, I managed to bring some conflict, antagonism, and unpleasantness to the proceedings, but not enough to make it really interesting and nasty. There was always some perky 'Little-Mary-Two-Shoes' to bring up the positive side.

After completing the program, I attended AA group interaction meetings for several weeks, in various locations, and then drifted away—not because they were depressing, but because they became excruciatingly boring. It got so dull that some of us had to have a drink just to sit through them. Not a good sign.

Contrary to all that's been said for centuries, there *are* alternative methods for dealing with substance abuse, other than total abstinence. Alcoholics are told, never to take a drink again, not even a "near-beer" or grape juice. Stay clear of places where liquor is available, and *away from people who drink!* You must stop "cold turkey" forever!

It ought to be noted, people involved in various types of substance abuse over a period of decades, who then abruptly cease, sometimes run a good risk of dropping dead before they would have in the natural course of events. Most people are more than capable of cutting-back, substantially reducing intake and shifting gears in general.

Chapter 25

PANORAMAS THROUGH KEYHOLES

On my birthday, I boarded a Finnair flight to Helsinki to rendezvousing with Heidi and Wilson Tait for a motor tour of Western Russia, then the Soviet Union. GQK's reaction to my Russian visit was relayed through mutual friends to whom she voiced her concern, "The combination of the Communists mentality and David's mouth don't bode well. I may never see him again."

The Taits bought a new Audi in Germany, to be broken in—no pun intended—on the roads and byways of *Mother Russia.*

Helsinki is a clean, pretty city and easy to leave behind. The only city I can remember being in for several days without seeing a single attractive person. Taking into account in former Communist bloc countries, few, if any, of the locals focused on you directly or made any eye-contact, they looked past you, or downward—many were nice to look *at*—not so in Helsinki.

Heidi, Wilson, and I drove the short distance to the Russian border, across into Vyborg, where Soviet officials ordered us to an inspection facility. We didn't have the customary "Intourist Guide," their term for two-legged surveillance and monitoring. The Taits and I were *on our own*, so they weren't taking any chances.

We assumed communication wouldn't be a problem, we had a pocket Russian dictionary, and between the three of us we could speak reasonable English, German, French, and Spanish. The difficulty came with the dictionary—the Russian words were *written* in Russian!

At the border station each piece of luggage was meticulously inspected, every article examined. The Audi's interior then strip-searched, the seats, floor carpeting removed, upholstery peeled away, the engine checked more carefully than any mechanic would bother to do. The car was elevated, its undercarriage probed, tires poked, every nook and cranny scrutinized. After all our personal and mechanical possessions were laid bare, to the Reds' credit, they put everything back in place *exactly* as it was, you wouldn't know our luggage had been opened or the car the car had been touched.

To further insure our safe passage, unbeknownst to us during the inspection, our vehicle was accessorized with additional technology. Henceforth, any problems or complaints expressed would be duly recorded, should we get lost or go astray, the power-that-be-would know exactly where to find us—*help was on the way*!

St. Petersburg, then Leningrad, after dark it was immense, sprawling, and foreboding. We couldn't even find the district our hotel was in on the *Intourist* map. In desperation, we pulled up to several older men playing cards outside a café to explain our dilemma, naming the hotel, hoping they would point in its general direction. Then one of the locals walked to the car, indicating the back seat.

"I think he wants to get in," Heidi exclaimed. KGB?

Would we ever be heard from again? On the other hand, at the rate we were going, we probably wouldn't be either way. The man spoke no recognizable language, simply gesturing right or left. The city was a maze at night, poorly lighted, few boulevards, mainly narrow winding streets and wide alleyways. Many minutes later our passenger pointed ahead to one of largest buildings I'd ever seen. We pulled up to the entrance, and our savior got out and started to step away. Wilson and I bolted after him, thanking him waving rupees. He wouldn't accept money, not even a bottle of vodka. He nodded politely, turned and walked into the night. Whoever our rescuer was, he's not been forgotten, I hope he was around when the Berlin Wall came down.

The hotel was immense, the rooms small, with a commissar at a desk on every floor as you stepped out of the elevator. Heidi and Wilson would bet me each night as to who could find the hidden bugs and/or camera in or respective rooms first. An important rule is not being observed as searching for the detecting devises if located— not indicating your find, especially if you plan to tamper with them. If you enjoy performing in front of a camera, it must appear you're not aware of its presence, just being plain ol' uninhibited.

In the elegant cavernous sparsely-occupied hotel dining room, the equally impressive menu offered a choice of fifty entrees. It was our custom when traveling, to order something different, so we could sample cuisine off each other's plate. The dish Heidi ordered wasn't available that night; Wilson's first choice wasn't either; they were out of what I wanted. Our second choices were "nyet,"—rejected or attributed to typographical errors. We finally asked the waiter, what *was* available, he pointed to two items on the list of fifty. We were curious about the other forty-eight? The waiter shrugged, "Maybe someday?"

After our feast we attended the Kirov Ballet. It wasn't an enthralling production, none of us were particular ballet fans, but our grogginess that evening far exceeded that normally experienced by one in a captive audience. Regardless of how hard we tried to stay awake our heads slumped. The last thing any of us remembered was the hazy form of dancers leaping and pirouetting about on stage, then nothing. The next thing we knew, we were jolted awake by applause as the company took their final bows and curtsies.

You don't have to be *James Bond* to know the difference between feeling sleepy and being drugged. What possible motive or reason would they have to drug us, we had no idea? To a ballet lover, it would have been frustrating as hell.

We'd been cautioned not to attempt any deviations from our specified route, if we did, we'd be stopped within thirty kilometers. Leaving Leningrad, we inadvertently took the wrong fork off a round-about, twenty kilometers later we found ourselves at the *Summer Palace*, which wasn't on our itinerary, but we were delighted. After an unplanned tour of the beautiful complex, we merrily resumed our drive south. Ten kilometers later we encountered a road block consisting of military vehicles and a dozen soldiers with weapons drawn.

Assuming it was a routine security check, we pulled up and were stunned discover we were the target of the deployment! We tried to explain contritely, we must have taken the wrong spoke outside of Leningrad. They were having none of it! Heidi, Wilson, and I were ordered out of the car, escorted to a guard shack and interrogated in Russian. None of the uniformed personnel appeared to speak or understand a word of English, German, French, or Spanish. The moment they left us alone for minute, I started into a diatribe on the evils of Communism and *how was it possible, that many Bolsheviks could be so stupid as to not speak any civilized languages.* Heidi gestured frantically, indicating they were outside listening. So what? They couldn't understand what I was saying. Heidi rolled her eyes at my naiveté, "It's a ploy. They understand everything we're saying."

Instead of being intimidated by serious situations of that nature, as any rational person should be, I became irritated and indignant. A *"You fools, how dare you!"* sort of attitude set in.

When our inquisitors returned, we went along with their strategy, confiding to each other very audibly, "There's no point in trying explaining that we inadvertently got on the wrong road. They know damned well by now we're not guilty of any crimes against the State. They're a fair and just people, they'll handle it their way."

Their way, took two hours before they released us, and then punished us anyway, not allowing us to take a direct lateral route to get back on the right course. We were ordered to go all the way back to the Leningrad round-about, then, get on the correct road!

After a night in an medieval hotel in Novograd, with bugging devises literally dangling from the light fixtures, we made our way to Moscow along the two-lane main highway with nothing but military trucks and farm vehicles, we rarely saw a civilian automobile.

Upon our arrival in Moscow we received an official reprimand from a bureaucrat at a desk in the hotel lobby, informing us, we'd exceeded the speed limit en route to the capitol city! What was he talking about? Sure, we passed around a few slow-moving trucks, but speeding? They had it all figured out, we'd left Novograd at nine-forty-five a.m., arrived in Moscow at 4:30 p.m. Had we driven at the assigned speed, we wouldn't have arrived until 5 p.m.!

Knowing our guardian angels were expending all that manpower and technology to guide us on our way was a big comfort. The sheer big-ness of the buildings was exemplified by the military museum in Moscow, a monument to history presented subjectively. The thousands of World War II displays never included anything about the U.S., British, and their Allies on the Western Front. It was as though the Soviets won the war single-handedly.

In the early 80s, Russian business establishments didn't accept Russian currency as payment, only U.S. dollars, pounds, marks, and francs. In a Moscow parking lot, one young Soviet offered me a king's ransom for my jeans. Although flattered he'd want me out of them that badly, I had to decline. Where to go was another problem, as you stepped out of the hotel elevator, on every floor a commissar checked your ID—so much for unregistered guests.

We got into the habit of addressing the person at the other end of whatever listening, and/or possible surveillance devise they'd installed in our hotel rooms, even if we couldn't locate them. We'd ask how they were, tell them where we were going, the approximate time we planned to return, should they perchance lose track of us. In Smolensk, between Moscow and Kiev, I was convinced a tiny hidden camera was trained on me from the ceiling molding.

In a moment of compassion for the poor bastard sitting in a dank room with nothing to do but look at a monitor, I figured he might appreciate some entertainment, so I decided to give whomever it was a show. He never thanked me personally, but I like to think it gave him a more positive view of Americans.

Kiev, now part of the Ukraine, was in pleasant contrast to other places we visited. There were hills with patches of green and even flickers of sunshine.

Greatly relieved at the prospect of departing the restrictive U.S.S.R., we arrived at the Romanian border. The car was given another thorough going over, this time to remove, rather than install, the tracking devises placed in it two weeks prior. Romania turned out to be as anally retentive as its big neighbor, only sloppier, less efficient and more primitive.

Ours was the only vehicle at the Romanian border, so, waiting a half-hour for someone to emerge from the guard shack was puzzling. Upon investigating the cause for the delay, we were relieved to find out someone would be with us as soon as they finished the card game!

My narrative aside, Heidi and Wilson were wonderful traveling companions and it was a fascinating, worthwhile experience. One I'd do again if given the opportunity.

Fiesta por la Familia Grande

Many in our family took more than a cursory interest in our heritage, there was a good deal to take pride in and our forbearers had seen to it—there was plenty to be interested in. A family reunion took place in San Diego the fall of 1982—not just immediate members, the whole enchilada.

In light of my dubious lineage and unorthodox background, being selected as co-chairman of the three day event, seemed an unusual choice. My primary function was that of a host *master of ceremonies*, the co-chairperson, Cousin Susan Smith, took care of the incidentals. All she had to do was oversee the entire event, set the agenda, make all the arrangements, take the reservations, handle the finances, and coordinate the whole affair for eighty or so family members.

When Gladys Quarre Knapp was referred to from the dais as the *Grande Dame,* her reaction to the intended tribute was negligible. As her eyes scanned the banquet hall, she hissed, "There's got to be someone here older than me!"

A special luncheon was arranged for the whole group at the *Casa Bandini* in Old Town. Afterwards, photographs were taken of us on the steps of the historical landmark house, which appeared in the *San Diego Union Tribune*. I only recognize a dozen of the assembled, but all and all, not a bad looking lot. Interesting to note, the descendents of the Bandini, Carrillo, Estudillo, Arguello, Del la Guerra clans, with a smattering of Figueroas, Sepulvedas, and others with streets named after them—in general appearance, could just as well have landed on Plymouth Rock. The generations of *mixed marriages*, outside the family was clearly evident.

If not the *Grand Dame*, GQK couldn't help but convey an image in the grandest of *Duennas'* tradition.

It's Now Official

Larry Bukzin advised, future plans warranted incorporating the production company as a legal entity with a board of directors, stock holders, annual meetings, agendas, budgets, accountability—my reaction, "Do we have to Larry?"

"I think it might be a good idea," he responded in a manner not encouraging a whole lot of debate.

What to call it? GQK made a simple obvious suggestion, *The Montecito Company, Inc.* The problem, there was a ninety-eight percent chance the name was already taken, but it couldn't hurt to request it. To everyone's surprise, it was granted. The Montecito Company, Inc., officially became a California corporation in spring of 1982.

The newly formed company got off to an auspicious start with Richard Ross and Heidi Tait as producers. We were soon involved in two overlapping productions. I'd seen Simon Gray's *Otherwise Engaged* in London some years before, vowing to mount a production of it with me in the principal role. The play, when done right, is brilliant absorbing theater.

The younger-than-young, first-time director, Dennis Erdman, came highly recommended. His hiring wasn't based entirely on my paternal nature or blind faith, I figured, if push came to shove, Dennis would be easier to intimidate than an established director—a gross error in judgment on my part.

By opening night, only three members of the original cast we'd agreed on remained. Behind Dennis' politely deferential, almost obsequious façade, there lurked an exacting and demanding taskmaster. If a scene didn't go well in rehearsals, Dennis would either over-verbalize his displeasure, or simply look at an actor with resigned disappointment, what we call *"You really plan to do it that way?"* expression.

Rehearsing a scene I wasn't secure in—a theatrical euphemism for *not having really learned the lines*—I was slow picking up cues, instead of a clipped terse exchange of dialogue there were beats of silence while I tried to remember what to say next. During one extended pause, Dennis smiled, "Jump right in, David, whenever you're ready." Subtler than yelling, "Learn your fucking lines!"

Dennis further solidified his position by firing an excellent actor and personal friend to whom I'd offered the role—without consulting me. Seething, I reminded Dennis, it wasn't just a matter of protocol, the contract stated, *"No member of production team, may be hired or dismissed, without the express knowledge and approval of the producers."* Dennis claimed he *had* discussed it with a producer. Well, it wasn't Heidi Tait or me, we didn't operate that way. Leaving only…

I met Richard Ross in New York during the NBC days; he was living with one of the actresses in the show. He had a good deal of technical and production experience, fiscally responsible and appeared to have a nice way about him. I brought him into *The Montecito Company* as vice president to handle the daily operation, some shares in the company, and full producer credit alongside mine, although we weren't co-producers in the fifty/fifty sense. It took several projects to realize the company's V.P. was essentially a competitor, not a collaborator—a foe, not a friend.

A week into rehearsals, Dennis remarked, "You know, David, you're actually quite good in this." *Quite good* wasn't going to quite cut it, so I decided to replace *me*, thus eliminating the "vanity production" label, and the sleepless nights riddled with acute anxiety. Bowing out would also serve to absorb some of the negative energy of my many detractors, before, rather than *after*, the play opened. "Maydays" for a *Simon* replacement went out. Rescue arrived two days later, when Granville van Dusen walked in.

During auditions, telepathy develops among those casting the show. An actor walks in who everyone undemonstratively senses is perfect for the role, quick looks are exchanged, "Please God, now, if he can just act."

Granville—*Sonny*—van Dusen acts so superlatively, you never see a trace of it. Within a week he had *Simon* down pat, the subtext and enigmatic layers I had struggled with, he absorbed with little visible effort.

By the time the play opened, Marianne McAndrew, Stephen Johnson, and Thomas Harrison were the only members of the original cast remaining.

GQK attended opening night, as the *chairperson emeritus* of The Montecito Company, performing her "power-behind-the-throne" role flawlessly, confiding to a new arrival, "I have no idea what we're in for, you never know with David."

Her uncertainty was kindled in the second act, when *Simon*'s lady friend, in a fit of peak, yanks off her blouse, exposing her bare breasts. GQK looked at the actress like the embarrassed parent of a cheerleader who forgot her panties, quickly glancing apprehensively to check the audience's reaction, then satisfied no one had gone into cardiac arrest—giving a look of relief—was worth the price of admission. This reaction from a lady who while watching the stage production of *Hair* noted aloud, "She's not a natural blonde." This embodiment of motherhood who at the *Folies Bergere* in Paris, laughed uproariously when a lady of the ensemble wiggled her bare *titties* and derriere in her non-pulsed son's face!

"Come on, Mom, you've seen a helluva lot more than that," I reminded.

"Yes, but my name wasn't in the program as '*Chairman of the Board*' of the company producing it," she laughed.

Two mornings later, Mama called early, "You must be feeling pretty chipper this morning."

"I just got up, Mom, do you know something I don't?"

"I certainly hope so—Read the *Calendar* section in the *Times*, page two, under the heading 'Theater artistry at its best.' Congratulations."

The effort and trauma was worth it, "Otherwise Engaged" received rave reviews:

"A must see!" – Variety; *"Should be seen and reseen."* – Hollywood Reporter; *"A glowing compelling production, a perfectly crafted jewel"* – Dramalogue; *"Great style, taste and thought. . . an auspicious debut for The Montecito Company."* – Herald Examiner.

To the author's knowledge, that was the last evening GQK would spend in a legitimate theater.

Digressing

Nine years later, Granville van Dusen and Marianne McAndrew surpassed their performances in *Otherwise Engaged* in another production for The Montecito Company directed by Stewart Moss.

An eight-character autobiographical play entitled, *A Bed Facing North.* Described by critics as; *"The real thing! Glistening with relevance," "David Knapp's play is brilliant riveting drama," "Funny poignant," "Delicious malice of* Virginia Woolf,*" "Compelling and haunting," "Gripping impact," "An ode to love in the turning years," "Exceptional writing, acting, and directing," "Cast to perfection," "Every theatergoer's ideal!"* and *"Knapp's play and van Dusen's acting belong in a Tiffany setting!"*

Regrettably, the play's glowing reviews were offset by the author's timing—four years too late for his mother to read them.

As most rational people, I kept the good reviews in a scrapbook. GQK recommended I keep *all* the reviews, advising, "You don't have to show the bad ones, but it's important for *you* to know they're there." Having seen mostly stunning pictures of Mama in her collection, I wryly remarked, "Rather like you keeping an album of bad photographs?"

"You can't keep a record of things that don't exist, dear," she countered.

There was no lack of material in my case, so, I took Mama's advice. Over the years, I've come to enjoy the really bad notices and I read them to friends—not the innocuously-negative ones, they're not much fun—but the scathing, venomous, "scorched earth" variety, especially those by critics with a personal ax to grind, who desperately want anything you do to fail.

Clever critics, intent on writing a bad review, will invariably attend the evening *following* the opening night, almost assured, they'll see the worse, sloppiest, lack-lustre performance of the entire run! This "theatrical tradition" may not mean a truly bad evening, but you can bet your house, what you see on stage the second night, won't be remotely up to previous night, or any subsequent ones.

On these nights, an actor's timing takes a holiday, lines they've known for weeks desert them, they don't listen, they simply wait for cues, and reactive moments are lost. This contagious condition usually begins with the first actor on stage in the first scene, then spreads like a malignancy to the other actors throughout the show.

Attempts by other actors to revitalize the pace, generally result in forced energy. A theatrical locker room at half-time, a coach rallying a team trailing by a big margin, its star quarterback just carried off the field, and half the team suffering the effects of the chicken-gone-bad they had for lunch. As the producer *and* author of a project, one is doubly vulnerable to the "slings and arrows" of spiteful critics, it comes with the territory—sometimes deservedly so.

***

During the *Otherwise Engaged* production, Leslie Moonves asked me to co-produce and finance a play with him, *Girly Girly and the Real McCoy*—the author, Jack Colvin, would also direct. The line producer, Sheila Guthrie, was the kind of lady you want with you on every production. On an ironic note, I initially asked Jack to direct *Otherwise Engaged*, at which time I was given a severe lecture on my drinking habits, and told he'd only direct it if I abstained—being a realist, it was a deal-killer, ending further negotiations.

Normally, I don't get involved in projects where the key elements are already in place, wanting to be part of the decision making process, not the result of it. Knowing those involved and having been "otherwise engaged" during the initial phase, I made an exception.

Jack was prone to heavy dark material, *Girly, Girly* was no exception. The play about the seamier side of showbiz was an intelligent, well-crafted work with a small cast headed by Karen Valentine and Robert Mandan—two consummate pros.

Jack is a very talented veteran with a track record open to suggestions—at least, he listens. I'm not assumptive in saying, we both believe at some time, someone-somewhere-somehow, might come up with a better idea, than ours.

No one is nicer to work with, or more adorable than Karen Valentine, also a damned fine actress. I'd worked with Bob Mandan on *Soap*, a superb comedic actor and compelling in not-so-funny moments.

I found it impossible not to like Leslie Moonves—no matter how hard he fought it—and I respect his ability. He sorely put me to the test with *Girly, Girly and the Real McCoy*. He pretty much served as an absentee executive producer, having much bigger fish to fry at the time. I don't know if he still feels a difference of opinion or approach is tantamount to treason or betrayal, but back then, he called daily in a rage about one thing or another. In a few cases it was justifiable from his perspective, in other instances, it was unreasonable and over-reactive. I was made to feel like a *production associate*, not a *co*-producer—exactly as intended. In light of Leslie's career ascendancy, that characteristic may have been exacerbated—on the other hand, his present position is in *Bonne Homme* magnanimity. Then, it created a divisive atmosphere, resulting in two separate opening night parties.

What Leslie's irascible style did get him was a pressure job involving mega-overtime—as president and C.E.O. of the largest network in television—while I got to leisurely write this book?

Otherwise Engaged and *Girly Girly and the Real McCoy* opened a few weeks apart to opposite reactions. *Girly Girly* was crucified by the critics and shunned by audiences.

There was no cause to gloat, it was a noble project, a quality production considering the minimal budget, with outstanding performances—it deserved better. I suppose there's a thin line to the downside of life—what's dramatic? What's depressing?

Otherwise Engaged was nominated by the L.A. Drama Critics, winning a *Dramalogue* award as Best Production, two actors including Marianne McAndrew, were cited as "Best" in their categories, and Robert Z. Zentis won for "Best Design."

Bill Watters arranged for *Dramalogue* to do a cover story on The Montecito Company, adding further credibility to our projects.

GQK hosted her last large soiree during this period, taking over *Penelope's*, an excellent restaurant across the road from the bird sanctuary in Montecito. The dinner for Clare Boothe Luce was made up of six tables of eight, with roast venison as the entrée. Identifying the main course might sound superfluous, but it played a key role that evening. If venison is overcooked, it simply becomes dry deer meat, so, the chef asked that the meal be served promptly at eight—*Cocktails at seven, please be on time!*

Clare was a staying with Jean and Maggie Louis. Jean was an Oscar winning designer for Columbia Pictures, the other houseguest was their close friend, Loretta Young, who Jean later married after Maggie passed away. With little enthusiasm, GQK included Miss Young on the guest list.

"I had the impression you and Loretta were friends."

"Loretta and I are cordial acquaintances, calling us friends would be a stretch."

I asked if there was a problem.

"No-no, we just don't particularly like each other," she shrugged.

"You look enough alike to be sisters," I noted.

"Years ago we did, when we were contemporaries," Mama grinned. "Now, I understand she's much younger than I." The truth lay mid-way, Miss Young was twelve years younger than GQK. Loretta's ex-husband, Tom Lewis, had been a casual friend of mine in the Brentwood days.

GQK, with her forty other guests, waited anxiously for the guest of honor and her party to arrive. By seven-thirty, GQK began to get antsy, by a quarter to eight, she was fit to be tied.

After a ten minute grace period, with venison drying in the oven, we had to sit down. Twenty minutes later, the hostess seething, in came an embarrassed and apologetic Clare, Jean, and Maggie—oblivious to it all, in swept Loretta.

Mama, apprised of the fact Clare and the Louis' were ready on time, but Loretta arrived late from L.A., then took two hours to prep, she affixed a smile, and empathized, "Oh, don't I know, Loretta, with each year it takes longer to do everything. Thank heaven, you were even able to make it."

Clare was impeccable, taking my arm, she asked to be taken to each table and introduced to any guest she didn't know. She was unfailingly gracious as we made the rounds.

***

During this period, GQK was visited by a relative, a sweet woman barely in her forties, with three ex-husbands, twice that many heavy relationships-gone-awry and three children. She'd consistently struck out with romantic relationships as far back as anyone could remember and had nothing nice to say about any of the men involved.

GQK listened to her litany of woes then asked, "Have you ever considered falling in love with someone you *do* like?"

Chapter 26

BEEN THERE, DONE THAT

In the latter part of 1983, GQK's oft-times eccentric behavior began a transition into an erratic mode—at times, idiocratic. She seemed constantly preoccupied, her mind focusing on matters unrelated to the subject at hand. An undercurrent of insecurity and uncertainty developed, not at all in keeping with her persona. What had been attributed to age, attitude, and absent-mindedness was evolving into a more serious diagnosis.

Concern increased when mother drove to the grocery store, purchased a list of items, returned home, then, several hours later, drove back to the grocers, returning to the house with the same items she'd purchased earlier. Those periods would come and go, a good part of the time she appeared to be lucid and facile. The two Rolls were involved in a number of fender-benders. She claimed the dents and scrapes were the work of resentful hippies and parking lot attendants. I accepted that, being a victim of cracked windshields, punctured tires, and key gashes since '64, but only at election time.

Many learned the hard way, a Republican bumper sticker is an invitation to vandalism—while noting, Democrats don't seem to have this problem, which may be indicative of something. The point being, neither of GQK's cars had bumper stickers, she did her part to insure Reagan's reelection that year in other ways.

During the campaign, to determine her thought process, I'd ask questions along with little spot quizzes. Half-seriously, I posed a question, not expecting a wholly coherent response, "Why are you such a staunch Republican?"

"Because we live in a *republic,* democracy was never the plan*."* Mama's simplistic answer was more than I'd bargained for.

She continued, "'Democrat is a misnomer. If you believe in economic redistribution, creating a dependency on government with social programs, you're a *Socialist.*"

I was stunned by her mental-resuscitation, although short-lived, when I commented, "That was a very profound assessment."

"What was, dear?" she responded.

The Republican's whelming victory at the polls, may have played a covert role in Mama's appearing to be in a period of remission, there were no significant mishaps for over a month.

The first manifestation of something gone radically awry came during a holiday visit to Honolulu, her first in years. We were comfortably ensconced at the *Colony Surf,* all her old friends had planned parties for her through the New Year—luncheons, cocktails, and dinners every day and night. Although delighted to be surrounded by old familiar faces, she wasn't always sure as to whom they belonged.

Less than a week after our arrival, I went to fetch her for another round of festivities and found her seated on the bed, half-dressed, in tears. "What's wrong, Mom?" She looked at me plaintively, wanting to know, "Why am I here? I want to go home. I want to be with my dogs." I reminded her of the welcoming she'd received, citing the effort her friends made on her behalf, the activities planned for the following week, she replied, "Please, take me home." It was Christmas Day!

Booking a flight was no problem. Christmas is the quietest day of the year for the airlines. Calling friends, trying to explain what I didn't understand myself, *was* a problem. They were sympathetic and would relay the situation to the others.

Mama and I were back in Los Angeles that evening. Once in the guest room at the Marmont House with the menagerie, she perked up, as though nothing out of the ordinary had occurred. She remained in festive spirits as I drove her to Montecito the next morning.

No Picnic in June

1984 was also a year of more conflicts than resolutions. GQK grew more sedentary. It begins with shortened distances between home and destination, any kind of substantive traveling becomes history. Length of trips diminished correspondingly from months away to a week or two, maybe? Eventually just going into town or to a social function becomes an ordeal.

Larry Bukzin called from New York justifiably concerned over the number and amount of contributions GQK was making to various questionable political organizations. She'd always been generous to charitable and worthwhile institutions—attesting to this is a larger-than-life painting of Gladys Quarre Knapp hanging in the entrance foyer of the Scripps Clinic in La Jolla.

Rationalizing Mama's erratic behavior became serious when she turned things on, forgetting to turn them off. Everyone at some point, forgets to turn off lights, TVs, hoses, sprinklers, and faucets, but they rarely have the potential consequences of gas burners, fireplaces, and a car left idling in a garage.

Hiding things, being unable to find them later, is common, but showing up at the right place on the wrong night for a social event, or forgetting you'd invited half a dozen people for dinner on a given night and having to serve frozen noodle casserole, was disconcerting for her—as it was for me on occasions.

***

One thing became imperative, GQK could not be allowed to drive, she was a danger to herself and others. In the past, citations for traffic violations were attributed to left-wing resentment on the part of the officer. In one instance, she was pulled over through four lanes of traffic. "You were going over seventy-five," the cop explained.

"So was everyone in front of me and behind me, officer," Momma point out.

"I can't cite everyone, ma'am," he replied without thinking.

"Why did you pick me?" GQK was interested to know.

The cop still hadn't adjusted his thinking-cap, "Well, ma'am, your car kinda' stands out."

"You're saying, I'm getting a ticket for driving a Rolls-Royce?"

"No, ma'am, for speeding."

Momma turned to me and loudly hissed, "This is bullshit."

The cop leaned in ominously, "What did you say, ma'am?"

I said, referring to *you,* officer, 'He's a Bolshevik.'"

When GQK informed him she wouldn't accept the ticket, he threatened to arrest her.

"Then you'd better call for a back-up," her grip tightening on the wheel, "It's a matter of principle now."

"Very well, ma'am."

Through the side mirror, I watched the officer return to his car with Mother's driver's license and get on the radio. After an exchange of information, looking frustrated, the officer returned—he'd just received an emergency call. Momma, triumphantly didn't say a word as we drove off. Many years later, I still wonder what transpired over that police radio.

I discovered having a driver's license revoked to be as difficult as trying to get one after a couple of DUIs—this is common knowledge, *luckily*, I had no first-hand experience.

It took a good deal of correspondence and visits to the Department of Motor Vehicles before convincing them, an eighty-three-year-old lady, with a growing number of tickets and reported traffic mishaps, was no longer fit to drive.

Once official, came the hardest part, explaining to mother, an avid motorist, she was no longer allowed to sit behind the wheel of a car. The news was met with outrage and defiance; she would *drive* to the Motor Vehicle Department to show those SOBs how well she operated a car! I thought had she done that some months ago, it might have expedited the whole revoking process. I knew if I hid the car keys, I probably wouldn't remember where, or the wrong person would. Disconnecting the car batteries seemed the only option.

***

In eight months, GQK underwent three extensive medical examinations, including a CAT scan with no specific diagnosis. The Scripps Clinic in La Jolla was ruled out, as the trip and change of venue might further destabilize her.

Two days after the fourth exam, the doctor-in-charge informed me, the experts had now confirmed, Mother had Alzheimer's disease! I wasn't sure how to respond, I'd heard of Alzheimer's and Parkinson's, but really didn't know them from Epstein-Barr—or whether it was a cardiovascular, neurological, or a thyroid condition.

In the early eighties, the medical community knew even less about Alzheimer's than they do now—which isn't much. The causes, treatment and duration are still being determined. Was Alzheimer's simply a new medical term for senility or dementia?

"Not quite the same thing," the doctor replied.

"What's the difference?"

"Well, we're still working on that," he admitted.

"Is she going to suffer?"

"No, not physically at first" he answered with more certainty.

Was there a treatment? They were making breakthroughs, I was told.

I wanted to know how long Mother would be functional, semi-ambulatory.

"Difficult to tell, maybe six months, possibly less," was the prognosis.

"Do you have any idea as to her life expectancy, doctor?"

"Hard to pin down. She's in excellent shape for someone her age, all things considered—it could be anywhere from ten months—to ten years."

Many doctors believe the deteriorating effects of inoperable conditions intensify, disproportionately faster, *after* an official diagnosis, than prior to. Victims tend to succumb sooner if they're aware of the seriousness of the situation. "Especially, if they dwell on it," one M.D. emphasized. This isn't the case with victims of Alzheimer's, once it takes over, they're past the point of ever being aware of it, hence, it can actually prolong a life—the inability to think erases anxiety and stress.

I called Larry Bukzin with the news, sensing the housekeeper, with her ear to the ground, had probably beaten me to the punch. Larry and Margie knew more about Alzheimer's than the medical fraternity. Margie's mother would live with it for over a decade. I could tell from Larry's tone it would be no picnic in June.

The very real and practical issue of the estate itself now had to be addressed. I wasn't cavalier or altruistic enough to think things simply work out for the best—not without some personal attention. Trying to broach the issue delicately, without appearing to be a Machiavellian, scheming heir-apparent, was greatly accommodated when Larry intuitively suggested with words to the effect, "David, I hope this doesn't sound insensitive, but we have to face the fact, your mother is no longer in condition to control the estate." Larry made it sound rational, reasonable, and right—had it been me, it would have probably sounded, cold, and calculating.

Now, co-executors Bukzin and I, along with the Santa Barbara lawyers, made a decision to act immediately. We all believed the administrative transfer of authority, should be done with Mama's full knowledge and consent, while there was still time.

Drifting

Mama half-seriously told me in the past, "If I ever get *ga-ga*, shoot me like a horse." I'd kid back, "Sorry, no-can-do, honey, we're Catholic."

On a visit, Fr. David Schuyler observed, "Gladys not remembering names doesn't concern me so much, what does concern me, is her not *knowing* them once she hears them."

The flashing red lights began to stay red. Sentences weren't completed, familiar faces took a few minutes to identify, if at all. The evasive responses of simple questions to which she no longer knew the answers were disturbing. In a relatively short period of time, she had to make a concerted effort to remember the right descriptive word, and proper nouns became a thing of the past, then, adjectives eluded her.

The initial transitional period as the mind deteriorates is the most traumatic for all concerned. The victim remains aware enough to realize something is terribly wrong, but they have no idea what it is—a surrealistic cloud envelopes the victim's thought-process and with it, emotional stability.

Slipping in and out of lucidity and dementia, results in a haze of confusion, frustration and self-directed rage, a feeling of vulnerability intensifies. No longer in control of their mental faculties, sensing conspiracies all around them, they lash out, unable to stem the impending feeling of helplessness, they're engulfed by paranoia—only it's not imagined, they *are* losing their mind.

Illuminating Shadows

Watching mother's decline was cause for more serious thought regarding work-related activities, as a result, my abstention from stage acting ended abruptly. Michael Cristofer's play, *The Shadow Box*, premiered at The Mark Taper Forum with an outstanding production directed by Gordon Davidson. One of the three overlapping stories, all set in a cancer hospice, struck a deep note—especially one role in particular. Keeping in mind, an octogenarian with Alzheimer's isn't as harsh as a man in his mid-forties facing inoperable cancer. The afflictions differ, but mortality remains the issue.

Despite the somber premise, the play manages to leave the audience uplifted, in a positive state of mind. The board at Theater East overcame skepticism about co-productions, and enthusiastically agreed to do one with The Montecito Company. The play required only one set adaptable to the three different stories and it affords nine actors an ideal vehicle to apply their craft. The proviso, all the cast be Theater East members, presented no problem; their talent pool offered more than enough. I don't believe anyone involved regretted the decision.

Jack Colvin summed it up, "Its commercial success is up for grabs, but it'll be prestigious, and probably win a lot of prizes."—high praise from Jack, who designed the production in a first class manner. Stewart Moss directing; myself and Jack Colvin producing, we set about the task of casting *The Shadow Box*.

I would play *Brian*, a bisexual writer dealing with a young lover, a neurotic ex-wife and his own imminent demise. Marianne McAndrew agreed to play the wife and Stephen Nichols the lover. Marie Windsor, Bobbie Jordan, Susan Quick, John La Motta, Matt Adler, and Del Munroe rounded out the cast.

Brian opens the play alone on stage with a three page monologue, directed to the audience, with no prior-establishing text. It proved an antitoxin for me, not a pressure point, and was the only opening night I wasn't terrified. When the show ended, Mama's observation decades before that moment of dead silence, before the audience reacts, means a job well-done, caused my vision to blur.

The Shadow Box was a bigger success than any of us anticipated. The critics were almost unanimously euphoric; all cast were singled out for their performances.

The word-of-mouth spread like wildfire. The evening affected people in a way which made it rewarding to everyone on and off stage.

Marie Windsor got top honors for her portrayal. She and her husband, realtor Jack Hupp, became special friends over the years. The informal dinners at their home attracted a guest list of major personalities in a relaxed, homey atmosphere. Marie's very successful film career as a shady-jaded lady, was totally obliterated off-camera, she shined! Her talent wasn't fully revealed until the latter part of her career, so, it was joyous to see Marie win several "Best

Actress" awards for her role. Receiving the company's second "Best Production" award, and Marianne McAndrew adding another acting award to her collection, made it all the more gratifying.

Chapter 27

HIGH ON THE HILLS

I wasn't looking for a new home when a realtor friend, Hubert O'Brien, suggested a house I should look at in the hills on the opposite end of the *Strip*. It was a stunning bachelor pad with no real yard to maintain, loaded with switches, buttons, and dials, which automatically controlled every element in the house, along with all mater of "recreational" components to assure an audio-visual record of all activity. I could only fantasize, it was a few years too late, and not conducive to the needs of five active animals. Hubert then asked if I'd mind accompanying him, "Just up the hill." He had to check another house he had on the market.

Doheny Estates is a group of hillside houses built in the early sixties by coordinated construction companies. An attempt was made to individualize the houses by juxtapositioning configurations and painting them different shades of beige. It had an aura of *"Trousdale on a budget."* The area commands a better view but lacked the charm and individuality of Lower Doheny Drive.

The house on a cul-de-sac off Doheny, eighteen-hundred feet and a mile and a half above Sunset Boulevard, at first glance, wasn't worth a second. A bulky top-heavy second floor added to one side of the structure above the garage made it look lopsided. Painted a curious shade of pumpkin orange, the landscaping pretty much left to Mother Nature, gave it a sad appearance—like its owner, a recent divorcee.

A small living room with a low cottage-cheese ceiling and sliding glass doors, adorned with decals, led to a cement patio, a shaggy lawn, and an innocuous swimming pool. A quarter of the property was steep unattended hillside, at the base, amidst untrimmed bushes, stood two magnificent trees, a pine and a cedar, about fifty feet high, something about the two trees struck a cord.

GQK had advised, before seriously considering a property, see how it shows at night. The night we did, half the exterior lights didn't function, realtor O'Brien asked the owner, why she hadn't replaced the bulbs, she candidly explained, "Bulbs aren't the problem, it's the wiring."

In spite of neighbors on either side, one had an exhilarating sensation of isolation, a feeling, nobody else was around—this remains so twenty years later, even then, I knew I'd probably spend the rest of my life there. I envisioned the dogs and the cat with plenty of space to explore. Larry Bukzin and Norman Volk flew out to have a look. Even so, I'm sure Larry was understandably thinking, *That schlemiel wants to pay this kind of money for a fixer-upper?*

Too Late Now

It was winter, due to reconstruction activities, central heating constantly being interfered with, other utilities undependable, noise and disarray, we postponed bringing mother down to see the house until it was habitable by her standards. By early 1985, her mental decline made it an exercise in futility. No longer being ambulatory, disoriented, confused, and not knowing where she was, weren't the kind of conditions under which to expose her to a new house.

Although GQK still recognized me, she wasn't certain in what context. Was I her son, a friend, relative, old beaux, or a former husband? At various times I was *Jack, Billy, Oz, Fred*, and some I wasn't familiar with.

I'm not adept at dealing with illness, I lack the nurturing and nursing skills, I make an effort to compensate, however, by being a lousy patient.

Mother had, if not a *Mother Earth*, a highly competent housekeeper and twenty-four-hour nurses. She was still sufficiently aware to warrant neighbors and friends coming by for visits, although the response they received varied. She still had enough pride to perk up when her hairdresser made his regular visits. The dear man was a walking encyclopedia of local goings on, GQK's being totally oblivious to all the "pearls of poop," in no way deterred his effort to keep her *au courant*. I suspect it wasn't all for naught, lurking in the hallway, someone was taking notes.

It's only reasonable friends and relatives be more conscientious with a sick person, if there's a chance of light at the end of the tunnel, the hope for recovery, or some definitive conclusion, in the foreseeable future. Knowing the end is imminent, little time left to share, is a unifying motive. The least desirable prognosis is knowing a long arduous road may lie ahead, leading nowhere. One can't avoid a tinge of despair if the end of the tunnel is enveloped in pitch darkness.

Chapter 28

A BED FACING NORTH

By winter of 1985, Gladys Knapp could no longer communicate on any level, all verbal interaction ceased. The words she couldn't remember became incidental, she had forgotten how to speak! Alzheimer's had rendered her mute. Seated on mom's bed one day, trying to coax some flicker of conscious awareness from her, I looked out the French doors at the foot of her bed, when I suddenly realized for the first time, her bed faced directly North! For seven years, neither of us had been aware of it. It was the obvious place, owing to the room's configuration, still things could have been rearranged.

I flashed back to an incident years before, when we checked into a hotel in London, GQK entered her suite and appeared disoriented. She walked around the bedroom. "I knew something was wrong," she announced, "the bed faces North." She wanted a different room, yet I persuaded her to accept the accommodation.

That afternoon, looking in the wrong direction, I stepped into the street and was knocked to the sidewalk by a passing car. Bruised and shaken, I narrowly escaped serious injury. The following day on Regent Street, a lorry came out of an alleyway and struck the taxi we were riding in causing substantial damage and a lot of attention.

Mama declared, "I'm changing rooms!"

To bring it up in Montecito at that point seemed gratuitous and too long after the fact, giving credence to the possibility Alzheimer's was hereditary.

The Appropriate Thing

From '84 to '89, the author became heavily involved with the *John Douglas French Alzheimer's Foundation.* The organization founded by Dorothy Kirsten French, in memory of her late husband, who succumbed to the disease after a long decimating battle. Dorothy Kirsten's operatic career was legend. Her *Tosca* was considered by many as arguably the most memorable at the time. Her voice and persona vividly brought her roles to life. She was quite beautiful, with a splendid svelte figure and sexuality.

She was dedicated, and not to be trifled with. To say she was tough as steel wouldn't be to over-state. She was a longtime social acquaintance of GQK's, the two ladies had enough in common to make it obvious why they never became close friends.

It seemed appropriate I become her "left-hand" man, social partner, co-host and partial underwriter. The major annual black tie fundraiser for the French Foundation, of which Dorothy was Chairperson, was held every April in the Grand Ballroom of The Beverly Wilshire Hotel. This ballroom is the fundraising mecca for more philanthropic, charitable, political, award galas, testimonials and tributes, than there are *Grammy* categories!

Sitting with Dorothy, six years in a row afforded an opportunity to resurrect my acquaintanceship with a man I greatly admired and hoped to see in the White House one day, Pete Wilson. We'd met in Washington through the Chuck Raysbrooks, when he was a California senator, and our association continued through his two terms as governor. Pete and Gayle Wilson were steadfast in their support of French Foundation. I never understood why his ability, savvy, character and record, didn't gain him national popularity. There wasn't anyone more eminently qualified to be his party's candidate.

Seated at Dorothy Kirsten French's table for the gala were the Wilsons, Barbara Bush, Bob Hope, John Forsythe, Peggy Lee, Robert *R.J.* Wagner, Jill St. John, and this one evening, a quiet army major in uniform. I didn't understand his role in the scheme of things. Army majors don't make enough to donate large sums to charitable groups. When I noticed the medal hanging from a blue and white ribbon around his neck, it came to me—his contribution was bigger than anyone in the room. He had been awarded *The Congressional Medal of Honor.*

For someone who gets a lump in his throat and teary-eyed every time he sees an American flag waving, or hears *God Bless America* or *The National Anthem,* being seated next to a man whose courage makes it all possible, is a humbling and thought-provoking experience.

Indulging in Exploration

It was my last day on a two-episode guest shot on *Scarecrow and Mrs. King*, a silly show, but fun to do, having a political ally in one of the show's stars, Bruce Boxleitner. Talking politics with someone "right" of me was a rare experience.

The show's director, Ivan Dixon, listened to Bruce and I having a discussion, commenting, "I thought only guys in the crew felt that way politically."

I'd been told Kate Jackson was *hell-on-wheels.* She must have had a tune-up before I worked with her, she couldn't have been pleasanter.

On the final day of shooting, I naively booked a 6 p.m. flight to New York as the first leg of an extended journey. A Hollywood axiom, if you've made other plans, fate decrees your one scene will be the very last one shot that day!

The following day I was apprehensive at the prospect of a twenty-hour flight, including two brief stopovers to Johannesburg, South Africa. Rushing to make a connecting flight at JFK, the British Airways agent lessened the ordeal when he asked, "Sir, would you care to be upgraded to the Concorde, we have seats available?" Before I could hug the master of English understatement, he added, "You'll have to hurry, it leaves in eight minutes." With winged feet of *Mercury* I made it.

The following day, thirty thousand feet over Central Africa, the airliner I was aboard experienced a sudden plunge in altitude. There was a surge of fear before the plane recovered moments later—my state of mind took longer. I'd been taught a supreme lesson on how to cope with panic by a lady lying semi-comatose eight thousand miles away.

Flashback

During the Cold War, at my bequest, GQK and the author were on a Pan Am flight from Frankfurt to West Berlin. She'd been less than enthusiastic about the side trip, never having gone to a Communist country during the years we traveled together. My visits to mainland China, the Soviet Union, Romania, Hungary, Poland, and other Eastern Block countries had always been done separately.

On this occasion, we were crossing the East German corridor into West Berlin, when the plane was struck by a bolt of lightning. We plummeted thousands of feet in less than two minutes, long enough and steeply enough for several passengers to cry out. Sensing the imminent peril, most on board believed we'd all be statistics in a matter moments. The urge to panic was overwhelming when I felt Mother's hand patting mine, her rosary ring in place. With calmness and a faint smile she said, "Well, darling, we've had some good times."

Moments later the plane leveled off and we landed intact at Templehof Aerodrome, outside West Berlin.

"Mom, you were magnificent up there, I wanted to panic," I admitted.

"So did I," GQK mused, "But I thought, if we *do* come out of this alive, don't look like a coward."

"I didn't think you cared what people thought," I joked.

"I didn't want to think of *myself* as one," she amended.

GQK had nothing to worry about. Her reasoning may not have been the noblest source of inner strength, but when self-control is seriously threatened in a crisis, the "If we *do* make it, how will *I* look?" worked for the author on several occasions.

In these instances, a big ego is an asset.

Back to the Past Present

South Africa got high marks as soon as I left Johannesburg, with one glowing exception. Chuck Raysbrook assigned to the U.S. Embassy in Pretoria, and his wife, drove up to take me on a grand tour of the surrounding area. The *Blue Train* to Capetown was the only experience comparable to the old days aboard the *Twentieth Century Limited* from Chicago and New York. Capetown and Durbin were splendid, the scenery spectacular, including many of the Anglo, and /or Dutch population. The natives seemed to be attractive, but only to each other.

Kenya was a unique and memorable experience, a book in itself.

Lingering in Limbo

Nothing had changed in Montecito; GQK was propped up in bed in the same position, with the same vacant expression, staring at the same spot she had six weeks earlier, only her sheets and nightie changed.

It was unnerving to see Gladys Knapp, Mom, so vulnerable and helpless, and at the mercy of others for every aspect of her existence. A woman, who heretofore was so aggressively mobile, on the go, and now incapable of lifting a spoon to her mouth—unaware of the procedure or necessity for doing it. Life begins being fed with a bib, your mouth dabbed for drool, but it's not a dignified way to end it.

The woman who so vehemently sought independence, went to such lengths to achieve self-sufficiency, now robbed of pleasure and purpose, pain and passion—life without strife, living, yet not alive, even her yesterdays taken from her. Had she known her final years would be spent in that catatonic state, she'd have opted for a cyanide capsule.

***

Our production with Heidi Tait and Stephanie Hagen, co-producing, Philip Barry's *Philadelphia Story* was enthusiastically received by audiences and critics. Under Norman Cohen's stewardship; *Tracy Lord* was magnificently brought to life by Carolyn McCormick, with Dori Brenner and John O'Connell, the perfect pair of enquiring reporters. Lisa Figus, Ross Evans, and John Furlong portrayed the senior family members admirably, and dishonoring his vow again, DHK as *C.K. Dexter-Haven*. The elaborate set by Robert Zentis, and stylish costume design in the small theater made everything on stage seem bigger and more imposing—in contrast to the backstage facilities which necessitated placing a *port-o-potty* in the parking lot behind the theater.

Among a few *opening nighters* who didn't seem to care for the production, regrettably, were the Phil Barry, Juniors. Not a case of preconceived negativity on their part, I like to think, Phil and Pat's disappointment was due in part to a very broad basis of comparison. The *C.K. Dexter-Haven* they saw was a far cry from a composite of Joseph Cotton, Cary Grant, and Bing Crosby in their experience.

Show business expressions become irritating—"*It was a fun show*"—but best describes, *The Philadelphia Story,* a company in harmony, on and off stage. The backstage atmosphere steeped with laughter and genuine camaraderie, a dozen cast members sharing minimal dressing room space, who went out after the show, en masse, for some serious partying, and continued to, off and on, after the show closed.

The Object of My Obsession

Meanwhile male menopause had me writhing in heavy emotional and physical mischief and misery. Over the years, GQK imparted sage advice in matters of the heart and libido, but by tacit mutual choice, we never indulged in clinical anatomical conversations about the birds and the bees. It was *after* they flew over, or you'd been stung, which concerned her.

The object of my obsession predicated the demise of our relationship, magnanimously leaving it up to me to formally end it. What had once been a glorious experience, became a prolonged ordeal, the termination process took over a year, of still-unspent passion, optimism and cowardice.

We weren't living together in the literal sense, only from sundown to sun up, three or four times a week. The problem was how and where the *other* nights were spent?

Typically, as things unraveled, the lights turned on, I had my blindfold securely in place.

GQK had cautioned me, "Declining relationships aren't democratic, when it's over for one, the other's vote doesn't count." She went on to emphasize, "Trying to debate or amend it is futile, you'll always be the minority. Pretending everything is fine, is like putting your head in the sand with your behind exposed."

Why anyone clings to a relationship when they're not wanted, was anathema to Gladys Knapp.

"You can't hang on to something that's no longer there," she reasoned.

"How do you really know?" I whined.

She looked at me as if I'd been in the sun too long, "When belaboring it becomes a bore."

"I guess I'm a bore." I concluded, with a hang-dog expression.

A tinge of irritation in GQK's tone, "Don't start that, dear, modesty doesn't become you."

***

Once again The Montecito Company got involved in a preset project, which it agreed *not* to do again. *The Normal Heart* by Larry Kramer, was a major off-Broadway production, not due so much to its merits, but to its timeliness, as the first play to draw dramatic attention and confront the AIDS epidemic. Barely a week into rehearsal the West Coast production at the Las Palmas Theater was floundering. The show desperately needed revitalization in order to open. In lieu of the eight "producers" listed on the credits, led by Josh Schiowitz—the only one doing any actual producing that I could see—how did this dilemma arise and why did they come to us after the fact, rather than at the onset?

The decision to co-produce it was due to several factors. By the mid-80s, I'd lost, or was in process of losing, a number of friends to the HIV virus. It was a matter of personal concern, a moral issue. A cast headed by Richard Dreyfuss, Kathy Bates, David Spielberg, Ben Murphy, and Bruce Davison, also served as an inducement, the latter, being a friend since the *Peege* days. The assurance of full production participation, from then on, closed the deal.

Not long after, it was gratifying to see Kathy Bates win the Oscar, and then, Bruce Davison's nomination in a role very similar to the one he played in *The Normal Heart.* Bruce gets many choice gay roles, but let the truth be known, in real life he's a raging heterosexual.

Mrs. Knapp Regrets, She's Unable to. . .

Mother's eighty-fifth birthday was reminiscent of a steadfast group of loyalists gathered around a deposed monarch. Those persevering souls who try to cheer a veteran candidate who ran once too often, for an office held too long.

The previous year, sixteen revelers helped Mama blow out the candles. She was confused, didn't know who they were, or why they were there, but she was sufficiently aware to enjoy the friendly festive atmosphere.

The four-score and five celebration didn't exist for GQK. Hubert O'Brien and John Laurent were house guesting, the Bartons and Lenore Adams were with us and the Bukzins flew out, as they had the previous years. I suspect they noticed the change more acutely than those of us having gone through a more gradual process. A year earlier, GQK, with her silver hair coiffed, sat up in her wheel chair, seeming to almost smile, consciously or not, she maintained a regal bearing. A mute flower you had bloomed at one point. In twelve months her physical decline was catching up with the mental deterioration. She sat slumped over in a catatonic manner; she was well-cared for but appeared slovenly, unkempt, and wholly unmindful of the presence of others. A once-beautiful flower now withered.

It became a pointless charade. For whose benefit or enjoyment was it? The forced joviality brought to mind those who pretend not to notice the person they're talking to has turned the lights out and gone to sleep—a depressing ordeal for a diminishing loyal group, beating their brains out, bracing themselves for a yearly obligatory ritual. It was easier for those who drifted off at the onset, buffered by the majority, they were less noticeable. Those remaining aboard after the others abandon ship, become increasingly prominent. When they finally donned lifejackets, it became more evident. The seven guests that night stayed aboard until the bow went under. This would be the last official birthday gathering. It seemed a safe decision; the chances of there being another were remote.

The only one who might have benefited from this grand *gignol* was the household manager, a.k.a. housekeeper, whom it served to remind all within earshot of her selfless commitment and dedication to Mother's well-being—and when I was out of the room, to emphasize the rigors of her position by casting volleys of aspersions about me to friends.

Loyalty and propriety aside, bad-mouthing her employer would attract eager listeners, but not earn the trust or confidence of potential employers. I've amassed enough flaws and vices on my own; I didn't need anyone else's two-cents worth of distorted, exaggerated supposition as to my hedonistic capabilities.

A heavily-mascaraed eyebrow raised in vilification for deeds not done, pleasures unattained, bacchanals unattended, and unspeakable acts unachieved, is not only fallacious, it is downright frustrating.

The housekeeper had little to complain about, living in affluence, a very substantial salary and all expenses, full-time nurses to do the serious tending of GQK; a maid *she* hired at our expense, to do her job so she could make runs to her *Beverly Hills* hairdresser in one of the three cars she was given over the years, in spite of a very unsatisfactory driving record and prohibitive insurance premiums!

Mama described the housekeeper years before as, "A perfect example of pretentious bourgeois—but she gets things done."

Ultimately, she made more silent enemies than I had verbose ones.

Flashback

Gladys Quarre Knapp embodied a family characteristic, something everyone in our widespread clan seemed to have without exception—a sense of humor. Humor varies, from ribald slapstick, to drawing room subtle. Gladys infused in me an ability to *think funny*. I believe one reason I wasn't a better student, was in finding a comedic side to everything, the more grave the situation, the funnier it was.

Mother's reaction to comedic situations was often funnier than the subject of her laughter—and more embarrassing at times.

A most embarrassing experience took place in a Munich Hotel Ballroom during a folk dance exhibition. Bavarian couples, the women, all overweight, in pigtails, those frilly blouses, horizontally layered skirts and clodhopper shoes; the fellows in silly-looking hats with feathers sticking out of them, ruffled shirts, lederhosen, thick socks that went on forever and North-Pole-hiking boots; all gleefully prancing and hopping about to the most God-awful accordion music—is there any other kind?

The spectacle sent Mama into a fit of giggles. All she could do was point at the locals' synchronized twirling like mechanical "coo-coos" in a clock. Suddenly, instead of dull, they *were* comical.

Mother by now was starting to lose it, trying to stifle hysteria, shaking, tears rolling down her cheeks, while I'm desperately fighting for control, as I now begin to see Bavarian culture, in new light, the dancers were uproariously funny.

"Mama, please, get a grip on yourself, this is embarrassing." I was glancing around apologetically to those in the audience, when I realized mother's condition was infectious, couples around us were covering their mouths, others were audibly reacting, unable to contain their laughter. They were looking at GQK, not the folk dancers.

Now aware of the commotion, the performers were not at all amused. The diversion caused their concentration to waver, they began to lose the ol' Bavarian rhythm and miss steps. We and several others had to leave so as not to further disrupt the festivities.

Pomposity was great source of humor to GQK. We'd been invited to a gala at the Metropolitan Club in New York, hosted by the Douglas Fairbanks, Jrs. The invitation read: *"White tie and medals."*

A mild blizzard struck on the night of the gala. Snow and ice covered the streets. GQK, in a long evening gown and full-length mink coat, (before they became unacceptable) and DHK in tails, ascended the steps to the venerable club amidst a host of social luminaries resplendent in their most formal attire. As we were about to enter, a police-escorted limousine pulls up, and out of it steps a *W. Averill Harriman* type in a velvet-collared chesterfield, with a lady dressed to the nines, bedecked in jewels—unfortunately she was only an eight—clutching his arm. They stride towards the front steps, when suddenly, the gentleman's patent leather pumps lost traction on the icy sidewalk, doing a pratfall in the best burlesque tradition and he lands flat on his keister taking his *insignificant other* with him. A swarm of on-lookers rushed to render assistance to the fallen couple. The crisis was compounded when, in an attempt to get the fallen pair on their feet, several affluent *would-be-rescuers* posteriors also hit the sidewalk.

Counterpoint to the gravity of the moment, Gladys Knapp reacted as one might to a slapstick farce, exploding into uncontrollable laughter. Not satisfied with her uproarious behavior, she beckons other guests to the entrance with "Hurry up. You've got to see this!"

Once, feeling proud of my cool in handling a near-calamitous incident, I bragged to GQK, "You have to admit, Mom, I'm not bad in a crisis."

"Yes, dear. Now all you have to do is work on day-to-day life."

You have to love a woman like that.

Chapter 29

END TO AN ENIGMA

Mid-morning on Friday, December 1, 1989, Kim Underwood, my assistant, answered the phone, it was the housekeeper in Montecito, with no preliminaries she told me, "Your mother just passed away."

Having anticipated this moment for half a decade, there was no sense of shock, but the reality stunned me. It took a moment to absorb. When an event you've been expecting for a long time finally occurs, there's an anticlimactic element—questions to be asked, answers required. Your job is to take charge. The *buck* is passed to you.

"I'll be right up. I don't want her touched until I get there."

As I put the phone down, tears welled up for several moments—then vaporized. I called Larry in New York to tell him what he already knew, then, Fr. David Schuyler, asking him to deliver the eulogy. Kim took over the long phone list; I got in the car and headed North.

I'd hoped, even prayed, for this day for Mother's sake, with no proprietary motives and nothing to gain and a fair amount to lose. I'd had control for five years, death taxes would claim over fifty percent of the estate and I was an orphan at fifty.

Ninety minutes alone in the car gave me time to organize my thoughts, concentrating on the funeral home, bringing her to Los Angeles, the church service, burial, and a reception afterwards—then the realization, all that was ancillary—*Mother was gone.* I felt a sense of loss, rather than grief, I needed to experience sorrow and emptiness, not just a void. GQK *died* years before her death, had to be the reason, for my stoicism.

I decided her final resting place would be Holy Cross Cemetery in Los Angeles, GQK had a strong sense of family and belief in her interpretation of Catholicism, I believed it more fitting she be laid to rest with other family members in consecrated ground in Los Angeles, her home base for half her life. Selfishness played a role, I wanted her in closer proximity for visits and communing. My archaic belief, the tangibility of physical remains are somehow more representative of a life, than ashes, is passé, impractical, environmentally-flawed, and more costly—but for the author, it's a kind of compromise to the finality of death.

I pulled into her driveway unsure about what was to transpire. The housekeeper greeted me with the two Retrievers. My stomach tightened when I entered Mother's room, closing the door behind me. Standing at her bedside, only her head and hands visible, her skin had the texture of cool marble. The angle of her jaw disturbed me, and she didn't look particularly at rest. Her expression conveyed a sort of annoyed inconvenience, as though breakfast hadn't been satisfactory—or was it a final reprimand?

An inanimate stranger, a still-life imposter, was lying in Gladys Knapp's bed, not the person I shared thousands of hours with, soared to the heights with, and took some nasty falls with. This wasn't the vibrant person we all knew. Who was this lady?

I went outside and walked around the house to the rose garden outside Mother's bedroom, where we had buried

Marilyn, Gloria, Jack, and Rosalie. I wanted to believe somewhere, a joyful reunion was taking place.

I watched the attendants roll the gurney with Mother's covered remains into the hearse. Could they adjust her mouth to soften her expression? A decision made easier, her casket would be sealed.

They followed me to the mortuary in Los Angeles.

***

Father Allen DeLong, then president of Chaminade Preparatory School, would say the funeral mass with Fr. Schuyler. I discussed the funeral service with my pastor at St. Victor's Church—which took negotiating. The Monsignor explained he would be happy to share the altar with Fathers Schuyler and DeLong, however, as pastor, *he* would deliver the eulogy, *allowing a perhaps unqualified stranger, chosen by a distraught relative, out of sentiment, could be potentially embarrassing.*

"Unqualified stranger!" David Schuyler was a close family friend for over thirty years, a greatly respected Catholic priest, an educator, and was one of the youngest Vice-Chancellors of a major archdiocese in the country. As for David Knapp being a distraught relative.

Encapsulating a lifetime, to convey a tiny essence of the deceased requires more than a ten-minute chat with the eulogizer or a hastily prepared biography. A formula eulogy, not applicable to the person being eulogized, does a disservice to all involved.

"With all due respect, Monsignor, you know nothing about my mother. Too many people knew Gladys Knapp, she gave too much to the Catholic Church, and a generalized tribute would be offensive to many." The Monsignor finally agreed.

***

On the day of the funeral, the housekeeper volunteered to drive down from Santa Barbara and pick up Larry and Margie at their hotel en route. Then rendezvous at my house. From there, we would go to the church in limos. She'd been to Marcheeta on several occasions, but that morning she couldn't find it resulting in all of us being late. Not the end of the world—but for your Mother's funeral? The housekeeper assuaged, "David, they can't very well start the service without you." I reminded her, "Mother didn't like to be kept waiting."

In the church, most of the people had already taken their seats. The pews were filling, when we roared up—a gratifying turnout for one who hadn't been active for over half a decade. Cousins Helen Young and Phillip Quarre accompanied me following Mother's casket up the aisle. Father Schuyler delivered a perfect eulogy, about a unique and very *human* being, not a litany of near-perfection, or pandering to sentiment. He set the tone from the beginning, "Gladys Knapp never drove, she motored." He looked down at me a moment, an exchange of brief smiles, conveying a legacy of remembrances. Father David then continued with what could best be described as, a haunting testament, solemn, insightful, affectionate, and humorous—the way GQK would have wanted it.

Leader of the choir group, a lady with a beautiful voice sang Cole Porter's *Night and Day* at the conclusion of the service, as Mama thought it the most beautiful popular ballad ever written. As we followed Mother's casket down the aisle, family and friends falling in line behind, from the choral balcony above, the *voice of an angel* filled the church with...

"Night and day, you are the one.
Only you beneath the moon and under the sun..."

Standing in the vestibule, greeting people as they filed out, many eyes were brimming with tears, while poignantly in the background,

"Whether near to me, or far,
It makes no difference where you are,
I'll think of you, night and day."

GQK was laid to rest in a muted peach-colored suede suit, the same one she wore in the funeral Mass card photograph, taken of her on our last visit to Sydney, Australia, a decade before. Around her neck, a simple gold necklace and medallion I'd given her, one she would always have with her, on the front, a perfect likeness of the face she so loved—on the back was inscribed, "Marilyn."

THE END

CPSIA information can be obtained at www.ICGtesting.com
Printed in the USA
LVOW112212261011

252281LV00001B/144/P